READ THE REVIEWS

"Finally . . . a great book on how to successfully implement today's leading-edge procurement technology. Written by three industry experts, *On-Demand Supply Management* is full of rich information and fresh new industry examples on how to make the business case, how to ensure your technology delivers, and how to reenergize your procurement organization, resulting in new levels of performance and sustainability. It's a powerful guide that all procurement, IT and finance professionals will want to read. Congratulations to Smock, Rudzki and Rogers for delivering this classic."

— **R. Gregg Brandyberry**, Vice President
Procurement
Global Systems and Operations
GlaxoSmithKline

"*On-Demand Supply Management: World Class Strategies, Practices, and Technology* is the major league coaching manual for business. After players are drafted, schedules arranged and lineups situated, the coach must teach the basics and the complex everyday of the season until the games are won. This volume of what to do, how to do it, and pure resource in the realm of technical supply management will be on the shelf of those in the know for many years as the first "go to" book for the best approach, solutions and measurement ideas in strategic supply chain management."

— **Leah Kalin**, CPM, CPIM, Director
Supply Chain Operations
BREG, Inc.

"If you are a CPO, CFO or CIO that is all about collaboration and creating true organizational excellence, *On-Demand Supply Management* is a must read. While vision, people and process are always fundamental to success, this book presents technology (appropriately selected and applied) as the fourth dimension that will separate the best from everyone else."

— **Brad Holcomb**, SVP and Chief Procurement Officer
Dairy Group
Dean Foods Company

"Insightful guide book to on-demand purchasing; helps to wrap the mind around the history and models of dealing with supply chains. The presentation inspires the development of in-place methodologies to deal with current supply chain opportunities. Great practical application!"

— **Gerry M. Hamilton,** IT Manager
The Brewer Company

"This book will make you think. Most of IT management has known for a long time that software and data can be of little benefit without a focused strategy for use. In the purchasing arena this book hits that nail right on the head and clearly outlines the principles of developing broad-ranging, effective, ethical and successful strategies for e-purchasing which transcend a specific technology generation. If you're interested in e-purchasing, this book will not just help you with effective strategy—it will also inspire you."

— **Glenn Bitzenhofer**
Former Interim CIO
Butler County Children's Services and
Former IT Director
Hewlett-Packard and Procter & Gamble

"*On-Demand Supply Management* nicely combines purchases best practices with new technology solutions. This integrated view can be a great resource for purchases professionals to more effectively and efficiently deal with the increasing demands and complexities of the global marketplace."

— **Roberto Magana,** Manager
Global Business Services Purchases
Procter & Gamble

"Don't read this book! Study this book and apply its insights! The authors apply their considerable experience and expertise to deliver a clear message of strategic choice to managers in all areas of the supply chain."

— **Lowell Hoffman,** Global Sourcing Solutions and
Adjunct Research Professor and Industry Fellow
Kenan Institute, Kenan Flagler Business School
The University of North Carolina at Chapel Hill

"As recently appointed Director of MRO Purchasing for the ZF North American Operations, I found this book, *On-Demand Supply Management*, to be extremely helpful and on target in the ever-changing world of e-tools. The emphasis on true spend analysis, supply management, and should-cost analysis will be used within the ZF North American Operations. In addition, the 'thought framework' for supply e-tool master planning provides great direction for e-purchasing tools."

> — **Mark C. Strominger,** Director
> MRO Purchasing
> ZF NAO

"This book is a balanced and valuable perspective on the rapidly evolving field of electronic tools for supply management. The authors are neither cheerleaders for technology, nor cynics. They provide evidence for the significant value that such tools can deliver, while emphasizing that even the best tools will deliver little value in the absence of well-designed businesses processes, skilled people, and effective change management."

> — **Jonathan Hughes,** Partner and Practice Leader,
> Sourcing and Supplier Management
> Vantage Partners

"Like *Straight to the Bottom Line™: An Executive's Roadmap to World Class Supply Management, On-Demand Supply Management* is a resource that supply managers should not go without. The role that technology and information play as a critical enabler of strategic sourcing will only increase. This book provides order and logic to this important subject."

> — **Robert J. Trent,** Ph.D.
> Supply Chain Management Program Director
> Lehigh University

ON-DEMAND SUPPLY MANAGEMENT

World Class Strategies, Practices, and Technology

ON-DEMAND SUPPLY MANAGEMENT

World Class Strategies, Practices, and Technology

Douglas A. Smock
Robert A. Rudzki
Stephen C. Rogers

Copyright ©2007 by Douglas A. Smock, Robert A. Rudzki, and Stephen C. Rogers

ISBN-10: 1-932159-62-2
ISBN-13: 978-1-932159-62-2

Printed and bound in the U.S.A. Printed on acid-free paper
10 9 8 7 6 5 4 3 2 1

Library of Congress Cataloging-in-Publication Data

Smock, Douglas A., 1948-
    On-demand supply management : world class strategies, practices, and technology / by Douglas A. Smock, Robert A. Rudzki, & Stephen C. Rogers.
        p. cm.
    Includes bibliographical references and index.
    ISBN 978-1-932159-62-2 (hardcover : alk. paper)
    1. Industrial procurement—Management. 2. Industrial procurement—Technological innovations. 3. Business logistics—Management. 4. Business logistics—Technological innovations. I. Rudzki, Robert A., 1953- II. Rogers, Stephen C., 1949- III. Title.
    HD39.5.S65 2007
    658.7'2—dc22   2006038386

Phone: (954) 727-9333
Fax: (561) 892-0700
Web: www.jrosspub.com

This book includes specific examples and case studies. In some of those examples, specific software solutions are mentioned because they are germane to the illustration. Had other case studies been used, quite possibly different software solutions and companies might have been mentioned. The mention of specific software companies in this book should not be construed as an endorsement by any of the authors.

Trademark notice: Greybeard Advisors LLC has trademark and service mark rights to the phrase "Straight to the Bottom Line."

TABLE OF CONTENTS

FOREWORD

A commonly asked question about Phillips Plastics Corporation is "How has Phillips been able to average annual growth of over 20% during the past 42 years?" An obvious part of the answer to our successful growth has been and continues to be our ability to attract additional business from existing customers in addition to developing new customers for our existing businesses. We also partner with customers who appreciate value, not just cost. Many of the themes in this book—such as long-term partnering, being customer-driven, early design involvement, and the value of technology-driven innovation—have been pillars of success and growth for Phillips Plastics.

In 1964, when we started Phillips Plastics, we didn't create a strategic plan that would position us to be a technology-driven company. The strategy really evolved: through the changes underway in the plastics industry at the time; the influence of my education in engineering; certainly by the growing use of plastic polymer processing technology; and of course, the need to make and sell parts to survive. Our start-up years were blessed with both new processing technology and development of new high-performance materials. We learned the value of being at the leading edge of manufacturing innovations and made a commitment to always utilize the best technologies as a competitive advantage.

This has been formalized as one of our corporate principles, which we still practice today: to invest in state-of-the-art approaches—including management style, equipment and people development—that enable Phillips Plastics Corporation to respond to the quality, service, and demands of the marketplace. Our foundation for decision making is supported by what I'll call our combined network of knowledge and resources. This network includes science, engineering, technology, finance, marketing, sales, product development, supply chain management, suppliers, information technology, customers, consultants, and others.

Achieving long-term business success requires the willingness to take risks. I had many lonely moments when we decided to become an early adopter of computer-aided design and manufacturing technology in the early 1980s. Now many supply chain managers also face difficult challenges associated with new technology.

Take the appropriate risks after the fundamentals are in place, starting with respect. We have achieved our success by working together with great effectiveness through our culture of respecting each other and respecting all the tasks we do. This applies to employees, as well as to all of our customers and suppliers. This is what we have done, who we are, and what we are—and it's still fun for me to be at work every day.

> **— Robert F. Cervenka**
> Founder, Chairman of the Board and Chief
>   Technology Officer
> Phillips Plastics Corporation
> Hudson, Wisconsin

PREFACE

In the late 1990s we were deluged with world-changing hype generated by the dot.com wunderkind. Reverse auctions, e-procurement, e-marketplaces, consortia—there were hundreds, maybe even thousands, of ideas generated by software entrepreneurs. Much of it was focused on the supply space, and very little seemed to be vetted with knowledge or understanding of the intricacies and complexities of the real buying world. You were not "in" unless you were into the lingo of electronic ordering, desktop buying to empower the user, automatic approval routing, and cataloging. The e-markets/e-consortia mostly went belly up (although some still survive with changed offerings). ERP vendors came into the fray to duel with procurement software providers, and the raging debate was integrated suite versus best of breed—which is still a debate, but a much less strident one. e-Procurement tools were accused of hype, disappointment, and wasted money by 2001, while reverse auctions became "the darlings" during the economic retraction at that time.

The purpose of this book is to put the priorities in order and then to outline where and how new technology may optimize supply management with the goal of becoming more "on demand"—that is, on demand in the sense of making your entire supply chain more responsive to changing market conditions and customer requirements. The on demand here does not refer to a software sales model. The intent is to convey understanding through descriptions of real purchasing practice, not software "speak." Two of the three co-authors are long-time executives at Procter & Gamble, Bayer Corporation, and Bethlehem Steel and are now actively advising businesses. The third co-author is a writer with considerable experience in purchasing media.

Technology investments make sense when companies are organized according to the principles outlined in *Straight to the Bottom Line™: An Executive's Roadmap to World Class Supply Management*. First, organizations—be they Fortune 500 companies or local government agencies—must recognize the value of the supply chain in improving performance in costs, quality, efficiency, innovation, and elsewhere. Companies must be organized to tap the value of the supply chain, appoint the right leaders, and constantly train their professionals. Emphasis should be on strategic, not tactical activities. Business processes must be integrated so that engineers and researchers collaborate with buyers and marketers. Core suppliers must be valued as long-term partners. The right types of metrics need to be in place and then be measured.

Once the foundation is established for those principles, a careful review of technology opportunities can begin. This book begins with spend analysis because you must understand your spend before you can optimize it. We then analyze the tools that can improve strategic sourcing, which is the cornerstone of advanced supply management. The next two chapters discuss electronic go-to-market tools, starting with reverse auctions and requests for information/proposal/quotation (RFxs) and then moving into use of advanced mathematics tools in optimization systems. Following these chapters are discussions of supplier relationship management, purchase to payment, contract management, product life-cycle management, should costing, services procurement, governance, and on-demand tools.

Two in-depth case studies of on demand are also included. The first is a look at IBM, the first major company to begin an on-demand transformation. The second looks at the U.S. tool and die industry, with the intent to show how even the smallest of companies can overcome intense international pressure through the application of better business practices and new tools.

The last section examines the crucial implementation issues that cause many new tools to stumble or create delays—getting the money, master planning, adoption, training, and measurement.

The primary audience of this book is mid- and upper-level professionals in procurement and supply management, including contracting and supplier relationship management. Secondary audiences include finance professionals because of their role in legitimizing the financial impact of the initiatives; information technology professionals because they are the internal enablers and often the approvers of these initiatives; and professionals in technical and manufacturing disciplines because of their required involvement in many phases, particularly those outlined in the chapters about product life-cycle management and should costing.

It is the hope of the authors that *On Demand Supply Management: World Class Strategies, Practices, and Technology* will provide a framework of action that will make companies more competitive in the global marketplace.

ACKNOWLEDGMENTS

The authors thank the scores of supply managers and executives at companies and organizations, from large IBM to tiny Midwestern tool shops, who contributed thoughts and ideas to this book.

ABOUT THE AUTHORS

DOUGLAS A. SMOCK

Douglas A. Smock is Editorial Director of GlobalCPO.com and "How Smart People Buy," which are sources of procurement analysis and best-in-class practices. He also covers technical materials for *Design News Magazine*, which has a global circulation of more than 170,000 design engineers. Previously, he was Editor-in-Chief of *Purchasing* magazine, which received five national awards for editorial excellence from the American Society of Business Press Editors while Smock was chief editor. No other publication in the field had ever won even one of these awards. During his career, he also served as chief editor of *Plastics World*, associate publisher of *Modern Mold and Tooling* at McGraw-Hill, and staff writer for the *Pittsburgh Post-Gazette*. He has won or supervised staffs that earned three Jesse Neal awards—the most prized award in the business press. He is also co-author of the best-selling supply management book *Straight to the Bottom Line™: An Executive's Roadmap to World-Class Supply Management*. He is a member of the Society of Plastics Engineers. Doug can be reached at: dsmock@globalcpo.com.

ROBERT A. RUDZKI

Robert A. Rudzki is President of Greybeard Advisors LLC, a firm that assists enterprises improve their near-term financial performance and their long-term business viability (www.GreybeardAdvisors.com). He is also a director of a privacy and security software company, is an Advisory Board member of several companies, and is a frequent speaker at professional conferences and senior management summits. Previously, he was Senior Vice President and Chief Procurement Officer at Bayer Corporation, where he led a nationally recognized transformation effort. Prior to that, he was an executive at Bethlehem Steel Corporation, which he led to recognition from *Purchasing* magazine as a "Best Places to Work" and to a top-quartile ranking in a best practices survey of 160 global corporations. In the course of his career, he has held various executive management positions, which included finance, accounting, procurement and logistics, business development, and P&L responsibility. He is co-author of the best-selling supply management book *Straight to the Bottom Line™: An Executive's Roadmap to World Class Supply Management* and is also author of the business book *Beat the Odds: Avoid Corporate Death and Build a Resilient Enterprise*. Bob can be reached at: rudzki@greybeardadvisors.com.

STEPHEN C. ROGERS

Stephen C. Rogers is a Senior Consultant with The Cincinnati Consulting Consortium—30 former Procter & Gamble executives—concentrating on purchasing and supplier management. He is also the Program Director of The Conference Board's annual SRM Conference and an adjunct professor and member of the Board of Advisors to the Management Department at Xavier University in Cincinnati, Ohio. During his 30 years at P&G, he had functional roles in purchasing, manufacturing, and marketing, with both domestic and global responsibilities, including development and expansion of global sourcing efforts, redesign of the Folgers Coffee supply chain, and leadership of P&G's worldwide purchasing training system. He was awarded a career Sourcing Award, recognizing his role as P&G's "father" of strategic sourcing and in delivering in excess of $1 billion of hard savings during his time there. He has written several articles and spoken at a number of forums on supply-related topics, is on the advisory board of a software company, and is a member of several *Who's Who* compendiums. Steve can be reached at: armo@cinci.rr.com.

Web
Added
Value™

At J. Ross Publishing we are committed to providing today's professional with practical, hands-on tools that enhance the learning experience and give readers an opportunity to apply what they have learned. That is why we offer free ancillary materials available for download on this book and all participating Web Added Value™ publications. These online resources may include interactive versions of material that appears in the book or supplemental templates, worksheets, models, plans, case studies, proposals, spreadsheets, and assessment tools, among other things. Whenever you *see* the WAV™ symbol in any of our publications, it means bonus materials accompany the book and are available from the Web Added Value™ Download Resource Center at www.jrosspub.com.

Downloads for *On-Demand Supply Management: World Class Strategies, Practices, and Technology* include free articles from GlobalCPO.com describing cutting-edge procurement and supply management best practices based on exclusive interviews with executives at industry-leading organizations; and PowerPoint presentations that provide guidance on how to select the correct supply management technology and tools based on your buying philosophy or strategy and type of supplier relationships and how to use it to drive value.

Part I

GETTING STARTED

THE DEMAND- AND TECHNOLOGY-DRIVEN SUPPLY CHAIN

Evolve or die.

— **Michael Powell,** Chairman
U.S. Federal Communications Commission
(to broadcasters)

Companies tend to go through evolutionary phases on a variety of topics. Some companies keep things "close to the vest" and try to do it all themselves. These companies may be very secretive about new product ideas and new business processes in the belief that they, and only they, could have such innovative thoughts. This hubris often inevitably results in a decline of the organization—hubris becomes arrogance, which generates myopia regarding the external environment (including customer needs), which in turn generates complacency. As Aristotle once wrote, "He who the gods want to destroy, they will give 40 years of prosperity."

Conversely the most successful companies tend to view themselves as constantly needing to reinvent themselves because of the changing needs of the marketplace. In that context, they often look for the "Holy Grail"—that combination of strategies, philosophy, and tools which enables the organization to promptly respond to changing market conditions in a manner that is good for their customers and good for their stockholders.

These successful companies often think of themselves as being quarterbacks of diverse teams, which are focused on fulfilling the ever-changing needs and wants of customers. These diverse teams include cross-functional internal resources such as marketing, sales, procurement, finance, IT, engineering, R&D, and manufacturing, as well as the resources of external parties such as suppliers. In other words, in world-class companies, suppliers are viewed as being a part of the solution in meeting the ever-changing needs of customers. If suppliers are viewed as a challenge and as being the problem, this perspective will limit what can be achieved.

PROCUREMENT AND SUPPLY MANAGEMENT

A Defined Role and Focused Objective

To have maximum impact on an organization's success, procurement and supply management must have a properly defined role. This role cannot be merely price reduction because such a narrow role severely shortchanges the impact that supply management can have. Supply management in world-class companies has a role that encompasses all key drivers of return on invested capital (ROIC). Key ROIC drivers include:

- Revenue enhancement opportunities, such as faster cycle time from new product concept to delivery to the marketplace
- Cost reduction opportunities, which are defined in terms of total cost of ownership and applied to all areas of external spend without exception
- Working capital opportunities, such as payment terms and inventory programs
- Capital expenditure opportunities, such as asset recovery initiatives and best-in-class capital project work

ROIC

Why is a broad, top- and bottom-line role that focuses on key drivers of ROIC important? ROIC drives shareholder value and more fundamentally it can be a factor in whether a corporation will live or die. If ROIC *exceeds* the weighted average cost of capital, value is being added to the company. If ROIC is *less* than the cost of capital, the lifeblood of the company is draining away. Diminishing ROIC is an issue of interest to not only the finance organization in a company, which is expected to monitor things such as ROIC, but also to the shareholders, Wall Street analysts, and anyone who relies on the organization for long-term support. This last point includes employees and their dependents, who expect to

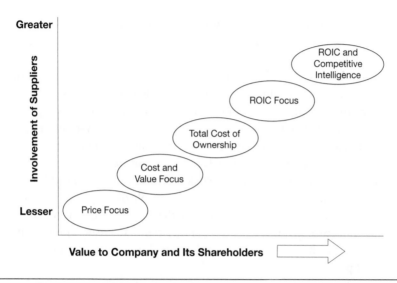

Figure 1.1. Do Not Leave Value on the Table.

have continued salaries and benefits and want pensions and retiree healthcare benefits as well. Therefore the ROIC of a company is not a theoretical concept—it is of real interest to many constituents.

Inclusive Supply Management Strategy

Companies that are stuck in a "price-focused" purchasing world are leaving significant value on the table (Figure 1.1). Only a role and an objective focusing on the drivers of top- and bottom-line growth can maximize shareholder value.

The objective requires an inclusive supply management strategy that actively involves key suppliers as partners in meeting the needs of the marketplace. In a rapidly changing world, an inclusive supply management strategy also requires not only the right role and objectives and the right strategy or approach, but also the right technology and tools that can speed the internal and external understanding and collaboration that are necessary for joint success. Done well, the right technology and tools can be features that distinguish a company from its competition—something all constituents of the company will value.

THE RIGHT FOUNDATION

Before continuing with an overview and debate of technology, the right foundation for success must be in place. Sustainable supply management success has several fundamental building blocks (Figure 1.2):

- First ensure that there is executive commitment to the strategic integration of supply management into the highest levels of corporate thinking, strategy, and operations.
- Establish a few of the right objectives, which are shared across the organization and which drive incentives and consequences.
- Pick the right leader—an individual who has the right skills and is an enabler of bright people—to implement twenty-first century processes, particularly strategic sourcing and supplier partnering. This leader in turn creates a leadership culture at all levels of the organization. He/she selects a structure that works in the culture of the organization and also ensures that the role of supply management includes cross-functional teaming with finance, technical functions, manufacturing, logistics, and other disciplines to create a process that "speaks with one voice" to suppliers. He/she embraces and embeds best practices.
- Last, but definitely not least, select and invest in the right technology and tools to support and enable all of the other building blocks.

Having all of these elements in place does two things:

- Creates a critical mass of momentum that can endure the inevitable ebbs and flows of corporate politics and organizational pendulum swings
- Provides the necessary strategic context for evaluating and selecting the right technology and tools

EVALUATION AND SELECTION OF TECHNOLOGY

In world-class companies, the process of evaluating and selecting the right technology and tools to support supply chain objectives is a collaborative process that involves supply chain leadership, finance, IT, and internal customers (e.g., plant operations). The evaluation should also ensure that the right strategic questions are asked. For example, a good, very relevant question is "Will the candidate technology, tools, and vendor(s) allow our supply chain organization to achieve best-of-breed performance and to deliver its full ROIC potential?" Questions about integration with existing ERP systems are relevant secondary questions, but they should never cause an organization to stop pursuing a best-of-breed enabler of the organization's aggressive supply chain objectives.

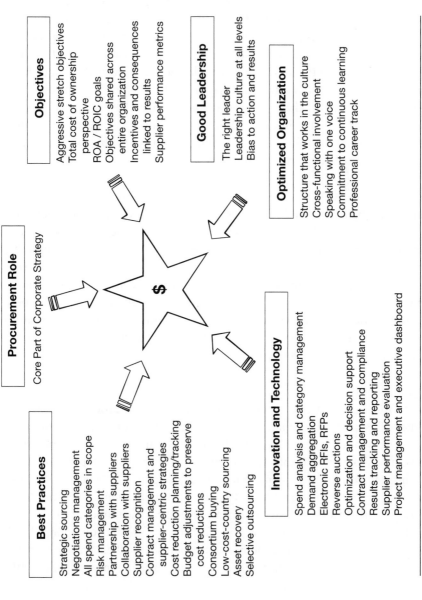

Procurement Role

Core Part of Corporate Strategy

Objectives

Aggressive stretch objectives
Total cost of ownership
  perspective
ROA / ROIC goals
Objectives shared across
  entire organization
Incentives and consequences
  linked to results
Supplier performance metrics

Good Leadership

The right leader
Leadership culture at all levels
Bias to action and results

Optimized Organization

Structure that works in the culture
Cross-functional involvement
Speaking with one voice
Commitment to continuous learning
Professional career track

Best Practices

Strategic sourcing
Negotiations management
All spend categories in scope
Risk management
Partnership with suppliers
Collaboration with suppliers
Supplier recognition
Contract management and
  supplier-centric strategies
Cost reduction planning/tracking
Budget adjustments to preserve
  cost reductions
Consortium buying
Low-cost-country sourcing
Asset recovery
Selective outsourcing

Innovation and Technology

Spend analysis and category management
Demand aggregation
Electronic RFIs, RFPs
Reverse auctions
Optimization and decision support
Contract management and compliance
Results tracking and reporting
Supplier performance evaluation
Project management and executive dashboard

Figure 1.2. Transformation Framework. (Source: From *Straight to the Bottom Line™: An Executive's Roadmap to World Class Supply Management.*)

Making the Technology Decision

Sometimes companies learn the hard way that the supply management technology decision should not be relegated to an overburdened information technology (IT) organization. IT has a very important role to play in the technology evaluation for a demand- and technology-driven supply chain. However, putting IT in the position of making the decision invites a decision that favors the unique functional objectives of IT—objectives that may be vastly different from the corporate imperative for the supply chain transformation to achieve best-of-breed improvements of the corporate top line and bottom line. Ultimately supply management and IT must engage in productive debate and understand the best way to support and achieve overarching corporate objectives.

Pitfalls

A common pitfall in the technology debate is to fail to distinguish between the strategic roles and activities and the transactional/tactical roles and activities. This distinction is important in the technology debate because different approaches may be necessary to optimize each role. For example, the strategic activities in support of corporate supply management objectives can be depicted as a continuum of interrelated capabilities (Figure 1.3). In recent years, several vendors have been successful in integrating these pieces into a closed-loop system offering, meaning the pieces "talk" to each other, which provides increased effectiveness and greater efficiency across the entire tool set.

Using the Tools

How the tools are used can vary greatly, depending on the procurement strategy and the philosophy of the organization regarding the role of suppliers. For example, the reverse auction tool has natural limitations and can be highly counterproductive in a situation that calls for a partnership approach to supplier selection and supplier relationship management (see Chapter 4, *Going to Market—Electronic Supplier Engagements,* and Chapter 5, *Optimization—Going to Market with Complexity*). Nevertheless, some companies have tried to force all, or virtually all, sourcing efforts through a price-focused reverse auction approach—at considerable risk of damaging the broader objectives of their corporation and their internal clients. "Different tools for different rules" definitely applies to the world of supply management.

Readiness

Table 1.1 provides a quick "litmus test" for an organization. Is the organization ready to partner with its suppliers? If so, is it ready to obtain maximum value from

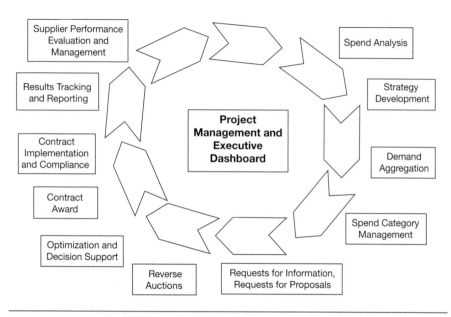

Figure 1.3. Integrated Supply Management Tools. (Source: From *Straight to the Bottom Line™: An Executive's Roadmap to World Class Supply Management*.)

its supply chain, both top line and bottom line? (*Note:* For a more complete review of the subject of partnering with suppliers and the benefits it provides, read *Straight to the Bottom Line: An Executive's Roadmap to World Class Supply Management* by Robert A. Rudzki, Douglas Smock, Michael Katzorke, and Shelley Stewart, Jr.)

After the Technology Decision

Too many protagonists in the technology debate believe that the battle is won (or lost) when the technology decision is finally made and the vendor has been selected. Certainly a major focus of this book is to provide an understanding of the issues and opportunities, to guide navigating the organizational challenges, and to ultimately lead to making sound decisions that facilitate corporate objectives. However, making a sound decision is not the final milestone. Successful *adoption* is the final report card. Sometimes companies make an absolutely sound technology decision, given their corporate supply management objectives, but then fail during adoption (see Chapter 18, *Adoption—The Real Measure of Success*). Suffice it to say that this failure is primarily a leadership issue. Therefore speed and thoroughness of technology adoption within an organization (and, as appropriate, with relevant parts of the supply base) will require the personal involvement of management.

Table 1.1. Are You Ready to Partner with Your Suppliers?

A Company Is Probably Not Ready If It ...	A Company May Be Ready If It ...
Believes that suppliers have nothing to offer beyond a rock-bottom price	Believes suppliers have expertise that can supplement in-house talent
Believes that "churning" the supply base for annual price cuts is the best way to manage suppliers	Believes there is greater value in structuring long-term relationships with shared objectives
Has a culture in which ideas must be "invented here" to have credibility	Has a culture that actively searches for the best ideas, regardless of who contributes them
Has a culture that insists on controlling all aspects of its supply chain activities	Has a culture that is comfortable with delegating to qualified parties
Views suppliers as part of the problem	View suppliers as part of the solution
Believes in holding information "close to the vest"	Is willing to communicate plans to key suppliers so that they can provide better service
Believes that only suppliers should have objectives	Believes that to maximize value from a key relationship, both customer and supplier should have objectives

Source: Greybeard Advisors LLC. © 2006. All rights reserved.

CLOSING THOUGHTS—TECHNOLOGY AND COMPETITIVE ADVANTAGE

The following chapters will examine how incorporating the use of supply management technology into advanced sourcing practices can lead to significant competitive advantage through the application of strategic electronic technologies, on-demand processes, improved supplier management, continuous sourcing, and collaboration with internal stakeholders and the external supply base. The potential role of several new software offerings as well as some old standbys will be described. Also examined will be the investment decision (including make or buy) and implementation challenges that occur within an organization, which typically result in victory or disappointment for a technology effort.

This book has free material available for download from the Web Added Value™ resource center at *www.jrosspub.com*

Part II

THE BASICS PLUS

SPEND ANALYSIS— START YOUR ENGINES

Prior to the spend analysis tool, we didn't even realize we had an opportunity. We didn't even know we had million dollar spends in some categories.

> — **James M. Cebula**
> Director of Global Purchasing and Travel
> Kennametal, Inc.

The journey to advanced sourcing begins with an understanding of what a company spends. For supply management professionals, spend data is the fuel that runs the sourcing engines. Spend information is the critical keystone in a sourcing foundation. A simple vision of spend analysis is that all of a corporation's purchases can be consolidated into large "pools" of like materials such as personal computers, office supplies, travel, and temporary labor. Then total spend can be leveraged and managed through the use of corporate contracts, and significant cost reductions can be achieved by using greater volume aggregation in supplier negotiations. Development of systems to enforce compliance with contracts goes hand-in-hand with contract management—despite the best intentions of engineers who favor tried-and-true suppliers or administrative assistants who find a "better deal" somewhere else.

Good purchasing managers in the twentieth century *thought* they understood their corporate spend. Yet extremely few were even remotely close. A typical process industry firm would consolidate major "direct" buys such as energy or styrene in the hands of a few purchasing experts (usually not located within the purchasing department), but would make no such effort for the myriad of "indirect" purchases, which often accounted for at least a third of total expenditures. Spend, of course, is significantly more difficult to mine in a large, complex company than in a very small one. A goal to manage spend better—whether at a tiny company or at a huge one—must begin with a desire to define the total purchases and then to do something about it. This is a simple statement, but until recent years it was a goal of only a very few companies of any size.

Until the 1990s, few purchasing managers at big companies had even elemental access to good information sources such as enterprise accounts payable data. However, in the 1990s widespread use of enterprise resource planning (ERP) systems created the first meaningful tool to gather data and study spend. Since 2000, specialized spend analysis tools have emerged, and the quality of these specialized spend analysis tools has subsequently grown by orders of magnitude almost annually. Today best-in-class organizations not only understand 95 to 99% of their spend, but they also update data frequently (at least monthly), can integrate new companies or groups quickly, and use cost-effective solutions. *How* the data is managed—or where the "rubber hits the road" in modern sourcing approaches—is the subject of subsequent chapters.

Spend analysis is a mandate for all organizations that spend money. The idea applies equally to Fortune 100 companies, tiny companies, the U.S. government, a town, and all of the organizations in the town. Once spend is understood, it can be managed. Then management of spend can be optimized. Gaining an understanding of spend is the first step in the development of meaningful sourcing strategies and supplier management (see Table 2.2).

THE KENNAMETAL, INC. EXPERIENCE

Consider the experience of Latrobe, PA-based Kennametal, Inc., the second largest supplier of metal cutting tools and tooling systems in the world. The Kennametal story is interesting because it shows that a combination of common sense, a lot of moxie, and some money can achieve dramatic results.

In 2001 management consultants visited the CEO of Kennametal and urged adoption of strategic sourcing, which could save the corporation at least 5%. (*Note:* High-level consultant presentations on sourcing are made to board of directors-level personnel—not chief procurement officers, who at times refer to these consultants as "the 5 percenters.") The CEO went to the CAO (chief administrative officer), informed him of the conversation, and asked: "Are you up to the 5% challenge?" The CAO responded positively, knowing that James M. Cebula, his CPO (chief purchasing officer), had some information technology background, a positive attitude, strong purchasing skills, and a lot of brainpower. Additionally the best-possible motivational tool was already in place—a CEO mandate to achieve results. At that time the purchasing organization's knowledge of spend was not great. Cebula commented: "We thought we understood it, but typically we only understood about half of it."[1]

The Company

Kennametal is a $2.3-billion company (fiscal year 2006), which is organized into global business units: Metalworking Solutions and Service and Advanced Materials Solutions. Primary purchases include tungsten, tantalum, titanium, cobalt, steel bars, steel forgings, and a wide variety of products and services that are not directly used in the manufacturing process, ranging from telecommunications services to travel services.

The Investigation

Investigation of the company's supply base by Cebula began with a review of all purchased products and services on the SAP system, which had been installed in 1996 as an ERP system. In 2005, the system was used by 150 company locations and had 4800 system users. There were 48,000 suppliers in the system, and 48,000 SAP documents were printed daily. About 8000 batch jobs were run daily.

Large companies with highly decentralized environments often have a large multitude of operating backbones that communicate poorly—if it all. However, Kennametal, by having a single ERP system, had a definite advantage. The spend team was able to capture spend on SAP quickly. The rest was elusive. According to Cebula, "We had a very difficult time finding non-purchase order spend. The CAO asked me four different times: 'What do we spend?' I didn't really have a very good answer."

Cebula began to look for outside help. A search of technology offerings resulted in the selection of Tigris Corporation (now part of Verticalnet), a privately owned, New York-based firm, which specialized in providing spend analysis solutions using a combination of strategic sourcing process expertise and cost-effective technologies—ideal for a company such as Kennametal that was dabbling in the area for the first time. The Tigris approach began with acquiring data extracts (or "flat files") from all relevant Kennametal processes, SAP being the largest and easiest to access. (*Note:* Flat files are text files stored in a computer. Flat files can be accessed through any text file editor such as Notepad and can be easily retrieved through automated systems.)

The next step was significantly more difficult. With the help of reports from the Tigris tool, the team took the data and normalized it. Normalization of the suppliers was not particularly difficult, but the categorization of spend was. "We had some key decisions that we had to make in order to get the data categorized," recalls Cebula. "One of the problems we discovered was that our accounts payable spend really had no line-item detail. But we were able to put a map between our general ledger account and SAP, which had a required field for every purchase order called 'material group.' As a result of that, all of our AP spend had a category. That took us from 40 to 80%."

For the final 20%—the onerous "last mile" of spend analysis—Cebula put his best people on a task force and the launch of a data "CSI"—a business "crime scene" investigation, which is the data management equivalent of the popular television show. The task force used a tool from Tigris that targeted uncategorized spend.

Product Codes

A service often used to normalize product codes is the United Nations Standard Products and Services Code (UNSPSC), which is a member-owned global initiative to establish product codes (Table 2.1). Current .pdf versions of the code and audit can be downloaded at no cost at www.unspsc.org. (*Note:* According to Cebula, the UNSPSC did not help much at Kennametal because the code only covered half of his product categories.)

Various efforts are underway to develop more industry-specific granularity in the global, multilanguage coding system. The Uniform Code Council (UCC), the code manager of the UNSPSC, and the American Petroleum Institute (API) are jointly developing voluntary global classification standards for the oil and natural gas industry. IDEA, an electronic commerce service provider jointly owned by the National Electrical Manufacturers Association (NEMA) and the National Association of Electrical Distributors (NAED), is working with the UCC, which marks the first time that the electrical industry has joined forces to develop a single global standard for classification.

The Classification System

Cebula used an alternate classification system and was able to achieve 95% normalization. "We didn't let 'perfect' stand in the way of 'very good,'" he commented. The Tigris tool at that time was state of the art, but it did not meet all of his requirements. "Once a quarter, we would get a report, but we had very little capability to drill into line-item detail," he said. Cebula describes how Tigris upgraded its tool by adding an online analysis component provided by its partner, Databeacon. "It was just a summary. Once we got the flavor of what we were missing we were able to take the next step, which was a hosted Internet-based tool.

Table 2.1. UNSPSC FAQ

What is the UNSPSC?

Developed by the United Nations Development Program and Dun & Bradstreet Corporation (D&B) in 1998, the United Nations Standard Products and Services Code (UNSPSC) is a hierarchical convention that is used to classify products and services.

What is the hierarchical structure?

The structure is shown below, with IT products used as an example:

Segment	43	IT broadcasting and telecommunications communications devices and accessories
Family	20	Components for IT or broadcasting or telecommunications computer equipment and accessories
Class	15	Computers, computer accessories
Commodity	01	Computer switch boxes, docking stations
Business Function	14	Retail

How are changes made to the code structure?

Any member can request an addition, deletion, or other change. Requests are posted on the group's website and are voted on by individuals (senior technical advisers), who are members who have agreed to assume this role.

What is the cost?

Membership is $250 per year. .pdf versions of the code can be downloaded at no cost. Versions of the code in Excel format are $50.

Source: Adapted from The United Nations Standard Products and Services Code (UNSPSC). Available at: www.unspsc.org.

That gave us the ability to drill down on demand, not only on the summary, but also on the line-item detail. That Databeacon tool was really a spreadsheet on steroids." According to Cebula another advantage was that the Databeacon tool had a very low cost from a licensing standpoint.

In 2005 Kennametal moved to a third-generation tool, a software package known as Cognos Supply Chain Analytics that runs on Kennametal's own servers. The big benefit is that Kennametal can perform all of the maintenance on the database internally. "Whereas we were getting 95% categorization every quarter, now we are getting 98% every month," said Cebula, "because it's obviously easier for our people to get exceptions into categories." Cognos Supply Chain Analytics is significantly faster than the previous application, in part because it does not go through the Internet. Integration of the Cognos tool into spend feeds was not a problem. Kennametal did the mapping internally.

The Results

To put "icing on the cake," the top sales officer at Kennametal saw the efficiency of the system for purchased goods and services and wanted the same capability on the sales side. The Cognos tool allows salesmen to pinpoint where they could best target potential customers based on data in the system. "They're using the same application in a customer-facing role," says Cebula. "Whereas we have a dashboard of global spend data, the strategic sales vice president has a dashboard of global sales data."

Kennametal is best in class in spend analysis. Yet James Cebula has one additional item on his wish list—and he is not alone. He would like to have the capability to integrate spend data from new acquisitions into the spend analysis cube more quickly. Currently integration of spend data from new acquisitions into the spend analysis cube takes 2 to 3 months. When referring to recent acquisitions by Kennametal, Cebula said: "Once (we onboarded data), we immediately identified millions of dollars in savings just by transferring spend at the acquisitions into Kennametal corporate contracts."

SPEND VISIBILITY

Benefits

Software allows spend to be analyzed by category, dollar value, number of suppliers, value to the company's bottom line, risk, or other factors. Sourcing strategies can be targeted based on priorities collectively developed by senior management. Spend visibility also allows supply managers to better enforce negotiating contracts. Identification of savings opportunities is an obvious benefit of spend visibility. Another more-recent benefit is improved compliance with financial and regulatory reporting requirements such as the Sarbanes-Oxley Act, through creation of a thorough, auditable record of all corporate spending. *Important:* Complete spend analysis is no longer just a best practice—it is a mandatory practice.

Companies that undertake spend analysis often discover that different business units or plants are buying the same products at a wide variety of prices. Good managers quickly convert all purchases to the lowest-price contract and then negotiate a new contract that leverages the higher scale. Quick rewards achieved through targeting of such low-hanging fruit have even fueled some mergers such as the combinations of Dow-Union Carbide and Compaq/Hewlett-Packard (HP). (*Comment:* Failure to quickly achieve promised synergies in purchasing, manufacturing, and other operations can lead to heavy pressure on the CEOs who led the charge such as Carly Fiorina at HP, who could not produce promised shareholder returns or profits.)

Limitations

Having described some benefits, there are enormous barriers to spend visibility in large, complex organizations—often bafflingly and sometimes seemingly insurmountable. For example, the CPO of one Fortune 1000 company with best-in-class supply management practices could not discover some $2 billion in spend after a thorough internal spend analysis, which was followed by a best-in-breed search by an outside vendor.

Data is often coded strictly for financial reporting or internal engineering classification (see Chapter 9, *PLM—Everyone Gets Together*). Data can be dispersed across an "alphabet soup" of unit-specific legacy systems that have been deployed over a period of years. Adequate classification systems may never have been entered in an existing ERP system, even though appropriate fields existed, e.g., as in the Kennametal case, when early systems often did not provide data frequently enough. *Important:* The early decisions made about how to approach spend visibility may be the most important decisions made in an organization's supply transformation. The amount of effort put into the process, the support received, the amount spent, the approach chosen, and who is hired to help can be make-or-break events.

RECOMMENDATIONS FOR SUCCESS

The following recommendations are based on the collective experience of the authors:

- Have an appropriate corporate-level officer on board as a first step.
- Think big. Adopt a scalable approach that can get the company to where it is desired to eventually be. Band-Aid fixes to existing inadequate approaches will leave a company "short" of its global competition.
- Develop a repeatable solution. In a "D-day approach," an army of outside experts spends months developing a spend view that is outstanding, but only for a specific moment in time. A company needs a solution that constantly updates data and quickly analyzes spend in acquisitions.
- Involve all departments that can play a role, including engineering and manufacturing.

- Ask the CEO to appoint executive sponsors to lead and monitor progress on specific parts of the project.
- Extract data from all accounting and payment systems across the company—such as from SAP, Oracle, and Ariba, Inc. software solutions; purchasing cards; MRO (maintenance, repair, and operations) systems; engineering data management systems; human resources data streams; electronic fund transfers; travel expense data systems, electronic procurement systems; and financial transaction systems.
- Select a comprehensive solution. Some approaches focus on internal accounting systems or on ERP data warehouses.

Solution Selection

When selecting a solution, an issue to consider is the approach used to classify data. Some CIOs and CPOs opt for manual systems, which is not a good idea. Manual systems are very expensive, are extremely time-consuming (often for high-level, strategic people), can lead to a million debates that bear little fruit, can create easy targets for opposition from within the organization, and are quickly outdated. Even with easy look-up tables, mistakes are numerous. Highly complex systems such as UNSPSC also have their own set of problems (e.g., as in the experience at Kennametal). The huge amount of spend that ends up classified as "miscellaneous" is evidence of the problems that are inherent in such systems.[2]

The authors recommend a combination of three approaches that complement the manual processes already in place, such as hierarchies for direct materials already developed through engineering data management initiatives:

Step 1. A good first step is the application of rules-based engines that mine general ledger accounts by using common elements of information to group records by supplier grouping and product type. Early efforts to use rules-based engines to classify spend performed well in detecting duplicates, but did not deliver great results, except for office supplies and other indirect categories, which do not require a high degree of granularity and can be easily grouped. Because spend data embedded in various systems is very abbreviated, rules-based engines that work for one data set may not work for another. Rules-based engines fail to perform well when applied to multiple languages at the same time.

Step 2. Add the application of automated classification technology (known as "machine learning" by some technology vendors). The most-advanced system uses artificial intelligence (AI) in which algorithms build models that interpret item descriptions and assign models.

General Electric (supplied by Zycus, Inc.) embeds the technology in its e-procurement system. As soon as a requisition is placed, the AI software proposes an eight-digit code. The person making the requisition can accept or reject the proposed code. A classification algorithm assigns a code in less than 5 seconds. The GE application runs on a shared Oracle system behind a firewall and bolts on to the company's spend data warehouse. The software is plug-and-play on SAP's newer Netweaver platform.

Step 3. An additional step to maximum spend visibility is matching data against content-rich, third-party sources such as supplier catalogs. Intelligent Web spiders can search these sources for additional content information that can help match a company's unclassified product items by looking for like words or descriptions.

Comment: The authors make no recommendations on specific suppliers of spend technology. However, looking beyond the specific tools to long-term business factors is important. The amount of turnover in the technology field is dizzying. Ensure that the company selected is likely to be in business in 5 years. Of course, always keep in mind that the point of spend analysis is strategic spend management that leads to cost reduction, improved quality, improved cash flow, and other benefits (Table 2.2).

Spend Knowledge

Negotiating leverage. Spend knowledge gives buyers significant negotiating leverage at the bargaining table. In the twentieth century, invariably the sales person came to the table with the best knowledge of the customer's spend. The sales person knew how much each division bought and what price was paid. Typically the buyer only knew the purchase history of his/her department or division.

Payment terms. Knowledge of spend creates knowledge of enterprise-wide payment terms with suppliers. Needed information is available to plan a logical, practical shift in payment terms (e.g., if a CEO launches a new push on cash flow).

Supplier scorecard. Supplier scorecarding is an important tool, which is significantly enhanced with spend tools. Supplier scorecarding allows focus to be on the most important suppliers. Then carefully selected metrics can be applied to achieve the desired results. (For example, Kennametal uses four different categories to rate suppliers: product quality is rated at 35%; on-time delivery is rated at 30%; total cost management is weighted at 25%; and payment terms are weighted at 10%. Within total cost management, price is one of the 11 categories evaluated.)

Table 2.2. Benefits of Spend Visibility

Spend analysis builds a framework for sourcing strategy that creates significant savings opportunities, including:

- Consolidates spend across the enterprise where there are no contracts in place—In best-of-breed companies the view of spend opportunities keeps expanding: production materials—travel—consulting services—legal services—marketing services, etc.
- Builds leverage across the enterprise for contracts already in place
- Identifies and stops "maverick" spending
- Consolidates business with the best suppliers, one of the most important opportunities in moving to an on-demand supply chain
- Identifies and prioritizes opportunities to consolidate product purchases through simplifying and making common (where appropriate) specifications for products, ranging from bottled water and boxes to polymer compounds and fasteners

Source: From globalcpo.com. With permission. Available at: www.globalcpo.com.

CLOSING THOUGHTS ABOUT SPEND ANALYSIS

The Kennametal operation has achieved cost reductions of about $16 million per year since taking the first steps toward spend analysis. Until that time, cost reductions had been more modest—about $5 to $6 million per year. Most of the savings have been generated by a dramatic move to corporate contracts and a focus on key suppliers. Cebula's benchmark is to achieve at least 85% of spend in a given category with the top five suppliers.[3] Other corporations have even more aggressive goals, e.g., 95% with two suppliers, with one being in a *dominant* position and another being an *opportunity* position. Business units want some control of their spend, often for very legitimate geographical and other reasons.

Cebula's approach is real world—it deals with a reality that many centralized purchasers face. He said, "When we began this process, we had in the area of 25 to 30 corporate contracts. By 2005, we had 85. Prior to the spend analysis tool, we didn't even realize we had an opportunity. We didn't even know we had million dollar spends in some categories."

The other sharp edge of the spend analysis "sword" is compliance. "We measure compliance to contracts and we challenge business units when we see noncompliance," said Cebula. "Why are you spending $24 for an item at OfficeMax when you could buy it under the corporate contract for $18 at Staples?" After instances of noncompliance such as this are called out to buyers once or twice, those individuals who had been buying based on convenience become significantly more focused on cost. Cebula's approach is again real world. Compliance at

Kennametal is not mandatory, except for software and personal computers. Kennametal seeks 85% compliance with other contracts. "We chose the 85% level because the last 15% can be malicious compliance." In other words, you can shoot yourself in the foot with the last 15%. "If there's an opportunity to buy something at a better price, and it's a loss leader, then we want to take advantage of that."

Cebula's spend journey began in the best possible way—with a CEO mandate. In July 2005, CEO Markos I. Tambakeras announced that Kennametal had earned a record $3.25 per share in the fiscal year that ended June 30. Net income was $119 million versus $74 million in the previous fiscal year, up 62%. He commented, "Despite difficult headwinds from rising raw material prices, Kennametal's team worked hard to generate EPS (earnings per share) growth of over 50% for the year, on top of 52% growth in the previous fiscal year."

That is one the best pats on the back a procurement pro can get.

UNDERSTANDING UNCLE SAM'S SPEND

One of the most mind-boggling examples of poor spend control is the U.S. government, which in 2004–2005 was assembling a massive spend database expected to channel billions of dollars of annual spend. This system is known as the Federal Procurement Data System—Next Generation. It is just one system within the Federal eGov Integrated Acquisition Environment (IAE) initiative. IAE is part of a program authorized in 2001 by President George W. Bush to move the U.S. government toward a more efficient electronic government. President Bush selected 24 projects. The IAE fits into the Internal Efficiency and Effectiveness portfolio.

According to a report prepared by J. Lisa Romney, who coordinated electronic business for Defense Procurement and Acquisition Policy, the program has three goals:

- To create a simpler, common, integrated business process for buyers and sellers that promotes competition, transparency and integrity
- To increase data sharing to enable better business performance decisions in procurement, logistics, payment, and performance assessment
- To take a unified approach to obtaining modern tools to leverage investment costs for business-related processes

"The IAE initiative is a portfolio of programs that support the contracting processes in the federal government, providing authoritative sources of data and common vendor engagement points," Romney said.[4] Federal buyers will use shared systems, including eMarketplace.

The Government Accounting Office (GAO) has issued several reports about the benefits of using a more strategic approach to procurement and spend analysis at the DOD. The Department of Defense (DOD) is a leader in the efforts to unify government buying. The DOD completed its migration of historical spend data to the next generation data system in December 2005. DOD has already begun the process of establishing machine-to-machine reporting to the new system.

UNDERSTANDING UNCLE SAM'S SPEND (CONTINUED)

More critical examination is now under way for opportunities in civilian spending at the urging of the U.S. Comptroller General. The targeted spend at five key federal agencies was $37.2 billion in 2003—Veterans Affairs, Department of Health and Human Services, the Department of Agriculture, the Department of Justice, and the Department of Transportation.

Three agencies have taken preliminary steps toward spend analysis. Veterans Affairs (VA) conducted an automated spend analysis of pharmaceutical procurement and improved spending practices to save $394 million in 2003. The GAO report points out that savings reports have not been audited, nor is any information available on the practices, such as net costing used to determine the savings. Teams at the VA are studying opportunities for national contracting of big-ticket equipment items that could save as much as $82 million per year. Last year the Department of Health and Human Services (DHHS) awarded contracts for office and custodial supplies that were based on spend analysis to three vendors. The Department of Agriculture also awarded an office supplies contract to one vendor. The Departments of Justice and Transportation have not yet begun to make any efforts in spend analysis (at the time of a GAO report to Congress in 2004).

LESSONS LEARNED

- Understanding spend is the first step toward achieving the benefits of lean sourcing that enable an on-demand supply chain and savings that can reach 5 to 10% of total spend.
- Because of the enormous internal obstacles that face a comprehensive spend study, having an executive mandate is a prerequisite.
- Having an auditable record of spend is mandated by financial reporting requirements.
- Increasingly capable automated tools improve the opportunities for a successful and repeatable spend analysis.

Web Added Value™

This book has free material available for download from the Web Added Value™ resource center at *www.jrosspub.com*

SOURCING STRATEGY—THE BRAINS BEHIND THE GAME

A leader needs enough understanding to fashion an intelligent strategy.
— **John P. Kotter**
Professor, leadership expert, author
Harvard University

The search for value and cost reduction from suppliers is never-ending, in part because the definition of value continually evolves over time as customer expectations rise (or sometimes even fall—how many times do we yearn for an old substantial version that morphed into a disposable?), but also because the markets, companies, and commercial circumstances surrounding that search for value constantly change. The outcome of a company's sourcing intervention factors into the dynamic market ebb and flow—to create an environment in which others react and the contrary forces of competition and collaboration sometimes redefine the value that suppliers offer.

The race in search of value and cost reduction is not a sprint, but rather an endless marathon. The same supply management leader who received corporate accolades for leveraging savings from spend analysis (see Chapter 2, *Spend Analysis—Start Your Engines*) quickly begins to hear the CEO's and CFO's relentless question, "What have the suppliers (read: *and you*) done for me lately?" Glory is replaced by even greater challenges. Low-hanging fruit is now gone, yet the expectations of senior management are that the spend management harvest has become almost an annual given. "How come you did so much better last year? Where will the next level of savings come from? Is there anything besides savings that suppliers can do for us? What about innovation or quality or quick response to changing customer expectations?"

Seasoned supply professionals who read this book will certainly recognize this attitude shift, which is driven by the dynamic nature of the competitive market game. As they read the chapters, they will also recognize that technology tools—and their application to a retuned supply base in search of "on-demand" value—revolve around applying electronic and Internet-based tools to the classic strategic sourcing process on various "spend pools" or categories. *Important:* The process, not the electronic tool (e-tool), is the key to ongoing value mining. Strategic sourcing today is almost blasé. Companies know about strategic sourcing and have multistep processes to accomplish it. (Doesn't everyone?) The number of steps can range from 5 to 15. Even if a company does not do strategic sourcing well, the hit to self-respect when admitting that this is the case is often just too hard to accept.

A. T. Kearney Procurement Solutions' (ATK) seven-step icon, which is the classic strategic sourcing process, is one of the basic models upon which the avalanche of electronic sourcing (e-sourcing) and procurement tools rests (Figure 3.1). Yet closer inspection of the sourcing process makes the distinction between strategic sourcing and sourcing strategy clear. The difference is much more than just a play on words. Exploring this difference and the role of technology and the Internet in that difference is the focus of this chapter.

STRATEGIC SOURCING VERSUS SOURCING STRATEGY

Regardless of the number of steps in a company's sourcing process (almost every company has its own tailored version), strategic sourcing is an ongoing effort to accomplish three things:

- To understand—the analysis of markets, suppliers, internal capabilities, needs, competitors, and industries
- To decide—the tactical "go-to-market" part, which is often confused with strategy—determination of which tool to use, e.g., request for proposals (RFPs), auctions, online negotiations, face-to-face interaction (*Decide* includes the supplier selection decision, the natural outcome of going to market that matches supplier capabilities to company needs.)
- To manage—perhaps the toughest to accomplish in a world in which the rules are not constant and the targets and scoring systems are changing as the customer expectations of value and the competition's actions shift

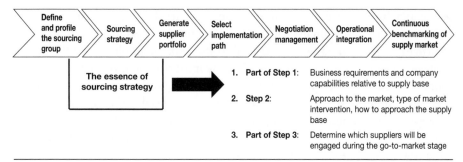

Figure 3.1. A.T. Kearney Strategic Sourcing Process.

Contracts, performance measurement, supply chain response, relationship management, and change management—tasks which are many and either complex or simple depending on the spend category and its relevance to the company's value equation—are the areas in which getting value to the bottom line really happens, but only if preceded by solid understanding and decision-making capability.

How technology can create advantage and value for understanding, deciding, and managing will be explored in this book, but for now sourcing strategy is the main concern and it falls in the *understand* part of the process.

Understanding Leads to Strategy

Using the ATK process in Figure 3.1 as a model, sourcing strategy is part of Step 2. Yet the strategy process is actually about thoroughly *understanding* what is needed, the goals for what is to be received from the supply base, and what the company is capable of supporting with its suppliers (part of Step 1); *analyzing* the potential suppliers, their industry, the power and collaborative dynamics in that industry between suppliers and buyers, and the classic supply/demand, macroeconomic and global implications—trade regulations, wars, protectionism, currency, etc. (Step 2); and *deciding* how to approach the market and which suppliers will make up the "market" that is approached (part of Step 3).

This process is called the skill of "linking" at Procter & Gamble (P&G), and it is the underlying purpose of strong supply management. In this section of the process the overarching approach to the supply market is set, and if done well, it will be set for 2 to 4 years into the future and have multiple go-to-market engagements across changing market conditions, with periodic renewals along the way.

Technology and Standard Processes

The question now becomes where does technology fit into the thinking/linking part of the process? Sourcing strategy occurs *before* suppliers are solicited and technology linkages are utilized, does it not? In part this is quite true. However, technology has created analytical tools and electronic access to treasure troves of information that if used well are critical to the *understand* phase and the *overall* strategic sourcing process. *Important:* Because most companies have tailored their sourcing process to their own culture, capabilities, and the skills of their people, very few rote sourcing strategy e-tools exist. Experienced sourcing organizations have evolved to a point that changing their process to an off-the-shelf e-tool version will simply require too much work in process retraining and vocabulary "brainwashing" to be efficiently deployed.

If a company has no common process or is just beginning to create a process, an opportunity for software to set the process exists, but to set a process correctly, sourcing consulting is a likely option. However, consulting does not come cheap, especially top-quality consulting. Consulting includes the consultant's own process, e.g., the ATK "seven stepper," the Accenture "five stepper," etc. Some processes have accompanying e-tools such as the ATK relationship with software leader UGS Corporation (a provider of product life-cycle management software and services that acquired the ATK eBreviate tools), but a "universal" software tool has not driven this process in most companies.

Several software suites do provide "generic" strategy assistance, sometimes using the classic Kraljic Grid 2 × 2 matrix developed by McKinsey & Company in 1983, which contrasts the strategic business impact on one axis and the complexity/risk on the other to suggest basic strategy choices such as leverage (competition), strategic (alliances), bottleneck (closely manage risks), and noncritical (automate or outsource) (Figure 3.2). Other software can provide some strategy direction. For example, the Verticalnet suite offers a "strategy coach" that helps a supply manager decide whether competitive market intervention or supplier relationship focus makes the most sense. Others such as the Ariba Category Management Module provide standardized processes.

Niche tools. It is in the more detailed analysis of the *understanding* phase in which technology makes its biggest impact. In addition to the standardized modules in purchased suites or the "homegrown" suites tailored to a company's process, focused niche tools are available to assist the strategic thinking and analysis efforts that are necessary to create a winning sourcing strategy. Niche tools focus on three areas:

- Analyzing suppliers and supply/demand balances in key markets by purchasing and using market-specific supplier analysis tools and Web-based market intelligence services
- Understanding relative dynamics between the "actors" in the supply chain, especially where power lies in the chain and whether that power

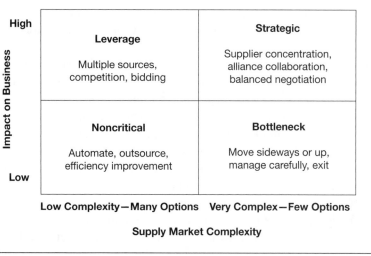

Figure 3.2. Classic Kraljic Sourcing Model.

structure, whether based on supply/demand, inherent assets, or intellectual property ownership, will influence how suppliers must be approached and even where in the supply chain to focus the strategy for greatest advantage (tier 1 or upstream or both)

- Using technology tools that reinforce the rigor in the strategic sourcing process overall such as the standardized or tailored process flows mentioned above (see Chapter 19, *Education—Training the Tools and Tools for Training*).

The use of technology in these areas is often highly tailored to the industry, a specific company, or an analytical methodology. One size rarely fits all.

GAINING UNDERSTANDING—SUPPLY AND DEMAND ANALYSIS

Once the internal analysis has been gathered (requirements, specifications, technical capabilities, resources, etc.), classic sourcing strategy requires an external environmental scan. The Web has made a buyer's search process far easier and with a broader reach than ever before. Many companies stop with Web searches—tapping Google or Yahoo! search engines to access supplier catalogs, websites, and particular supply capabilities half a world away, checking finances, reputations, current customers, and contact information. The advent of blogs and customer rating sites adds to the information available, making market analysis a light year more effective than just 5 years ago. Additionally some software and procurement outsourcing companies can add specific market expertise if their services are chosen.

There are some caveats in all this, however. Internet information requires some degree of due diligence because the information available can be as much rumor and opinion as fact and insight, depending on the source. (*Remember:* Company financials are not the same as blogs.) Data overload is a huge "watch out"—constantly shifting information can paralyze as well as energize.

Comment: The key to using the Internet's vast information reservoir without being overwhelmed by its sheer volume is to be able to take a step back and determine just what information is needed and then to focus on excellent places to find it. The challenge only a few short years ago was the opposite, i.e., "cast a wide net" to find enough good information to develop a sourcing strategy. Using rifle-focused searches versus shotgun-scattered surveys is more effective today.

Market Services Subscriptions

The ability to focus requires organizational experience and market savvy to be key parts of the supply management repertoire of skills. A particularly useful tool set is market services subscriptions that allow/use technology to comb through the enormous amount of information about a particular industry that is strewn about on the Web. Every industry has its own market services (energy, electronics, agriculture, metals, etc.), with some spanning multiple markets (e.g., Dun and Bradstreet financials that are built into many e-tools). Market services subscriptions can enhance both strategy formulation and strategic outcome monitoring in dynamic markets.

The key, however, is not the *subscribing* to market services, but rather what is done with them. As an illustration, the CPG (consumer packaged goods) industry relies heavily on energy- and petrochemical-based ingredients, ranging from natural gas that is used to dry paper and electricity that is used to make caustic soda/chlorine to the polyolefin plastics used in bottles, films, and nonwoven fabrics to the surfactants, solvents, polymers, and specialty chemicals used in product formulas.

In 2005, the world "erupted" for users and manufacturers of these materials, especially in the United States where the U.S. Gulf Coast energy and petrochemical industries were ravaged by increased demand, falling supplies, and damaging hurricanes. High feedstock costs erased decades-long low-cost-producer status (superseded by the Persian Gulf), and shortages/price spikes racked supply chains. High-density polyethylene reached $0.98 per pound—an unheard of level 2 years before—which was frightening to veteran supply managers who were caught in the

"Wal-Mart effect" of customer and consumer resistance to price escalation. Yet this experience was not a new phenomenon. The first two oil-triggered price shocks had come in the 1970s, but were somewhat artificial (a result of embargoes and the Shah's fall in Iran). This newer version was fabricated by a spider web of global proportions, which included huge Chinese demand, capacity that was restricted by recession in 2002, political unrest (in Iraq, Nigeria, and Venezuela), opportunistic pricing, trading speculation by commodity investors, and hurricanes.

For sourcing professionals who are tasked with developing an effective strategy to deal with these turbulent events, understanding and forecasting supply/demand balance and commodity costs and then formulating plans to blunt their impact represent huge challenges. Two of the many services available are Chemical Market Associates, Inc. (cmaiglobal.com) and Global Insight (globalinsight.com), services that are among the industry price forecasting leaders on a global scale in these markets. The purchase of their services brings a Web-based tool to the table that enables supply managers to both understand the market situation and, more importantly, with internal analysis, to create future scenarios across the range of potential market changes and underlying drivers that are necessary to formulate flexible strategic options. Effective sourcing strategies must deal with a wide enough range of market conditions to avoid constant direction changes and the accompanying internal cross-functional realignments (and frustration).

The Cargill, Inc. Experience

Roger Larsh is director of procurement for the North American Dressings, Sauces, and Oil business of privately held trading giant Cargill, Inc., which sells packaged goods to the institutional food industry (e.g., McDonald's, Wendy's, Outback, etc.). Larsh has spent his career in the agricultural commodity/petrochemical supply areas at Sara Lee and P&G before coming to Cargill. He is no stranger to agricultural or petrochemical volatility and the need to formulate strategies that navigate through price and supply ups and downs. The way in which his organization uses services such as Chemical Market Associates, Inc. (CMAI) to drive strategic interventions versus tactical reaction illustrates the value of astute use of these tools.[1]

Several of the divisions and businesses within Cargill subscribed to market services, but with no overall coordination or consensus on their application, which ranged from tactical forecasting to more strategic applications. As a member of Cargill's procurement leadership team, Larsh helped organize and focus the use of these market services tools for strategic interventions versus basic market monitoring. Sophisticated use of market services tools requires researching the mechanisms and data sources behind these Web-based models. (*Note:* Larsh traveled to CMAI headquarters in Houston to discuss how the models are constructed and ways to maximize their value-creating application.)

Market services gather data via a number of means, ranging from routine telephone/e-mail interviews to more rigorous data-based use of capacity utilization (short term) and relational product analysis (longer term), using relative prices and line-item detail to create forecasts and analyze historical trends. Yet forecast accuracy is not the strategic point—nor should accuracy be a counted-upon expectation. (*Comment:* If anyone could accurately and with certainty predict the future they could have made a fortune in the stock and commodity markets and be sitting on a South Sea island with a drink in their hand rather than working for a living.)

Larsh recognized that access to downloads of the data fueling the rigorous CMAI models and identification of potential relationships—by analyzing history—would enable an ability to create potential market scenarios to broaden the horizon and range his people used to drive market strategies. *Remember:* Sourcing strategy is not a "snapshot" go-to-market intervention, but rather a 2- to 4-year plan for how to deal with an industry, its suppliers, their suppliers, and the volatilities inherent in markets driven by supply/demand shifts. Hence tools such as those from CMAI allow key feedstock cost- and availability-scenario planning that can be transformed into flexible, yet clearly directed strategies for these types of commodities, instead of gut-wrenching reactive scrambles when a situation shifts in an unexpected direction.

Pitfalls

A pitfall some companies encounter when using market services is that they expect the market price forecast to be "future price-point accurate" (unlikely) and are shocked when some indices are restated due to recognition that the transparency of market price discovery was not perfect. *Important:* Recognize that market price indexes are as much educated guess (a "black" art?) as science—estimates are often based on a survey of prices, probably from a market researcher's telephone call.

As an example, consider this scenario. At one time, one of the co-authors had responsibility for developing market prices for plastics for a monthly trade magazine. The prices had been researched by the world's biggest plastics buyer at the time, the U.S. government, and had been found to be most accurate. As a result, government purchases of plastic bags were pegged to the price in the trade magazine. Yet creation of the estimate had been extremely subjective—based on size of the buyer surveyed, contract stipulations, exact specifications, market position of the supplier, etc. Additionally, during periods when prices were in transition, the point at which prices actually "settled" was unclear until the following month. Some suppliers really like it when prices are pegged to those types of indexes because surveyors rarely get to the real bottom of the market. *Remember*: There is no such thing as a "market price," but rather a great many individual prices, each tailored to the supplier/buyer deal involved.

Strategic Use

If today's "snapshot" is *not* a go-to-market sourcing strategy, then what does strategic use of market services entail? Continuing with the experience at Cargill, strategic means:

- Scenario analysis of business profit and loss risk that is based on a range of potential petrochemical prices that enables *proactive* strategies ahead of market moves rather than *reactive* tactics behind market moves
- Quicker reads on the relationships between items in the supply chain in differing circumstances (e.g., ethylene/polyethylene relationships at varying capacity utilization rates and historical feedstock prices)
- Use of scenarios in "should-cost" models of supplier products, not only to forecast price, but also to manage price impacts ahead of time (see Chapter 10, *Should Cost—From Spreadsheets to Science*)
- Hedging analysis, using statistical analysis of past prices and accounting correlations between products, to reduce price uncertainty to a level compatible with company profit and price risk tolerances, instead of letting fear drive hedging at the top of the market or trying to beat the market (a fool's errand at best and a recipe for disaster at worst)
- Material substitute analysis (e.g., packaging resin or structure), to focus interventions at either end of the supply chain—with suppliers on pricing and specifications or with customers on specification and package changes (The key is that the analysis looks at a *range* of scenarios *before* engaging a customer about specifications such that the recommendation addresses a full range of market possibilities to avoid rework or disappointment when/if markets inevitably rebalance.)
- "Free" half-day meetings with CMAI (or another index provider), to discuss markets on a face-to-face basis (This is "fuel" that feeds organizational insight and expertise—part of a market services subscription, but often never used.)

• Market view development across the company, which is then coupled with a tailored view for particular needs and risks at the business level (In Cargill's case, market view development across the company taps into an amazing amount of trading expertise and knowledge across numerous commodities.)

Therefore the key becomes looking forward to understand risk and the range of potential change, not counting on a service to "do the job for you." Long-term supply success requires building the skill base at a company to use the tools and having consultants who develop the ability of leaders to "do strategy"—which is when leaders (such as at Cargill) can create competitive edge.

Choosing the Tools

Each family of markets is different. Not all of them have outstanding price discovery and forecasting tools available, but many do. Savvy sourcing managers must be aware of these tools, understand the data gathering/modeling behind them, and then use the tools to understand possibilities, trends, and potential risks in their suppliers' supply chain by exploring market scenarios.

Comment: CMAI and some of its peers are good examples of companies that offer service-based tools that enable usable strategies. Their market intelligence supports understanding the breadth of the market that a particular sourcing strategy covers and recognizing when the market has broken through your planning limits to trigger timely adjustments.

GAINING UNDERSTANDING—SUPPLIERS AND INDUSTRIES

Tools that examine markets are only one part of the external environment scan that good strategy requires. Understanding suppliers within key supplier industries—especially suppliers that are or could be strategic to a firm—is equally important. Taking supplier relationships to a higher level is a seminal factor in becoming an on-demand enterprise. (See Chapter 14, *On-Demand Transformation—IBM*, for a discussion of the on-demand transformation at IBM.) Face-to-face personal interaction is critical in "knowing" suppliers, but having a way to monitor a supplier's overall corporate situation is equally vital.

Companies are in continuous change, whether due to major acquisitions and divestitures or product line modifications or more subtle changes in strategy or marketing. Personnel shifts are constant. Is a supplier's new vice president of marketing or a division's general manager someone with whom you have had dealings before? Was he or she with a supplier that you had a poor relationship with in the past? What experience and preconceptions might that individual bring to the supplier's broader strategy toward its customers and markets—and to your strategic relationship in particular? Financial status adds another element—overall profitability or cost structure can change quickly. More importantly, the status of the division, plant, or business unit that you deal with may not be "in sync" with the parent organization's situation. Keeping track of all this can be a full time job—and you still will not catch everything. Google and Yahoo! searches have made the task more instantaneous, but they have also made the avalanche of information even more unmanageable.

LexisNexis

Globally sifting through today's data and information to catch the actionable elements in time to do something with them is the difference between proactive and reactive supply management. LexisNexis (LN), one of the leaders in capturing public domain information, provides an Internet-based service that can do that. LN services capture news and make it more "digestible" for use by sourcing practitioners in strategy development and ongoing supplier relationship management (see Chapter 6, *Supplier Relationship Management—Bringing Home the Value*). (*Note:* In the ATK seven-step process, part of the pre-go-to-market phase in Step 3, "generate supplier portfolio," requires understanding your incumbents, their competitors, and potential new entrants.)

LN, a division of Reed Elsevier Group plc, which includes publications such as *Purchasing* magazine and *Supply Chain Management Review*, gathers information from myriad sources, working with clients to tailor the search and its delivery. Via the Web, delivery can either be push (arrives at user-determined intervals) or pull (user retrieves delivery on his/her schedule). Attorneys and academics are extremely familiar with the Lexis (legal) Nexis (business) tool box, which unlike many other sources, offers tailoring, not just research access.

Once information is in the press or registered in the legal system as public knowledge, what good is it to sourcing professionals? This is not the interesting "nobody else has figured this out" type of information that fortunes are made of, is it? You would be surprised. The Information Age has spawned a flood of data, information—even knowledge—that overwhelms people who have real jobs "fighting fires," even if they have a speed-reading degree. Public knowledge remains private because a lack of time and access keep it that way.

So how do service tools such as those offered by LN help a sourcing professional? Data mining, like oil or mineral exploration, takes time and effort. Yet unlike the easily unearthed material everyone can find, the data nuggets that can make a difference are easy to miss in the massive data flow. P&G, the huge consumer products company, has built its expertise the "old fashioned way" on fundamentals—principles, organization, education, skills, stewardship, sourcing strategy, and supplier relationships—and timely access to information is *foundational* to that effort. *Remember:* Information is the raw material of sourcing strategy.

The P&G Experience

P&G began to use LN well before the introduction of the LexisNexis Purchasing and Supply Chain Solutions service, which interestingly was not conceived by a purchasing person, but rather by Pete Wolf, an R&D section head. In the late 1990s, P&G was grappling with the challenges of localizing supply in China and globally innovating for multiple consumer income levels and product usage conditions (think about washing clothes in European washers at high temperatures, in U.S. washers with cooler water, and in parts of emerging markets using a bucket or a stream). Along with the goal of CEO A.G. Lafley to get 50% of the formerly insular company's innovation from outside its walls, these challenges occurred while Pete Wolf was on the technical side of P&G's fabric and homecare business (brands such as Tide, Dawn, Downy, Ariel, Fairy, and Swiffer). He was working with sourcing teams to eliminate specification complexity, create performance specifications, qualify new suppliers, and simplify supplier processes.

Wolf was familiar with tools that the newly entrepreneurial R&D department was using in its search for external innovation—one of which was access to LN databases for patent filings, legal actions, company information, etc. Wolf made a "connection"—timely commercial input into that process would make market success more likely. The more he worked with purchasing people, the more he understood that the same reservoir of data that R&D was panning for R&D "gold" contained nuggets of purchasing "gold" for use in strategic interventions, tactical moves, and supplier relationship management. Ultimately Wolf transferred from product development into purchasing to help lead procurement's expanded use of e-tools and Internet-based tools across businesses and spend pools.

P&G leveraged the R&D LN connection during a meeting at the Dayton, OH headquarters of LN. The P&G vision included news feeds that are targeted for particular buying desks and cover specific industries (e.g., petrochemical, pulp, molded parts and bottles, corrugated, etc.), specific strategic or potential suppliers (including financial, management profiles, mergers and acquisition rumors, patent strengths, etc.), and even preliminary best-practice benchmarking in sourcing, procurement, outsourcing, and use of e-tools.

An ongoing effort between the two companies created the forerunner of today's LexisNexis Purchasing and Supply Chain Solutions tool, which is based on basic news feeds and the LexisNexis Company Dossier product (already marketed). LN search experts interviewed sourcing managers and developed key word lists, which were later transformed into search criteria. If the resulting feed "missed the mark," they met again and refined the searches until purchasing customers were happy. Did every article found hit the mark? Of course not, but a list of headings permitted quick scanning of the day's feed and access of articles that looked relevant. P&G, under the leadership of Rob Patton, Wolf's successor, has broadened the range of feeds and refined content and delivery.

The Value of Information

A short example illustrates the potential value of the LN tool.[2] Russ Stewart is a P&G associate director of purchasing, who has held positions in North America and Asia and has experience that spans several spend categories ranging from chemicals to IT outsourcing. As strategy owner for an important material for one of P&G's global business units, his team's in depth analysis of the market and supply chain had recognized that the industry, which was made up of a few vertically integrated major producers and several feedstock processors, was driven not by the final product, but rather by an important feedstock that was much farther up the chain.

While scanning his tailored LN industry feed from his office in Cincinnati, Stewart noticed a short article in a Taiwanese English language newspaper announcing the opening of a local plant that could potentially make that feedstock. Timely communication with teammates in China and Japan resulted in a meeting with the potential supplier to understand the supply impact of the expansion and its proximity to feedstock-constrained Chinese suppliers. This was the beginning of an effort (completed by Stewart's successors) to develop Chinese suppliers which were key to P&G's success longer term. All of this resulted from a news feed of a small article in a local newspaper half a world away—from such small details can strategic interventions be built or missed. Access to public information coupled with sourcing skill and responsiveness truly can make a competitive difference.

GAINING UNDERSTANDING—BUYER/SELLER MARKET DYNAMICS

As the example above about using information illustrates, understanding why things happen with suppliers the way they do means understanding where the vital points exist in the supply chain and who has power over those pivotal points. This effort requires thinking skills. Most e-purchasing tools used to identify and capture value do not help people think through complex intercompany interactions. Are there strategy tools that do?

Cox's Methodology

Andrew Cox is the director of the Centre for Business Strategy and Procurement at the University of Birmingham, U.K., and head of Newpoint Consulting. He has become a thought leader on the implications of power in buyer/supplier interactions and the distribution of value when they interact. Years of research have led him to some highly provocative conclusions that run counter to many popular "seamless" value-sharing concepts popularized in the literature—provocative ideas such as more value is extracted by the company with power; or win-win relationships are not a likely long-term outcome; or a supply chain is a string of actors looking out for themselves, not an aligned community which is focused on the ultimate customer.

We may or may not agree with these conclusions, but that is not the point. Something in Cox's methodology rings true, at least some of the time. How many times have veteran supply managers sought out "partnerships" with suppliers, only to conclude a couple years into the relationship that win-win is elusive and the big "W" is falling on the supplier's side? Like marriages, supply relationships have honeymoons that are followed by the real world. The details of Cox's methodology including critical asset control and supply chain power regimes (supplier-buyer dyads) are well beyond the scope of this book—practitioners are better served by reading one or more of his books on the subject. Still, a simplified overview can help illustrate the relevance of relative power to sourcing strategy in terms of understanding where leverage lies in supply relationships.

The Concept of Power

In a nutshell, the concept is that power drives the distribution of value along the supply chain and that power derives from control of critical assets—intellectual property, regulatory position, imbalance of business reliance on the other party (supplier needs the buyer more than the buyer needs the supplier or vice versa), innovation, branding, physical assets, distribution channels, or high switching costs. *Important*: An examination of the relative power at each supply chain link (power regime) leads to an understanding of how power influences value appropriation along the chain. It helps explain a phenomenon such as the "Wal-Mart effect," in which retailer power drives supplier behavior, price, and (sometimes) profit reduction back through the chain. The goal of Cox's methodology is to identify where the power lies and then to try to reposition the relationship, either within the existing situation or by changing the set of suppliers or the type of item bought (substitutes) or through smart in- or outsourcing choices. Simultaneously, suppliers are trying to do the same thing (a point sometimes forgotten in the elaborate but naïve strategies that some supply organizations design).

One could jump to the conclusion that Cox espouses only an adversarial approach to supply chain value acquisition, but as he said in a conversation at the ISM Conference in May 2002 in San Francisco: "Just because you are dominant doesn't mean you have to be nasty." For example, Toyota, in addition to equity stakes in many suppliers, uses its power dominance to maintain "value preference" in the chain and in its collaborative business model to ensure that suppliers have at least a small "w" in the win-win equation. The result has been a competitive advantage over many Western automobile companies that have win-lose supplier relationships, the outcomes of which ripple back to undermine these car makers' supply chains via bankruptcies, forced mergers, and sales/innovation shifts away from automotive buyers. Toyota has climbed to the top of the automobile food chain, in part fueled by use of the somewhat benevolent but the always competitive pressure of its power dominance over its supply base. The heart of Toyota's supply chain behavior is the understanding that success also rests on a measure of success for its suppliers. This is a key tenet in building an on-demand supply chain.

Analyzing the Balance of Power

The astute use of power to achieve long-term value is part of the thinking that must go into sound sourcing strategy that delivers direction-setting beyond short-term market fluctuation. One of the tools that the Cox consulting group provides that helps the thought process necessary to use that power is the Oraculix Power Positioning Tool. This software tool is designed to help supply managers analyze the relative power between their firm and selected suppliers (using a 2 × 2 Power Matrix that contrasts the buyer's and seller's relative power; see Figure 3.3) and then to enable an assessment of the buyer's strategic options for moving to a more favorable power position that increases the likelihood of more value acquisition to achieve supply objectives.

The software forces analysis of the balance of power between the buyer and each supplier in a spend category and then plots all the suppliers onto the power matrix for easy visual comparison of the *current* state. It does this by posing a series of questions on five topics that must be answered:

- Relative importance of the product to the buyer
- Nature of the demand and supply flow (e.g., tight, loose, etc.)
- Power attributes of the buyer
- Importance of the buyer to the seller
- Power attributes of the seller

The questions require two levels of response—direct answers and an assessment of the quality of those answers (based on objective data, educated guesses, or

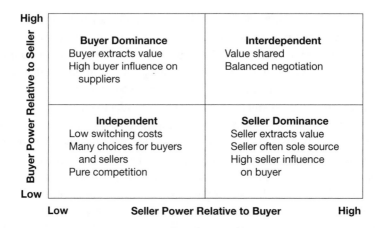

Figure 3.3. Cox Power Grid. (Source: Cox, Andrew, Sanderson, Joe, and Watson, Glyn. *Power Regimes: Mapping the DNA of Business and Supply Chain Relationships.* Warwickshire, UK: Earlsgate Press; 2000, p. 18; Cox, Andrew, Watson, Glyn, Sanderson, Joe, and Ireland, Paul. *Supply Chain Management: A Guide to Best Practice.* Warwickshire, UK: Financial Times/ Prentice Hall; 2003, p. 54.)

"don't know"). A key benefit of this tool is that it highlights what is not known as much as what is known. As Cox points out, "Analysis based on guesstimates and lack of data is guesswork rather than an objective analysis of the real buyer and seller power position." In fact, if enough answers are "don't know" the tool will not automatically provide an analysis solution, thus forcing more rigorous analysis.

Once the current state analysis is completed, the focus moves to the future via another series of questions on two subjects:

- Buyer's sourcing and leverage options
- Seller's marketing and strategy options

Quality designations and the ability to compare all suppliers against each other on the power matrix are also part of this stage, which results in a "before and after" snapshot. The model, based on insight from years of supply chain power research, suggests factors that the buyer could use to move toward more optimal positions as well as factors that the supplier could use to do the same thing from their side. Obviously, strong use of the tool requires knowledge of the concepts behind it, delivered through what Cox describes as "master classes" and workshops covering a range of topics (e.g., effective in-sourcing and outsourcing management, strategic source planning, etc.).

The software—a series of prompts, questions, and diagramming—is nothing special, but the questions, the knowledge behind them, the rigorous thinking and analysis necessary to answer them, and the research behind the improvement suggestions are special. Sourcing strategy is not simple. "Generic" options that pass for real strategy can shortchange results. Having discipline and the time to truly penetrate the supply situation is absolutely necessary for a company's strategic materials and services. The Oraculix tool, although somewhat resource-intensive, drives the depth of thinking to make a competitive difference for vital sourcing decisions.

CLOSING THOUGHTS—SOURCING STRATEGY IS A MENTAL GAME

Sourcing strategy is a mental chess game which is played before going to market. Sourcing strategy blends expertise with knowledge and intense analysis to formulate a value-creating game plan for use with the supply base. These sophisticated niche e-tools, coupled with skilled people, typically are not considered e-purchasing tools, nor, other than generic strategy "suggestions" or sourcing processes, are they offered by traditional software providers. These are deep-diving, somewhat niche-focused offerings that help a company change the game. Some types of tools are part of a wide range of similar offerings—many industries have their own equivalent of the CMAI Web Service or the LexisNexis Supplier/Industry Intelligence Solution, while others such as Oraculix are more unique. What separates the leading-edge players from the rest is not just finding these tools, but more importantly having the ability to use them as an integral part of their strategic sourcing process.

LESSONS LEARNED

- Processes, not e-tools, are the key to ongoing value mining.
- One size rarely fits all when applying technology to sourcing strategy.
- Sourcing strategy is a long-term plan, not a short-term go-to-market tool.
- Strategic sourcing, regardless of the specific multistep process being used, has three phases—understand, decide, and manage. Sourcing strategy emerges as the first important decision from the understanding phase.
- Highly tailored search tools can mine the Internet for useful supplier, industry, and market data.
- In designing supply strategies, companies must understand how power drives behavior throughout the supply chain.

Web
Added
Value™

4

GOING TO MARKET— ELECTRONIC SUPPLIER ENGAGEMENT

Reverse auctions can be a valuable tool; however, they cannot be a universal answer to today's needs in supply management.

— **Rob Handfield**
Professor of Supply Chain Management
North Carolina State University

One of the best ways to create interest and excitement about the cost-reduction potential of supply management is to show company management a picture (Figure 4.1). Figure 4.1 depicts the typical price curve of a reverse auction bidding event. A reverse auction is a bidding event which is characterized by competitive price visibility (with anonymity) such that suppliers can submit revised offers in an attempt to win the business.

As any software vendor will say, in only 30 minutes (or slightly longer if overtime periods are triggered), a company can experience 10, 20, even 30% or more in price reductions. How could anyone not be impressed?

Although not obvious, perhaps, is that to achieve optimum results with a reverse auction, thorough preparation and planning are required—sometimes for weeks or months in duration. Something that is also not obvious is that a reverse auction may be absolutely the *wrong* e-tool to use in a given situation. Simply stated, going to market is *not* a situation in which one size or type of tool (such as reverse auctions) fits all situations.

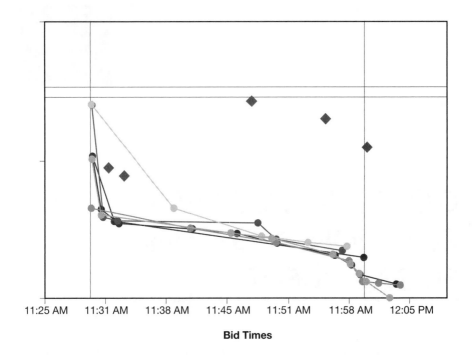

Bid Times

Figure 4.1. Classic Price Curve of a Reverse Auction.

During the latter years of Jack Welch's reign at GE, more than one company CEO reported to his procurement department: "I was at a meeting and Jack Welch said you should auction everything." Worse could be that after seeing a live auction that you had personally arranged, your CEO came to the same conclusion: "Let's auction it all." In spite of what your CEO might have heard from his peers, or seen for himself in limited demonstrations, reverse auctions may not be the right tool for many situations.

REVERSE AUCTION—STRATEGY CONSIDERATIONS

Before reviewing the pros and cons of reverse auctions and other tools, take a step back and review some fundamentals. First, successfully going to market requires developing market knowledge and determining an appropriate sourcing strategy. In other words, there is no shortcut to going through the discipline of strategic sourcing. The strategic sourcing process is a multistage, fact-based process that helps to determine—and execute—the appropriate strategy for adding value to a company.

e-RFI

An electronic request for information (e-RFI) is a tool that can be used in *preparation* for going to market. An e-RFI, just like a manual RFI, is a useful technique to gather market knowledge from the experts—a company's supply base. Using e-RFIs can speed up the process of soliciting information from current and prospective suppliers and enable easier compilation and comparison of responses. The key is asking the right questions in order to gain insights about the supply market dynamics and supplier cost components. (*Comment*: In the experience of the authors, typically RFIs are not used as often as they should be prior to crafting a request for a proposal, an RFP, or a request for a quotation, an RFQ.)

Some e-RFx (electronic request for [x], where [x] can be P, proposal (RFP); Q, quote (RFQ); I, information (RFI), etc.) service providers offer an ability to archive the information so that RFIs can be compared year to year or event to event. If the questions are well designed, a cost model of some of the supplier operations and purchased material ramifications can almost be built over time.

For example, to gather information about its printed film and paper spend pools, a large consumer products company asks numerous questions about types and sizes of presses/printing technologies, the cost to add colors, change cylinders, or digital-print copy, cylinder costs, engraving suppliers, stock suppliers with cost per ton and basis weight, escalation provisions if the cost of the stock goes up (e.g., the cost of low-density polyethylene, cartonboard, or label stock), press change over times and costs, line crewing, etc. By storing this information and comparing it year to year, several things can be accomplished—see progress or regression in the parameters, benchmark components of cost structure, and build best-of-best theoretical benchmarks across multiple suppliers to assess potential waste elimination potential.

Using Information

At times an almost line-by-line cost and time structure of major suppliers used regularly can be pieced together. Additionally, patterns should start to emerge that would be optimal in printing multiple specifications (e.g., a series of cartons or labels across different scents or versions of the same brand size of a particular product box).

The issue for most companies is that evaluating and understanding supplier cost data are easier if employee roles are stable over many years, which is not realistic in today's career-changing environment. Therefore, using e-RFx software and having the ability to easily store and compare/analyze the data between sourcing events provide the information required for improvement over time. Theoretically this was doable in the old spreadsheet days or on paper, but not easily. e-RFx tools make value analysis a part of the go-to-market "discovery" process—more can be discovered than just price. The archives also can be a training mechanism. A final thought regarding e-RFx tools—e-RFx tools can be an efficient and effective means of preparation for the next step in a sourcing process, whether it is reverse auction or something else.

Making Decisions

Based on market knowledge, a determination could be made that the market is "low complexity" and that many supply options exist. In that scenario, going to market with one or another e-tool such as reverse auctions or electronic sealed bids may be appropriate.

In other cases, the market assessment and the internal review might conclude that the impact on the business is too great (or strategic) and the supply market is too complex (i.e., few options). In that situation, a more thoughtful and collaborative approach to prospective suppliers is appropriate. In that scenario, a price-focused reverse auction may well be the wrong tool. More appropriate would be to devise a sourcing strategy that is based on a partnership approach or a sourcing strategy that utilizes a more complex decision-support tool such as optimization (see Chapter 5, *Optimization—Going to Market with Complexity*).

REVERSE AUCTION—THE BIDDING PROCESS

The Electronic Sealed Bid

An electronic sealed bid is a real-time, secure, Web-based, electronically sealed bidding process (using cryptography) in which a preselected group of suppliers competitively bid for a defined product. Using an electronic sealed bid is appropriate in situations in which price transparency is not advantageous or when a sealed-bid process will gain greater participation from the target supply base.

The Classic Reverse Auction

Considerations and Limitations

In many cases, however, there is tremendous value to all parties in having a price-transparent process—the classic reverse auction. When, specifically, should using a reverse auction be considered? Typically a reverse auction is used when a situation is characterized by:

- Price as the major criteria
- Many suppliers, with similar capabilities

- A commodity product/service
- Excess market/supply capacity
- A commodity/service that is not strategic to company business
- A company that is willing to change suppliers
- A supply base wanting the company's business

Reverse auctions also have some important limitations. Reverse auctions are difficult to use if:

- Non-price factors are important.
- Suppliers have different capabilities or products/services are not easily described.
- Suppliers have negotiating leverage (i.e., a seller's market).

Reverse auctions also cannot easily incorporate business constraints and business rules and typically require rigid descriptions of what is being offered as a business opportunity (i.e., the bid "lot" description is rigid). Because of the limitations of reverse auctions, optimization tools have a complementary role to play (see Chapter 5, *Optimization—Going to Market with Complexity*). Nevertheless, in the right situation, reverse auctions can be an important part of the company tool box.

Evolution

The reverse auction field came to life in the mid 1990s, when FreeMarkets, Inc. (later acquired by Ariba, Inc.) introduced its initial "full-service" offering, combining a reverse auction software platform with consulting assistance. A number of large companies became early adopters of full-service reverse auctions.

More recently, as reverse auction tools became easier to use and the tools gained credibility, "self-serve" or desktop reverse auctions became more commonplace. In the desktop approach, a sourcing professional can literally run an auction from his or her desktop computer, without the assistance of a consultant, which makes the use of reverse auctions for relatively small sourcing events possible (e.g., under $10,000 in annual business).

Experienced users of these self-service tools find that providing a menu of reverse auction options to their organizations makes sense. Often the decision to use self-service/desktop versus full service is based on an assessment of the relative complexity of the supply market plus an assessment of the category expertise internally available in a company (Figure 4.2). If the company has reasonably good category expertise in the target sourcing group and the supply market is not unduly complex, then a self-service or desktop reverse auction may be quite effective.

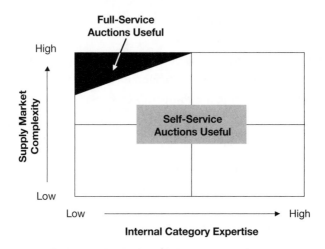

Figure 4.2. Full-Service versus Do-It-Yourself Auctions.

Prequalification

Preparing for a reverse auction typically includes prequalifying the suppliers to be invited to the auction. Some companies allegedly include *non-qualified* players—suppliers that they *know* will never be awarded the business—in an effort to increase the competitive pressure on the qualified bidders. Using known non-qualified suppliers as "mechanical rabbits" to increase competitive pressure on other suppliers is unethical.

The perception of ethics is heavily influenced by how the ground rules are laid out, the transparency of the ground rules to all participants, and adherence to the ground rules during and after the event—important to note because in the world of reverse auctions, fully prequalifying bidders may not always be possible. Some companies conduct auctions in which all bidders are not prequalified because fully prequalifying bidders up front is costly and impractical. In these situations, the ground rules of the auction are clearly laid out up front to all participants. Incumbents know that some suppliers are not fully prequalified, but that the customer's technical staff had assessed these suppliers' operations and believed that their qualification would be feasible or likely. The ground rules involve explaining that if a new supplier that is not fully confirmed as qualified should win an auction, one of two things could happen—incumbents will get a partial award at their last bid price for perhaps the first 3 or 6 months while the full qualification process continues or the new supplier wins only a qualification for future consideration, but no final award of business for this event. However this topic is handled, the key point is to have clear, well-explained ground rules, which are executed without variation.

Bid Lots

The strategy relating to designing and presenting bid lots is a crucial part of the reverse auction strategy. Some companies might "nest" requirements in some cases—by putting an unattractive item with an attractive item, for example. Lotting strategy can contribute to ensuring that competitive tension builds and is maintained with progress through the various lots in the bidding calendar.

Transparency

The most prevalent form of reverse auction offers participants full visibility and transparency into the actual pricing behavior of the bidders, without revealing the identity of the individual bidders. In situations with a good number of competitors, this type of transparency can increase the competitive dynamics. In some cases, however, avoiding price transparency may make sense, e.g., if there are only a few bidders or if the company does not want the bidders to know the winning price. So-called rank auctions or masked bidding can be used in this situation (Figure 4.3).

Bidding Techniques

An important technique that will help avoid confusion and rework is to issue an invitation to participate, which includes a detailed contract template. When suppliers bid, they will be bidding not just on the requirements, but also with full awareness of the contract terms and conditions.

Another useful technique is to have discussions with suppliers in advance of the auction to clarify the requirements, specifications, the bidding approach, and the technology. Doing this well with suppliers will first require an investment of time in internal discussions. If an event is the supplier's first reverse auction experience, it may be necessary (and worthwhile) to provide system training and allow the supplier to test the system in advance of the live auction event.

Also the technique of providing suppliers with a contact person during the auction is prudent—just in case they encounter difficulties during the live auction.

CLOSING THOUGHTS ABOUT RESISTANCE

Some suppliers, or even certain categories of suppliers, may express extreme reluctance to participate in reverse auctions. In some cases, the hesitation is the result of poor commercial experiences with other prospective customers. In this instance, communication with a reluctant supplier(s) is critical to success. In a nonthreatening manner, ask exactly what is of concern to the supplier about the

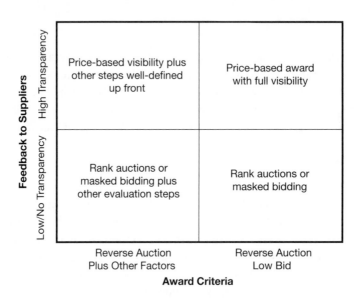

Figure 4.3. Strategy Choices—Feedback and Award Criteria.

company's plans. In some cases, the supplier may be making assumptions that are incorrect. The supplier could have been the "mechanical rabbit" described earlier. Assure the supplier that if their participation in the auction is well done, there is a strong likelihood of being awarded business.

Hesitation may be based on a hope that the customer's sourcing approach will change if one or more suppliers indicate that they will not participate in a reverse auction event. If suppliers are resisting, thinking that the plan to use an auction approach will be dropped, assure them that the organization has done its homework, is committed to this approach, and will be awarding future business based on the performance of those suppliers who participate in the auction. Expect "back-door selling" and "end runs" to occur—ensure that all key contact points in the company "speak with one voice" on this topic. If a supplier senses weakness in anyone they talk to, the supplier will not give up easily. On the other hand, if a supplier hears a consistent, firm message when talking with contacts in the company, resistance often fades.

In general, suppliers have become much more sophisticated in their responses to reverse auctions. In the early days of reverse auctions, customers often witnessed pricing behavior that could best be described as irrational and illogical. Now it is uncommon for suppliers to not respond rationally. Why? Experience and self-preservation are key reasons. Often suppliers have learned the hard way about the high cost of failing to understand the dynamics of reverse auctions and the high cost of failing to invest time and effort in planning their auction strategy.

As a result of the increasing sophistication of suppliers, there is an increasing premium on buyers to develop solid go-to-market sourcing strategies and to execute these strategies well.

Comment: A classic internal debate regarding reverse auctions is triggered when the procurement department decides to not accept the low bid due to one or more non-price value considerations. Price-based reverse auctions elevate the price dimension to a high level of visibility, which makes deciding to not award the business solely on that basis a challenge. This shortcoming of reverse auctions—in some situations—has spawned the field of optimization, which will be discussed in Chapter 5 (*Optimization—Going to Market with Complexity*).

REVERSE AUCTION—THE RULES OF FAIR PLAY

1. Mean it if you do it. Significant supplier resources are devoted to preparation for reverse auctions. Intend to award business at the end of the process.
2. Conduct no reconnaissance by auction. Do not use the auction process as an attempt to gather market intelligence. Doing so is an insult to your most important partners.
3. Allow no outside quotes. All deals must be made according to the stated rules and conditions.
4. Keep out the shills/rabbits. Only invite participants if you are absolutely willing to do business with them.
5. State all terms and conditions up front.
6. Ensure that all participants receive the same information and clarifications in a timely manner.
7. Award business quickly and inform participants of the auction results. The actual award, of course, is confidential, but inform participants that the process is complete.
8. Do not change the structure of lots after the bidding is completed. You made the rules and you must live by them. Bids are made based on the lots as structured. Changing the rules is a breach of trust.
9. Set realistic price expectations. If realistic price expectations are not achieved, inform bidders in a timely manner.
10. Hold suppliers accountable for what they say they will do.

Source: Adapted from *Purchasing*, February 6, 2003. With permission.

Web
Added
Value™

This book has free material available for download from the
Web Added Value™ resource center at *www.jrosspub.com*

5

OPTIMIZATION—GOING TO MARKET WITH COMPLEXITY

Out of intense complexities intense simplicities emerge.
— **Winston Churchill**
Former British Prime Minister

As Chapter 4 has described, going to market using electronic bidding tools, whether e-RFx or reverse auctions, capitalizes on the transparency, efficiency, and communication capabilities of these tools in markets worldwide to leverage competition and extract value (savings). Going to market using electronic bidding tools works well for spend categories in which specifications are clear and other factors in the value equation can either be qualitatively weighed into the sourcing decision or assured by rigorous qualification, verification, and ongoing quality/service management. In fact, several users of reverse auction best practices actually use requests for proposals (RFPs) to set a base price and to iron out the many non-price variables so that after everything else has been determined the auction itself can be about price/cost alone. Yet many companies still struggle to effectively weigh total value. Hence there is the concept of "expressive bidding," which includes non-price attribute weighting systems within the electronic bidding tools and which is touted as "advanced sourcing" or "optimization." Many tools have these types of weighting systems, which work when the value assessment is not too complex.

Alas, however, sometimes the world is just too complicated! Some spend categories have a level of complexity that requires buyers to "dumb down" the evaluation process, either to meet reverse auction lotting requirements, to cope with the sheer size and breadth of responses to a massive RFP bid package, or to give a more precise understanding of the tradeoffs between competing value components, especially when the *non-cost* and *price plus cost* aspects (price and cost are not the same) simply cannot be balanced out easily.

So just what is "advanced" optimization? Entire magazines are devoted to "optimization," and the word can mean just about anything to anyone. In this chapter, optimization refers to advanced optimization as a supply management solution for complicated bidding processes. The technology tools that have emerged to deal with high complexity are known as optimization tools. At their foundation, these optimization tools rely on two things:

- Extremely sophisticated mathematics, known as combinatorial science, which is made up of capabilities such as mixed integer programming, decision tree branching, and other bounding algorithms (in other words, "big-time" science and math)—The sophisticated mathematics is Byzantine to the practitioner, but is necessary for the high-speed solutions of huge problems with many competing requirements and constraints.

- The "right" computer hardware and software systems—A user thinks the software is easy to use on a personal computer, yet the software contains calculations that are supported by enough "oomph" to get high-speed solutions done.

Optimization burst on the scene in 2004 and 2005, when use of these tools was reported in the general press. Yet leading-edge companies such as Procter & Gamble (P&G) and Motorola had been exploring the use of these tools well before that time (e.g., in 2001 and 2002). By 2005, magazine articles,[1] research study papers,[2] and awards (e.g., the 2004 first-place award to Motorola, with its provider Emptoris, and the 2005 finalist finish of P&G, with its provider CombineNet, Inc., in the Franz Edelman operations management competition) identified use of these tools as a catalyst for the next quantum leap in sourcing after the go-to-market tools. As with most new things, marketplace buzz blended truth, hype, visionary potential, and the early results with far too little "battle-scarred" perspective.

TOOL ADOPTION—BARRIERS TO OPTIMIZATION
Software Capability and Complexity

One expert source has declared that only two software companies have "real" optimization, another source has listed seven, while at the time of writing this book, the authors could only personally vouch for three—which is the first barrier to widespread use of optimization—much more of a barrier than its cost, which while not cheap does deliver huge return on investments (ROI) paybacks. Despite identification of an average 12% incremental savings (median of 9%) and the typical user's estimate of 3 to 12% over other online tools, a June 2005 study has stated that only one in five companies were using optimization and only a third were planning to do so by mid-2007.[2] The range in this study was an amazing 3 to 45% savings! Most users focused primarily on transportation sourcing, an area in which, uniquely, sourcing managers seem to "get it," given the complexity of lane structures and service requirements.

Early bid optimization tools were complex to use, focused on a small number of very discrete spend categories (such as transportation), and required significant category and systems expertise to create allocation scenarios. Optimization faced the fate of many other e-purchasing tools. Software companies, quick to jump on the bandwagon—some legitimately and some on the fringes—sometimes put marketing before substance. Enticing descriptions of the "optimization" term appeared everywhere:

- Flexible expressive bidding
- Advanced sourcing techniques
- Optimized e-sourcing
- Expressive competition
- Powered by an optimization engine

One software company spokesperson said, "The algorithms are out there. You can get a linear programming algorithm for $100. Linear programming and similar algorithms aren't new: what is new is applying them to sourcing. Companies will argue that their algorithms will deliver a superior result, but the skill lies in applying a given algorithm to commercial procurement in the real world."[1]

Embedded in this statement is truth—the skill to apply the power of optimization is indeed the difference between using the tool and leading-edge redefinition of a supply problem. Yet today's world is far past simple $100 linear programming models, even though that application of math is technically "optimization" with a small "o." Math and software programming are the intellectual property behind fierce competitive marketing-claim superiority battles between providers. Similarly to auction/e-RFx tools, self-service and custom optimization applications exist, depending on the problem complexity level and the using company's need, but the blending of them with $100 "optimization" tools requires that due diligence, both commercially and technically, be vital to making a good selection. Adding to the challenge is the fact that feasible "answers" pop out, which are not always intuitive. In addition, other prerequisites exist, particularly spend analysis (see Chapter 2, *Spend Analysis—Start Your Engines*) and confusing anecdotal user comments.

Three key factors have driven solution providers to improve functionality to address these issues—two from their customers and one internally:[3]

- Maturing auction use forced supply management executives to look for total cost-based negotiation methods.
- Tightening supply market dynamics required supply management to deal with dramatic cost escalation and supply outages amid sellers' markets.
- Improvements in solution usability and capabilities made optimization more practical for more companies and spend categories when incorporated into their e-RFx process.

Solution providers have made improvements in usability via pull-down menus, wizards, and utilities to create and test multiple scenarios in their bids, to provide more intelligence about more spend categories to supplement user knowledge with generic spend information, and to provide an ability to invite specification alternatives and more supplier-friendly bidding bid bundling/unbundling capability—all without substantial provider consulting help. Companies that have "penetrated" provider claims have been able to overcome the "confusion barrier," but as is often the case with software tools, the companies that did not do so and were "burned" have long memories, so the barrier remains. Additionally, just adding optimization to other bidding tools often gave the incremental 3 to 12%, which is not a game-changing shift.

User Maturity, Expertise, and Philosophy

Capturing truly "blockbuster" results from an optimization-driven redefinition of the allocation problem is the second barrier, which separates leading edge from just applying "real" optimization tools. The maturity, expertise, and philosophy of a supply organization using real optimization tools can result in amazing results (Figure 5.1).

Why? To drive dramatic incremental value, optimization fundamentally changes the perspective of the go-to-market experience of suppliers much more than optimization changes the buyer's perspective. Unlike reverse auctions or requests for quotes (RFQs), in which the buyer structures how suppliers bid and the bid package often has an obligatory, polite, "mushy" statement to "Please provide alternative offers that you believe will provide value," optimization lets a supplier into a buyer's world. The key to success is for suppliers to have access to the depth and nuance of a buyer's requirements (far beyond just specifications and average demand) and then to be encouraged to begin tinkering with that knowledge by adding a similar depth from their side about things the buyer could not possibly know.

Maturity	The ability to balance best practices such as simplification with the need to add complexity when and where it provides substantial value
Expertise	In-depth knowledge of markets, suppliers, and business, which is combined with experience to select the right sourcing tool for the right situation
Philosophy	The recognition that suppliers must be segmented; that suppliers are more than a place to extract value and squeeze margins, depending on their segmentation position; and that a level of trust is necessary before suppliers will begin close collaboration and business option development

Figure 5.1. Organizational Drivers Enabling Maximum Optimization Benefits.

In essence, suppliers do the lotting instead of, or along with, the buyer, resulting in huge numbers of alternative bids for things such as price discounts, capacity/response options, specification changes, inventory levels, and time horizons. Events can generate 30,000 quotes, e.g., such as an Alcan transportation event did when using Verticalnet software that delivered impressive results (two times expected savings).[2] However, in this type of close collaboration, if spend usage and demand patterns given to suppliers to use are incomplete or inaccurate, even a great optimization tool will provide disappointing results. "Garbage in garbage out" is still alive and well, so accurate spend and demand analysis remains critical.

The Maturity Factor—The Motorola Experience

Perhaps Motorola's success will help illustrate the maturity factor.[4] Motorola's journey was completed in a relatively short time period because business events at Motorola required them to "put their foot to the accelerator" to avoid what, in 2004, then-President/COO Mike Zafirovski and then-CPO Teresa Metty described as "The Perfect Storm." (*Note:* By the end of 2005 Zafirovski and Metty had left Motorola.)

The 2001 telecommunications industry bust combined with Motorola's specific situation to create "The Perfect Storm," but unlike the fishing boat in the movie, Motorola came through as a much stronger player, and the use of go-to-market tools including both basic and advanced optimization was an important reason why Motorola did. Three forces came together in Motorola's "storm:"

- The telecommunications collapse, including bankruptcies of key telephone customers (remember WorldCom?), which resulted in a collapse of the telecommunications equipment market that led to extreme telephone price deflation (demand fell a third worldwide)

- A product portfolio made up of relatively expensive, overengineered, aging products, which lacked key features that consumers and customers expected (As the market plunged, Motorola dropped faster because both halves of the value equation—cost and performance—were going the wrong direction.)
- An internal resource "squeeze," resulting from downsizing that was occurring before complex, high-cost structured internal processes had been redefined in a strongly decentralized, engineering-driven culture (Face-to-face sourcing processes with equally stressed suppliers could take months of time that Motorola simply did not have.)

Metty, who had joined Motorola from IBM's procurement turnaround team under legend Gene Richter, explained in a presentation to the Edelman judges that purchased goods and services make up well over half of Motorola's cost structure. The need to reduce the supplier side of Motorola's cost equation fueled a major effort to use go-to-market tools. Motorola quickly progressed through on-line bidding from reverse auctions to RFPs/RFQs (both individual and multistage) to optimization—for both relatively simple and extremely complex items. Given the Motorola business crisis, downsized procurement ranks, and tight administrative budgets, the 5-year goal was to drive up to 90% of their spend to on-line go-to-market tool sourcing events. By 2004 the number was between 60 and 70% and growing.

The Motorola effort utilized a tool set from software provider Emptoris. The tool set was dubbed MINT (Motorola Internet Negotiation Tool). The results were incredible—over a 3-year period, Motorola saved $600 million! About 600 trained sourcing professionals ran over 700 MINT events (using reverse auctions and RFQs, with RFQs being the dominant application with and without optimization) across every major worldwide geographic center in the company during those same 3 years.

Metty said, "We needed a solution that could handle the very large and complex semiconductor sourcing events to the smallest one-time prototype buys. We needed the ability to analyze and optimize our purchases like we never had before. We needed to do things that humans couldn't accomplish and do it quickly." In a nutshell this is an excellent description of the "on-demand" value potential of these go-to-market tools. The impact of optimization in these results is particularly impressive when considering that $200 million of the 3-year $600-million savings total was attributed to optimization[5]—fully a third over and above basic electronic bidding tools and over many spend pools that had been professionally sourced for years.

Generating results of this type with an e-tool set means doing a lot of things right—having major adoption; training people to use the tool; selling and training suppliers; having trust to invite suppliers into the business to create options; and having savvy to apply the right bidding approach to the right spend category. Motorola also had all three of the organizational qualities previously described as necessary to maximize the benefits of optimization (see Figure 5.1)—*maturity* to recognize suppliers as a means of help rather than a place to "steal" value, which led to the selection of a range of bidding tools; *expertise* to understand which tool to apply where; and a *philosophy* to build enough trust to let strategic suppliers "see" into their business to fuel options that created the $200-million incremental savings.

Yet part of the *maturity* organizational barrier is more subtle than just viewing suppliers as help and giving them details of the business. Optimization requires embracing and then leveraging complexity, which "flies in the face" of years of leading-edge purchasing truth. The best in class embrace simplification and standardization—supplier consolidation, tier 1 supplier purchase and assembly of components (manufacturing outsourcing), reduction of specification options, and individual spend focus. The act of "doing optimization" is, in many ways, counterintuitive because a company must consciously add complexity and allow supplier ideas to create diverging options just when traditional thinking says to converge before going to market. Motorola has handled this paradox well.

In addition to MINT, Motorola's need for product and component simplification to overcome years of independent engineering-based product and component design required "waging war" on complexity. Factors such as average part count, test time, industry standard components, and component reuse across products were improved.[6] Motorola simultaneously innovated its way out of its aging product portfolio issue (the raZR telephone is an excellent example). MINT balanced the simplification of previous face-to-face and spreadsheet go-to-market processes, while optimization counterintuitively added complexity where it added significant value. *That is maturity!*

The Complexity Framework

So what kind of complexity lends itself to major optimization events? Optimization is not needed for every situation. Although incremental savings are probably available almost all the time, real blockbuster results come when the complexity of the situation not only requires sophisticated computer algorithms, but also requires sophisticated supply manager skills and creativity to explore the "what if world" of potential scenarios to create a set of potentially feasible options. This is the difference between the value available in the 3- to 12% average player and the high-side +45% best-in-class users.[2]

Creative options are compared with (1) the *lowest-cost-feasible solution* to understand the impact of business rules and supplier suggestions and (2) the *theoretical lowest cost* (no constraints other than supplier capacity) to understand future waste-elimination opportunities. This is when user skill drives value creation. It is an ability to recognize when the exploration of complexity, innovative new configurations, or unique allocation combinations across supplier tiers can drastically reduce total cost of ownership to unlock new value. A way to visualize this concept is to think of it as a three-level "complexity framework" (Figure 5.2):

Level 1. Fundamentally large problems—problems which include large numbers of using locations, producing locations, specification variations, demand patterns, and even preferred suppliers, but which are primarily cost driven. Evaluating all the options across the allocation problem involves too many possibilities for an individual to examine in a reasonable length of time. Optimization provides a rapid "what-if" capability that allows buyers to query the system and to see cost boundaries more clearly. Level 1 optimization usage embedded in reverse auction and RFP tools delivers the incremental 3 to 12%. Typical examples include single business unit printed packaging or MRO categories and large globally shippable commodities with multiple supplier and user locations.

Level 2. Large problems with multiple internal, external, and non-price constraints—problems which add the complexity of numerous internal customers with different needs, regulatory constraints (trade rules, government rules, safety rules), functional specification requirements and/or corporate policy constraints (social responsibility, localization, etc.), and multiple value factors to the sheer size parameters of Level 1. Optimization combines the skill to engage these internal customers and their needs, but still leverages enterprise-wide spend in dealing with all of the business rules. "What if" scenarios expand beyond allocation options to include exploration of new horizons by relaxing some of the non-price "rules" and by comparing the resulting cost and non-cost business outcome. Level 2 begins to differentiate base optimization skills and those of the leading-edge companies as the complexity scale increases. Examples include large single-mode transportation cost/service/capacity tradeoffs, cross-business unit commodities such as labels or cartons with huge numbers of specifications, languages, and substrates, and at times even relatively simple commodities with very complex internal user-preference requirements.

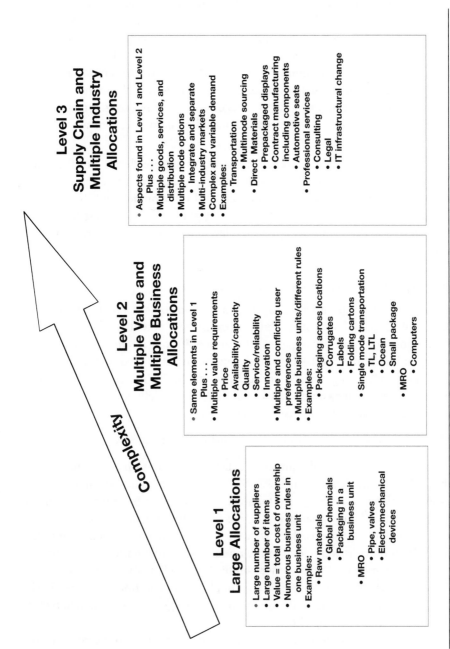

Figure 5.2. Understanding Sourcing Complexity. (Source: From Cincinnati Consulting Consortium. With permission. © Steve Rogers.)

Level 3. Requires having skilled supply managers who can reconceptualize a problem by expanding the option analysis to multiple industries within a supply chain. In effect, optimizing is done across the related vertical material families and services in a given supply chain, and it has a more horizontal perspective that includes a number of Level 1 and Level 2 allocations. Examples include contract manufacturing, including purchase of some components along with the service; temporary labor across multiple categories in multiple geographies and languages; and IT infrastructure, including hardware, software, support, and services.

Real-world problems tend to have elements of all three levels, but the complexity progression framework helps in quickly evaluating where optimization technology might have major application to "find value on demand" by embracing system complexity rather than trying to simplify it instead. These tools provide a way to "break complexity apart" and leverage the pieces into a reassembled whole.

The Complexity Factor—The P&G Experience

Arguably, one of the premier users of optimization tools is Procter & Gamble (P&G). Unlike many companies, P&G recognized the potential of optimization beyond transportation early on, in part because of its long strategic sourcing history, beginning in the late 1960s with the appointment of George Perbix as vice president of purchasing for the entire corporation. Perbix, considered P&G's father of modern purchasing, was CPO until 1985. He defined a value equation that is more far reaching than just price considerations:

$$Value = Cost + Availability + Quality + Service + R\&D$$

Under Perbix, P&G used homegrown custom optimization programs as early as the mid 1970s, the first of which was DECAL (the Detergent Carton Allocation program), which leveraged printed folding carton spend across multiple business units. Computing being what it was at the time, the data was input via punch cards. (Yes, quaint as it seems, there were such things.) To have enough computer power, allocation runs were done in the middle of the night after the company's two major operational systems (order, shipping, and billing on the customer side and accounts payable and receipts on the supplier side) had finished, so the business would remain running while the company's computer was consumed by the carton optimization-solving effort.

About midnight, a cadre of buyers would be given access to the entire company mainframe capacity until about 6 a.m. the next morning to run only a few allocation "what ifs" using linear programming models. Allocation analysis took days and weeks. By the 1980s the company's systems were efficient enough to run during the day (e.g., BASS, the Business Allocation Support System). When P&G began its global sourcing and low-cost-country work in the early 1990s, it was supported by C-BOS (the Chemical Buying Optimization System), which incorporated the many suppliers, using locations, and the total-cost-of-ownership components (e.g., price, freight, duty, handling, and currency) necessary to optimize global allocations.

The BASS and C-BOS programs, however, were resource-intensive to maintain internally. So during the same week in 2002, when two conference attendees (co-author Rogers and P&G's Purchasing Innovation IT leader at the time, Dennis Begg) both saw the CombineNet tool at two different conferences, Rogers and Begg instantly grasped its potential for multiple spends. Within a year, P&G was using the CombineNet tool across all three levels of complexity:

Level 1. The perfume chemical industry includes a myriad of chemical materials (more than 3000), numerous globally dispersed suppliers, the purchase of both individual materials and blends, and shipping to P&G perfume plants, which in turn ship to other P&G using sites, as well as direct supplier shipment of finished perfumes to those plants. P&G is one of the world's largest users of perfume in its many beauty and homecare products. Therefore, the buying task is enormous, requiring an entire section of purchasing, logistics, import/export, and technical service people, who are all involved in sourcing support. (*Note:* The CombineNet tool was P&G's first non-transportation use of a purchased optimization tool. The tool provided major cost and efficiency gains, leading to use of the tool on other direct and indirect spend pools.)

Level 2. P&G is also the largest truckload shipper in North America. Its transportation challenge encompasses over 50 production locations, over $750 million spend, 2500 to 3500 trucks daily, and an average 650-mile haul in over 7000 lanes with 120 suppliers (80% for hire and 20% customer pickup), with both drop and hook and live unload delivery—all of this before the acquisition of Gillette. Value is comprised of cost, on-time delivery, capacity access, transit time reduction, minority supplier involvement, and numerous shipping and delivery site preferences. Success concerns much more than just cost reduction. Servicing P&G's powerful retail customers is imperative and an important precursor of becoming a "full-bore" on-demand organization. Optimization has reduced costs and allowed carriers to help P&G respond to customer requirements while dealing with changes in governmental over-the-road driver hour regulations.[7]

Level 3. Important drivers of business for both P&G and retailers are the prebuilt displays of P&G products that are used for weekly end-of-aisle merchandising events. These displays are "solutions," which cut across an entire supply chain—finished product from P&G/contract manufacturers' plants, packaging materials and components, display assembly, and multiple transportation routes from manufacturers to assemblers to customers. Because of the scope of P&G, tens of thousands of display specifications each year—developed by both P&G and its customers—have the potential to change frequently. (Have you ever seen exactly the same display in a store more than a few times?) By using optimization[8] P&G has been able to find the "sweet spot" between:

- Buying the entire system (all of its parts—both goods and services)
- Buying individual parts
- Buying bundles of parts
- Buying a mixture of parts and bundles
- Then adjusting that "sweet spot" to changing market conditions

In its first display optimization event, P&G discovered that its optimized solution was 15% lower than the option of individually buying the parts and a massive 30% less than the more intuitive choice to have a tier 1 supplier handle the entire system—a configuration that typical supplier tiering consolidation efforts recommend.

At a purely strategic level, after running the display optimization event, the resulting configuration was such a discontinuity that P&G reconvened a 15-person cross-functional sourcing team and spent 2 days revamping the sourcing strategy using insights from the display optimization event as "intellectual raw material."

In 2003–2004 P&G saved over $300 million just from "big bang" optimization events, beginning a trend of nine-figure annual optimization savings on spends that had been previously put through the strategic sourcing process and repeated use of go-to-market tools (see Chapter 4, *Going to Market—Electronic Supplier Engagements*).

More importantly, however, is that the use of these powerful tools allows response and rethinking in the hands of people who "get it" about their use. When

Hurricane Katrina slammed into the U.S. Gulf Coast in August 2005, not only were P&G and its suppliers' manufacturing and warehousing operations impacted, but also the short-term (and perhaps long-term) customer channels and locations were changed. Tactically rebalancing the truckload delivery system and factoring in Katrina's impact became a strategic intervention of great value that was not measured by cost alone.

CLOSING THOUGHTS—SUPPLIER RELATIONSHIPS AND OPTIMIZATION

Implicit in this discussion is that optimization is supportive of strong supplier relationships because suppliers are invited into the business and encouraged to use their creativity as much as they can or want to. Motorola and P&G recognized that they needed and wanted suppliers to play key innovation and improvement roles in their business.

This point was never more clearly made than at a 2002 Conference Board Supply Chain Conference Workshop, which was hosted by CombineNet, Inc. in Chicago. Another CombineNet customer, presenting the use of optimization technology in ocean freight allocations, commented that the tool had a positive influence on supplier relationships. At that point, a workshop participant interjected, "This looks like a reverse auction in disguise with all these multiple bids driving competition up and prices down!" Before the presenter could respond, another participant spoke up: "That isn't true! We were a supplier in that event and were so impressed that we are now using the tool with some of our key suppliers on complicated spends. We felt that it was very different than an auction because it let us put our best foot forward by offering alternatives that we thought up." The first participant responded, "Well, winning suppliers always like the process. Talk to the losers." To which the participant from the ocean freight company replied, "We didn't win. We lost." When a losing supplier endorses a buyer's go-to-market tool, the endorsement is a compelling one indeed.

Said another way, optimization tools can create a platform that both enhances supplier relationships and creates strong competitive pressures for complex spends. However, leveraging supplier relationships and strong competitive pressure to the utmost requires a blend of art and science, both taken to a deep level and across a breadth of applications. This blend drives the search for "on-demand value" (Figure 5.3).

A Blend of Art and Depth and Breadth

Art

Depth
• Supply market intelligence
• Supplier relationship trust
• Cost knowledge

Breadth
• Cross business spends
• Cross spend pools
• Supply chain view
• Internal linkage

Value

Science

Depth
• Advanced math analytics
• Business rule evaluation
• Scenario building
• Solution speed

Breadth
• User friendly
• Collaborative interface
• Flexible bid options
• PC Web access

Figure 5.3. Successful Optimization Tool Usage.

This book has free material available for download from the
Web Added Value™ resource center at *www.jrosspub.com*

SRM—BRINGING HOME THE VALUE

Business is a cobweb of human relationships.

— **H. Ross Perot**
Billionaire, Computer Industry CEO

When putting together a proposal for this book, our first outlines had no chapter about supplier relationship management (SRM), and the suggestion to add one precipitated a debate. Not including a chapter about SRM may lead some to question, "Why not?"—quickly followed by, "SRM is a hot topic. Everyone 'does SRM' and any book about software tools which delivers value from supply strategies has to discuss SRM, doesn't it?" Obviously, the authors agreed, as evidenced by the inclusion of this chapter, but there is also ample reason why the debate happened.

SRM—THE GENESIS OF CONFUSION

SRM has become a big area of e-purchasing hype. As Dave Hannon, Managing Editor of *Purchasing* magazine, has pointed out in an October 2005 *SRM Report*, an informal poll shows that purchasing people are "… confused about where SRM begins and ends and how the mishmash of software labeled 'SRM' can help them in the day-to-day process of managing strategic suppliers."[1]

Many people throw the term SRM around, but no common, universally agreed upon definition exists about what SRM is or what it does. The software industry has not helped clarify the issue and probably has done much to make understanding even more tangled. Everyone agrees that "doing SRM" is important, even mandatory, to adding value in procurement, but "what does doing SRM actually mean" is a question that can have many different answers. The lack of a common vocabulary in the supply management field once again fuels the uncertainty of SRM.

Before leaping in and trying to define SRM, first take a step back from, as Hannon puts it, all the "mishmash." More than one thing seems to be occurring.

The Practitioner Side

At the Conference Board's first Supplier Relationship Management Conference in March 2005, co-author Steve Rogers was talking with two supplier relationship managers from a major MRO company. These managers were troubled by some of the presentations that had been made that day by purchasing people—their point being that a purchasing organization does sourcing, not SRM.

Companies may see and place SRM differently within their operations (e.g., the MRO company has an SRM group that is separate from purchasing). At some companies contract managers, also not part of the sourcing organization, conduct supplier performance management, not the deal makers. At yet others, both sourcing and SRM are conducted by purchasing. The IT organization that often interfaces with SRM software providers frequently has yet another take on SRM as being an extension of the ERP data backbone.

This variability within organizational boundaries creates very different customer user groups for software vendors to target, including the CIO's (chief information officer) organization where a sales pitch can easily end up, and can make the inclusion and exclusion of various tools under the SRM umbrella logical in one case, but not in another.

Something that practitioners do mostly agree on, however, is that SRM is not only about information and data—it is also about people and relationships (hence the "R" in SRM). On the IT or finance/accounting side, information and money/performance flows are what managing a relationship is all about. Because many but not all purchasing organizations report to finance, the definition of SRM becomes tailored by organizational reporting lines—but with no consensus across different companies about where SRM fits operationally. "Truth" is situational, often based on company philosophy, culture, history, and structure—none of which facilitates agreement on a common definition for SRM.

The Software Side

The other thing going on is on the software side. Technology continues to evolve—and rapidly at that. Additionally as the complex data stream from the upstream supply chain is "cleansed" and organized, software is enabled that looks beyond transactional to tactical and sometimes strategic interventions.

When writing the second edition of their book, Gerald Antonette, Larry Giunipero, and Chris Sawchuk asked the software supplier Entomo, Inc. to provide an SRM chapter (which subsequently came from papers written by Sunil Pande and David Lapidus).[2] The chapter described five levels of SRM:

- Transactions
- Communication and Collaboration
- Exceptions
- Data Mining and Reporting
- Analytics

According to Antonette, Giunipero, and Sawchuk (2002), the most tactical areas, especially transactions, were the areas most commonly used, while the most strategic area, analytics, was the least used—and many of the advantages of SRM sounded extremely tactical. The "sell" for SRM was in small-dollar-value components such as reduced expediting costs, increased buyer productivity, reduced requisitioning and dispute costs, and decreased inventory levels—all mostly transactional and material-management driven. Antonette, Giunipero, and Sawchuk predicted that technology would reverse that, and since 2002 it has continued to do just that, with increasing technology and user sophistication.

The real value of SRM tools must be justified less by making the supplier interface more efficient and more by what companies actually can do with that efficiency to drive externally created value. The trouble is that the increasing sophistication of SRM technology brings as part of the suite definition the original tactical tools such as supplier portals, automatic ordering, and material tracking systems with no "translation" to indicate where these systems fit into the overall sourcing process. Sometimes touting these elements creates enough noise to drown out the elements of over 75% of the value available—material cost/waste reductions, response time contraction, and top-line sales growth from supplier innovation. Instead SRM becomes an easy umbrella under which software suppliers can link everything from invoicing and ordering to sourcing and supplier scorecards.

Added to this history is that the SRM software competitors have arrived at this point from very different places and thus use different product- and module-naming terminology. SAP AG and the three Oracle Corporation platforms (Oracle and its acquired PeopleSoft, Inc. and J. D. Edwards lines) have their roots in ERP; SAS Institute has its roots in BI (business intelligence); i2 Technologies, Inc. and Manugistics, Inc. have a SCM (supply chain management) operational planning and logistics focus; and Emptoris, Inc., Frictionless Commerce, Inc. (now part of SAP AG), Verticalnet, and Ariba, Inc. began as sourcing/procurement applications.

No wonder software products do not help achieve definitional consensus. As of this writing, SAP, the Oracle PeopleSoft line, and SAS call their entire suite of tools SRM; Oracle embeds SRM (which sales literature describes similarly to the PeopleSoft functionality) as a module in procurement; the J. D. Edwards Oracle Suite uses the term "supply management;" i2 uses the term "sourcing and procurement;" and Ariba offers a "supplier management" module. Even within the ERP vendors, the three Oracle platforms each have a different number of modules (Oracle has 8; PeopleSoft has 11; and J. D. Edwards has 4 as of this writing—all with slightly different names). SAP's single suite still touts 4 major modules, consisting of up to as many as 11 submodules. All of these suites, modules, submodules, and terms result in a cacophony of names, functionality bundles, and marketing approaches. Practitioners are left wondering what SRM software really is and what it can do for them (as in Dave Hannon's apt moniker "mishmash").

Yet if supply management professionals can cut through the vendor names and claims to translate the functionalities into what is needed to manage their supply base, there is great value to be had. However, from the experienced practitioner's vantage point, SRM is probably a misnomer for the full range of the e-tool suite. These comprehensive tool boxes are probably better named "e-procurement" (to be discussed in more detail in Chapter 7, *P2P—Where e-Procurement Meets Accounts Payable*).

SRM—FROM THE PRACTITIONER'S PERSPECTIVE—A DEFINITION

So just what is SRM? Looking at SRM from a practitioner's view, the answer is found in the recollections of Tom Stallkamp, creator of one of the most famous SRM initiatives—Chrysler's Extended Enterprise and its SCORE system: "Our idea was to establish a closer relationship with our outside suppliers to make Chrysler more competitive as we struggled against intense pressure." Implicit in that statement is that SRM deals with the *relationship* with a supplier once the sourcing decision is made. SRM is not about changing suppliers, but rather about leveraging their abilities. In other words, SRM is the management and optimization of an *ongoing relationship* once the strategic sourcing is completed.

At the strategic level, SRM drives how a buyer and a seller interact to deal with marketplace dynamics and customer requirements that are not static, but require constant commercial and operational tweaking. Hannon[1] calls the interaction "SRM the Process." Other experts concur. Pierre Mitchell, longtime buy-side software and operations analyst (now a director with The Hackett Group) defines SRM as: "Once you've done your strategic sourcing work, how do you best collaborate with the suppliers you've got? It involves leveraging technology like supplier portals, scorecards, collaboration tools, and so forth. I see it as the collaboration with the supplier mostly."[1]

Jonathan Hughes, Sourcing and Supplier Management Practice Leader at Boston-based, alliance consultant Vantage Partners is even more emphatic. Hughes compares the emerging SRM software tools with their customer-facing predecessors, e.g., CRM (customer relationship management) initiated by Siebel Systems, Inc. (now part of Oracle). The idea is for the software to integrate all of the supplier- (SRM) or customer- (CRM) facing information residing in various functional silos within the company. However, Hughes points out that CRM is more intuitive because tracking all of the data points helps to better understand what a customer wants, which links back to decades-long marketing and sales disciplines that are core to company management. "With SRM," Hughes says, "the case is somewhat less straightforward. With customers the overwhelming goal is sales. But is the best supplier the one from whom you buy a lot at low prices? Not in an analogous way (to sales revenue/profit with customers). Typically a high-volume, low-price supplier is a commodity vendor: relatively easy to replace and by most measures not a source of competitive advantage."[3]

Hughes sees the essential insight of SRM as viewing suppliers as sources of competitive advantage, not just cost centers, which leads to a need to tap into ongoing relationship elements extending well beyond the sourcing choice—especially for strategic suppliers providing (or with the potential to provide) value beyond the basics of price, specified quality, and on-time delivery. Hughes' definition of SRM also revolves around the "post-deal" interaction, including the qualitative boundary between buyer and seller. The "currency" is agility, flexibility, innovation, performance tracking, and improvement planning, which is a significant change from early SRM, which meant ordering, auctioning, or invoicing. Do these latter elements—ordering, auctioning, or invoicing—play into the relationship? Yes, but for practitioners they are no longer the driving force.

SRM—e-TOOLS

Throughout this book, several e-tools that software providers often include under SRM are identified as separate parts of an overall "on-demand" search for value using software and the Internet. Given the SRM definition of "an ongoing relationship management after the sourcing decision," the focus in this chapter will be on two sets of software tools. First is a subset of the broader SRM or procurement suites—supplier performance management—which deals with information, scorecarding, and data-based management of supply base results. Second is a collection of niche tools (much like some of the sourcing strategy tools described in Chapter 3), which is focused on personal and institutional relationships between companies—supplier relationship support. The sum of the two subsets gives a working practitioner view of SRM, which is different from the software industry definitions that result from a work-enablement, not a work-doing perspective.

SUPPLIER PERFORMANCE MANAGEMENT—DATA, TRACKING, AND METRICS

Supplier performance management revolves around using data to understand the results of a company's goods and/or services buy, timely tracking of actual supplier performance, and the use of metrics to improve basic foundational elements (e.g., cost, quality, service, and lead time), plus the tracking of the economic outcomes that result from sourcing decisions—in other words, are the "go-to-market tool savings and operational improvements" actually there? Having the ability to use data is where the software suppliers' definition of SRM "nails" a key need. By using transactional data to build information that can actually be used, these solutions drive business results that are directly linked to supplier performance.

Software

At the May 2005 Institute for Supply Management International conference in San Antonio, co-author Rogers was speaking with a well-known software supplier, trying to understand what SRM is and what the tools do. He asked a sales person if there was someone in the company's sourcing or procurement operation with whom he could speak in order to understand how the company used their own tool. The salesperson sheepishly responded that the company did not use the tool yet because the company was too busy launching the tool with their customers. (*Note:* Always ask a service supplier this question: does the company use its own product? If not, ask further questions to understand why or walk away and find a company whose practitioners do use the company's tool and can help you to do the same.)

SAS Institute, Inc. (pronounced "sass," not the letters S-A-S as in Scandinavian Airlines) cannot be accused of selling, but never using, the company's SRM tool. SAS, whose genesis is BI, highlights its SRM suite on its website with a case study explanation of what the tool has meant to their own business.[4] For SAS, use of its suite begins with spend analysis and management, to understand where volume leverage and maverick spend reduction can improve cost, and then moves to the "supplier performance management" half of our SRM definition. Vendor scoring elements of the SAS tool are combined with spend analysis to illuminate not just which suppliers have a lot of spend, but also which suppliers provide the total cost of ownership that sourcing decisions expected. Additionally, these measures help reveal (unlock) non-price reliability and customer service (internal and external).

Perhaps one of the more interesting aspects of the tool's use is that SAS tracks information from its minority- and female-owned suppliers, leveraging that information when SAS sells SRM software to customers struggling with tier 2 diversity spend initiatives, adding this sourcing information to the SAS software product's overall value. Procurement at SAS has used its own tool to make the leap from cost center to revenue source. Furthermore, marketing people can see both the buying and selling interface with companies that are both customers and suppliers to SAS—a blend of SRM and CRM into a holistic manageable picture of the entire relationship.

Similarly, pharmaceutical giant Bristol-Myers Squibb (BMS) uses an SRM tool suite from Frictionless Commerce to automate and report the full range of BMS sourcing and supplier management processes. Internal policy mandates that in order to get credit for their work, sourcing people must enter all sourcing savings projects into the Frictionless SRM tool suite. This tracking system provides an understanding of not only individual contributions, but far more importantly the organizational progress against business goals, both internally and supplier by supplier.[5] Interestingly, the BMS example also highlights the fact that companies do not always feel compelled to use one suite for every interaction that pertains to their suppliers. In the case of BMS, the Frictionless tool interacts with their SAP ERP, Ariba Buyer e-Procurement, and ECOOutlook Web-EDI systems. BMS was probably pleased when SAP AG bought Frictionless in May 2006, which brought two BMS platforms together under one umbrella. (*Comment:* Use of one tool versus multiple tool combinations will be discussed in Chapter 7, but for now the point is that SRM tools provide information about the supplier relationship to help drive top- and bottom-line results.)

Supplier Scorecards

Supplier scorecards are perhaps the most frequently documented aspect of performance management. A benchmark report in 2005 outlines a compelling case for proactively using supplier scorecards:[6]

Relative Performance Improvement	Program (%)	No Program (%)
Price	23	13
On-Time Delivery	23	11
Quality	21	5
Service	21	17

According to the report, the most common metrics available in software scorecarding systems are:

- On-time delivery
- Quality of goods and services
- Price competitiveness
- Contract compliance

Nonquantifiable Factors

Yet to maximize the relationship potential, delivery, quality, price, and compliance measures must link to several other measures, which are far less convenient to capture in a software system—innovation, supplier responsiveness, and technical capability. Hence, the overall relationship requires melding technology-driven and human-driven information generation and assessment.

Maybe this challenge is part of the reason why only about 50% of the companies in the 2005 benchmark study actually "do scorecarding" to drive supplier performance—of the 50% that do, 16% use the metrics to weed out suppliers with low results, rather than creating action plans for performance improvement.[6] A 2004 benchmark study on the subject of supplier performance cites a remarkable 61% better performance when companies create joint action plans by sharing scorecard information with their suppliers versus only using the information to internally judge their suppliers.[7] Considering these compelling business cases, why do only 34% of companies use scorecards to drive improvement planning? The reasons are often internal:

- The integration of quality or delivery performance data from separate systems
- The decentralized functional silo ownership of different parts of the performance picture
- The "big bang syndrome," in which a company is overwhelmed by an attempt to push all suppliers into a program at once rather than using gradual inclusion over time

- The "procrastination syndrome," in which a company starts gradually and then never follows through

The 2005 benchmark study also notes that companies that measure over 25% of their suppliers deliver significantly better results than those that scorecard less than 25%:[6]

Improvement Area	<25%	>25%
Quality	16%	26%
Delivery	16%	25%

Investment of resources and time to institute the data-driven side of supplier performance management, while also carefully setting priorities on which suppliers and metrics are automated, has an advantage over using subjective, recent event-influenced, internal user and supply management "gut feel" supplier management. Data turns into information, which can overcome opinion and emotion to both focus improvement efforts and to communicate excellence to suppliers.

The human element makes the tools hard to implement because both transactional data scores and nontransactional qualitative metrics are needed to obtain the holistic view that gets the best results from suppliers—especially strategic ones. Still, the "data side" supplier management tools provide quantitative insight that empowers the other half of "practitioner" SRM—supplier relationships, which are built on human interactions, not only financial and physical transaction measures. Having the data allows prioritization and internalization of value focus. For the best in class, scorecarding, supplier savings tracking, and supplier intelligence tool modules are the foundation upon which full SRM capability is built. Supplier relationship support tools will finish the job.

SUPPLIER RELATIONSHIP SUPPORT—TOOLS AND THE PEOPLE PART

In an early 2006 conversation, Bill Moon, UPS Vice President of Procurement and Supplier Diversity, and a 38-year "Brown" veteran, described the SRM dilemma best: "We are working to decide how SRM fits with our strategic sourcing methodology." He also described how sourcing and the data-based tools that track sourcing are important, but so are the "people" relationships behind those data points. Always remember, it is the people in a supplier relationship who make the decisions to support (or exploit) their customer and it is people who ultimately deliver performance for both parties in a relationship.

The second tool set supports and builds upon traditional interaction—face-to-face meetings, telephone calls, e-mail, and sometimes rumor control. Tools such as those described in Chapter 3 (*Sourcing Strategy—the Brains Behind the Game*) apply here as well—recall the LexisNexis tool that helped often over-worked sourcing managers to keep up with public domain reports about critical supplier changes? Could an executive resignation or a financial result change the nature of a relationship? Early knowledge of and actions in response to such changes can mean continued success instead of a gradual drifting apart of a joint value-producing alignment.

Relationships and Sourcing Strategy

Andrew Cox's Oraculix Power Positioning Tool (discussed in Chapter 3) can make a difference in SRM. Cox relates a client's experience with a low-complexity component supply base. The company recognized that the classic relationships of the "generic" four-quadrant Kraljic model did not accurately describe the power relationship with the company's suppliers. The conclusion that a simple component was in the leverage quadrant, available from many suppliers, had led to years of bidding events. Once sourced multiple times, a consistent pattern of 1 to 3% savings per event had emerged.

The tool's probing questions, however, raised insight at the buying company that this particular business allocation pattern had resulted in the company having a series of low-bid suppliers, several being major companies that did not see the buying company as a particularly strategic customer. The nature of the relationship had shifted from a leverage situation to a relatively independent power relationship, with little supplier interest to collaborate at a deeper level to find value.

The buying company subsequently changed its sourcing strategy and sought out smaller suppliers who saw the buying company as a strategically important customer, thus achieving a stronger power position. (*Comment*: This is an example of the tool's sourcing strategy use. The SRM side emerged in the execution of a new strategy.) The buyer selected three smaller suppliers and leveraged its enhanced power to influence these suppliers to search for more value. In return for long-term contracts, each supplier provided open-book cost access and agreed to supplier development efforts that the larger short-term-contract "generic leverage" suppliers had refused. Within 2 years, waste elimination and process improvement initiatives had achieved a 15% cost reduction, a 25% on-time delivery improvement, and a 21% product quality improvement—easily eclipsing the traditional approach.[8, 9]

Interpersonal Interaction and Partnersmith

Another set of SRM tools enables the interpersonal interactions that actually make the business decisions in relationships. Vantage Partners LLC applies its appropriately named Partnersmith tool to extremely complex relationships (large outsourcing arrangements) or companies with highly autonomous decentralized business cultures. The point of this type of tool is not to have data precision or accounting accuracy, but rather to facilitate the use of *relatively accurate* data in the boundary-crossing internal and external workflows that allow the timely collaboration that is needed for success.

Unfortunately, one outcome of spend analytics and Sarbanes Oxley Act compliance is a level of paralysis that strikes companies until they have accounting-grade-accurate, real-time, fully integrated data solutions. Although having accurate, timely, integrated data solutions is necessary for governance (see Chapter 12, *Governance and Risk—Living in a Regulated and Dangerous World*) and certainly is advantageous for day-to-day product flows, managing ongoing relationships can use recent, roughly accurate, relative comparison data to deliver results. Two examples illustrate how results flow from accomplishing business tasks with the Partnersmith tool.

The J&J Experience

Medical and consumer goods giant Johnson & Johnson (J&J) is a highly decentralized company—its many subsidiaries operate independently. Although corporate scale is significant, central sourcing groups have little authority to mandate a business allocation in this culture. The sourcing organization saw potential to deliver more continuous improvement and innovation by identifying and using a cadre of high-quality clinical research organizations (CROs) to leverage scale and more tightly connect a network of decentralized divisions and therapeutic areas.

Partnersmith addresses two key challenges within J&J[10]—first was how to see the whole clinical "elephant" across all of the J&J organization versus individual unit snapshots, and second was how to make individual clinical groups comfortable with using a peer company's CRO for their studies. Because performance and capability were still unknowns for some company using groups, a mix of structured data (spend, volume, schedules) and unstructured data (assessments, opinions, reports), which was scattered in little pockets across the company, had to be assembled and discussed.

The J&J example raises an important aspect of all "on-demand" tools—data entry is not free. Data entry requires a combination of people (wages, either internal or outsourced) and software (maintenance fees). Often the results from these combinations require data pragmatism, not accounting accuracy.

J&J suppliers enter much of the data, which J&J periodically audits and then implicitly audits during the natural cross-business unit discussions that Partnersmith encourages. Entering good data is in the suppliers' best interests because future business is tied to the "performance unknown" question and the audit by J&J precludes opportunism. Johnson & Johnson uses supplier-provided data to create synergy across clinical operations at a lower cost in a decentralized culture. (*Comment:* "Asking suppliers for the data" has a negative stereotype because doing so is simply not good practice. Although this is true, the pragmatic reality is that with the right audits, supplier data can jumpstart stronger leverage of relationships for both cost and performance. Waiting for perfect data can be a long wait sometimes.)

The BCBSRI Experience

The Partnersmith tool can also design complex workflows that are necessary to manage complicated outsourced services contracts. Healthcare insurance companies such as Blue Cross Blue Shield of Rhode Island (BCBSRI) have outsourcing relationships that include major back-office operations such as billing claims. Anyone who has tried to decipher a hospital bill understands this "maze."

BCBSRI uses the Partnersmith tool to help manage the complexity of back-office operations. In 2003 BCBSRI outsourced its back-office IT infrastructure, claims handling, membership services, and application development along with 600 people to Perot Systems Corporation.

A complex outsourcing arrangement cannot be a static arrangement. Instead an ongoing process of negotiation and adjustment is absolutely necessary to sustain value as business conditions change. Through the use of several modules, including Partnersmith Issue Management and Escalation and Contract Amendment Tracker, BCBSRI and Perot Systems came together to make key decisions, escalate and resolve claim issues, handle work scope changes, and jointly govern the relationship in a complex and dynamic space with regulatory change. The tool set supports process clarification plus individual and organizational skill development in a complicated environment that requires significant person-to-person interaction and adjustment to change. It helps develop how the work is done.[11,12]

- **Strategic Fit**
  - Future vision and value proposition
  - Aligned metrics of success
  - Competitive advantage
  - Customers' needs

- **Chemistry/Cultural Fit**
  - Trust, culture, and teamwork
  - Quality of relationships
  - Cultural integration and respect
  - Leadership commitment

- **Operational Fit**
  - Alignment of systems, structural connectivity
  - High-performance processes
  - Integrative mechanisms
  - Fast time implementation

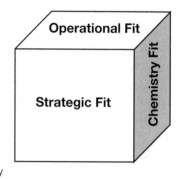

© Robert Lynch
The Warren Company

Figure 6.1. Lynch's Three-Dimensional Relationship Fit Model. (Source: From The Warren Company. With permission.)

Gaining Insight—Niche Tools

SurveyMonkey

An example of e-tool support for supplier relationships is so simple that it could easily have been dismissed as not even belonging in this chapter. SurveyMonkey (SurveyMonkey.com Corporation) is survey software that allows almost anyone to gather data. In the hands of a relationship expert, who adds experience, sound perspectives, and processes, the simple SurveyMonkey tool can make a big difference.

Robert Porter Lynch is the principal of The Warren Company, a small alliance consultant that flexes its capacity through a network of knowledgeable resources (including co-author Rogers on occasion). Lynch, Chairman Emeritus of the Association of Strategic Alliance Professionals (ASAP), was an early pioneer in the alliance field—both marketing and supply sides—long before alliance became a commonly accepted business vehicle. Years of research fueled Lynch's development of a simple, relatively short survey tool (about 30 questions) administered via SurveyMonkey. The survey results are loaded into a spreadsheet to create graphs and visuals to be used with buyer/seller partners. The questions are mapped against a "three-dimensional fit" relationship model (Figure 6.1):

- Strategic fit—the joint value proposition
- Operational fit— performance delivery and economic viability
- Chemistry fit—cultural compatibility, both individual and organizational

A technology/hardware company had outsourced a number of back-office processes to a provider with a global "footprint" (India, Eastern Europe, North America, etc.). Although the relationship had been largely successful at the operational level, the real strategic fit behind the arrangement was accessing the outsourcing company's process innovation in purchase to payment (P2P) and customer order management (COM) processes. The relationship's strategic fit in these areas had been frustrated and handicapped by contractual issues concerning budget and cost responsibility for investments that would be necessary to pay for those innovations.

Using the SurveyMonkey tool to ask his research-based questions, Lynch sampled key stakeholders across internal buyer boundaries (business units and functions), geographies (Asia, Europe, and the Americas), work processes (P2P, COM, and finance and accounting), and internal supplier boundaries (customer support and innovation development). The companies subsequently brought their various groups together in a governance meeting using the survey results to reenergize and refocus efforts.

Expectation outages were pinpointed, including the very different definitions of the meaning of innovation that each party had. Lynch cautions that in addition to carefully tested and refined questions, responses of the companies need to be compared (keeping individual responses confidential) and the consultant/facilitator must avoid hypothesizing about why the answers are what they are. Explanations from the companies of the reasons behind their responses fueled insight between companies and across their internal boundaries.

The result was a watershed engagement at the business unit level—creation of a new joint value proposition and resource focus on both operational improvement and innovation opportunities to move performance to a higher level. The result is not a "group hug," but rather hard-headed, business conflict identification and resolution.

Sounds like consulting, not software, doesn't it? True, but using a simple e-tool that gathers worldwide input can supercharge the application of strategy and process knowledge to a relationship. More importantly, a simple tool gets real issues and feelings on the table, putting the customer and the supplier in charge of dealing with them—which is the first step toward ultimately delivering results.[13]

General Idea Software

Another tool uses off-the-shelf software to enable today's version of the well-known Chrysler SCORE system in which suppliers submitted ideas that reduced cost and provided breakthrough innovation to the automaker prior to the

Daimler acquisition. A General Idea Software tool is used by Bristol-Myers Squibb (BMS) for its "Idea Bank," a repository for supplier-generated productivity-improvement suggestions. BMS, like Chrysler, realizes that ideas are nothing if they just sit upon arrival. BMS uses an aging report and clear senior-level insistence on timely idea feedback to augment the technology and avoid missed expectations that hurt relationships.[14]

These relationship support tools represent an emerging set of niche software tools to help manage a living, breathing organism made up of people from two companies. Relationships are often unstable due to change inside each participating company and the outside world. To endure over time, constant adjustment, interpersonal interaction, and new idea generation are necessary ingredients. A number of software companies offer products, including several that can be found on the Association of Strategic Alliance Professionals (ASAP) website (www.strategic-alliances.org) under the "About" tab's alliance directories section. Whether these tools will ever have the sales potential to become part of larger tool suites is certainly debatable. It is too soon to tell, but the tools have undeniable ability to support sustained results from the interface between structured financial/performance metrics and the often unstructured people side of SRM.

CLOSING THOUGHTS—SUPPLIER SEGMENTATION AND APPLYING THE TOOLS

So after all the discussion, what is SRM? Before answering, no discussion of SRM would be complete without some mention of supplier segmentation,[14, 15] which is the classic triangular differentiation of relationships into routine, tactical, preferred, and alliance relationships (Figure 6.2).

The challenge in SRM is to use the right tools to manage each type of relationship. A typical large company has tens of thousands of suppliers, a few of which are strategic and a multitude of which are not. The full range of SRM deals with three types of suppliers—the critical strategic few, a meaningful group of midsized suppliers, and a seemingly endless "tail" of small-spend, infrequently used vendors. Most SRM performance management tools deal with the first two groups. Relationship support tools focus on the top strategic few—a group in which the investment of time and effort have the biggest payoff. The enormous long "tail" that includes 80% of the suppliers and about 10% of the spend is a very different problem, which is solved more by sourcing than by SRM. Viewed from that perspective, spend analysis, tactical procurement, and supply base rationalization tools do apply to SRM, but more to reduce numbers and to automate transactions.

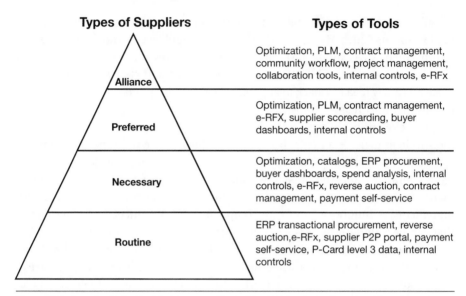

Types of Suppliers

- Alliance
- Preferred
- Necessary
- Routine

Types of Tools

Optimization, PLM, contract management, community workflow, project management, collaboration tools, internal controls, e-RFx

Optimization, PLM, contract management, e-RFX, supplier scorecarding, buyer dashboards, internal controls

Optimization, catalogs, ERP procurement, buyer dashboards, spend analysis, internal controls, e-RFx, reverse auction, contract management, payment self-service

ERP transactional procurement, reverse auction,e-RFx, supplier P2P portal, payment self-service, P-Card level 3 data, internal controls

Figure 6.2. Supplier Relationship Types—e-Tools Should Match the Relationship.

Perhaps the various uses of the tools to manage many types of relationships and activities are one of the reasons why SRM is a fuzzy term, but for practitioners SRM is managing the relationship post-deal. Managing the relationship after the deal is done needs transactional data to aggregate into operational metrics (areas in which suite-based SRM scorecards and project tracking provide foundation governance). Simultaneously SRM must support human relationships and interpretive communications behind higher-level strategic decisions, expectations, and emotions that make up the relationship (areas in which niche tools that assess attributes and perceptions play a role).

Each company must plot its needs (savings, innovation, quality, reliability) and resources (money, people and time) against the range of available tools and then choose the tools that will make the biggest difference. Many companies forget the people side, but companies that integrate niche tools with strong quantitative software suites can create advantage that is hard for competitors to replicate.

LESSONS LEARNED

- SRM is the management and optimization of an ongoing supplier relationship once sourcing is completed. SRM has two facets—supplier performance management and supplier relationship support.
- The label SRM is used in widely differing ways by software providers.
- Buyers that scorecard supplier performance achieve better results.
- Several e-tools, including online surveys, can augment supplier communications and partnering.
- The challenge of SRM is very different when dealing with strategic suppliers, an area in which resource and time investments have high potential for payback, than when dealing with the myriad of small routine suppliers, an area in which efficiency and risk protection against outages are the objectives.

This book has free material available for download from the
Web Added Value™ resource center at *www.jrosspub.com*

P2P—WHERE e-PROCUREMENT MEETS ACCOUNTS PAYABLE

The devil is in the details.

— **Gustave Flaubert**
French novelist

In purchasing and supply management, P2P is an acronym for "procure to pay" or "purchase to payment." Another acronym with the same meaning is R2C—requisition (req) to check. P2P is the transactional flow that surrounds an order that is sent to a supplier, the fulfillment of the order, and then payment for the product.

As the preface to this book has described, e-procurement began in the hype of the dot.com boom in the late 1990s. Many companies started with e-procurement of indirect spend and found doing so was much tougher than the magazine articles and software ads had depicted. Even worse, some procurement leaders were "stained" by the damaging perception of senior management—an indelible picture of a struggling, million-dollar IT investment to save a few pennies on the pens and pencils stored in office supply cabinets. Not a good mental image for the people with the purse strings who were looking for a strategic intervention.

Through it all, the P2P pathway automation of e-procurement kept quietly plugging away, ultimately undergoing perhaps the most improvement in terms of capability and foundational importance. The nomenclature, however, is still fuzzy, with some SRM suites looking more like e-procurement suites and most e-procurement suites having SRM modules (see Chapter 6). The original transactional P2P Internet interfaces—requisitions, purchase orders, delivery receipts, payment approvals, ledger postings, and funds transfers—are still the backbone for a host of evolving powerful purchasing tools. Not much imagination was required for software suppliers to add sourcing, contract, and compliance components to the horizontal process of the early tools.

e-Procurement suites, regardless of their specific product names, are e-tool lineups that mirror corporate supply management processes. Throughout this book discrete elements of the broad e-procurement tool set (spend analytics, go-to-market reverse auction/RFx, contract management, SRM, etc.) will be examined, but this chapter will return to the genesis of these e-tools and discuss how e-procurement has survived, even thrived, for companies that "get it."

P2P is the ultimate multifunctional process, cutting across users (requisitions and desktop buying), sourcing (deal making to reduce cost or increase value), departments/functions (Finance and Accounting, money tracking and funds transfer; Accounts Payable, paying bills; Human Resources and Internal Controls, setting/enforcing policies), and ultimately the suppliers themselves (to "make it all happen" in the real world). A December 2004 benchmark report highlights continuing e-procurement improvements well:[1]

- Basic requisition-to-order functionality—Matured requisitioning, approval routing, and reporting are comparable across most software solutions.

- Broader suites that more effectively tie the process together

- Improved catalog approaches requiring much less maintenance and providing more standard, intuitive user screens.

- Dramatically reduced product cost (e.g., a 75% license fee reduction since 1998)

- Availability of believable, realistic sourcing and internal efficiency savings for use in investment justification

Performance Area	Before e-Procurement	After e-Procurement
Maverick Spend	38%	14%
Savings on Maverick Spend	—	7%
Requisition-to-Order Cycle	20 days	4 days
Requisition-to-Order Costs	$56	$23
Spend under Purchasing	56%	69%

This capability is now something that is within reach for many companies, not just the well-funded elite. Plus, the return is clear. For many companies the journey to e-procurement is by no means over, but progress is obvious, with improvement areas becoming more visible and attainable. Hard work is still required, but it will be with far fewer unexpected missteps caused by immature software or overconfident implementations.

THE BUILDING BLOCKS OF e-PROCUREMENT SUCCESS—A KITCHEN TABLE

Like a kitchen table, successful P2P has four legs:

- User-friendly interfaces
- Solid sourcing behind the interface
- Policy development and compliance
- Supplier enablement to make it work

Successful P2P also has a table top, which is constancy of purpose or, said another way, steadily continuing execution. P2P success is not for the impatient or for the easily distracted.

Yet, according to the December 2004 benchmark report, the various P2P e-procurement applications had only a 40 to a 60% penetration by late 2004 and were projected to increase to just 55 to 75% by 2007. The range is caused by variation between particular elements, with catalogs at the top and items such as invoice reconciliation and automatic payment applications toward the bottom. The report listed many of the same traditional "challenge" areas that long-plagued implementations as barriers—supplier catalog management, user adoption, policy enforcement, non-catalog spend management, and the task of simply maintaining the e-procurement application.[1]

Leg 1—User-Friendly Interfaces

Bottom line, the interface must be easy for users. "Easy" means easier than telephoning Costco or Staples and picking up the goods on the way home after work! If a computer desktop application is confusing or frustrating, users simply will not tolerate it. The battle then moves from implementation to insurrection because in many cases users can be quite inflexible. This situation leads to an interesting phenomenon. Several tool suites, especially those from ERP suppliers, would seem to be natural sole-supplier applications, thus avoiding integration costs. Yet an enormous number of companies implement a procurement vendor's tools on top of an ERP vendor's underlying systems.

Companies using multiple software solutions cite user unfriendliness and the "underwhelming-ness" of some ERP system tools as reasons why they pay for multiple software solutions. (*Comment*: Perhaps this is the same reason why SAP acquired Frictionless Commerce, Inc. in May 2006 to improve its then relatively weak e-sourcing tools?) Another reason is that e-procurement tools (e.g., Ariba e-Procurement) were purchased and installed before the completion of base ERP implementations and/or before the availability of ERP provider procurement or SRM applications. Still another reason is that integration costs continue to fall as middleware improves and tool providers include specific modules that more easily link with other suites, leading to lower cost implementations and quicker results. (*Note*: Frictionless Commerce, Inc. was certified as an SAP NetWeaver partner just 4 months before the acquisition.)

Whether through acquisition or internal application improvement, ERP products are improving, leading to intense budget and supplier choice battles. A CIO and CFO can be highly resistant to a "users dislike the interface" argument to justify six- or seven-figure investments and internal IT integration resources for a two-supplier solution. Meanwhile CPOs and functional budget owners counter with the point that if people will not use the system, the results will falter at any price. For example, 55% of companies cite employee adoption problems as the biggest P2P automation problem.[1] *Remember*: P2P functionality requires user involvement at levels in which personnel turnover is significant, necessitating ongoing training and "resale" of the system to new arrivals.

Leg 2—Smart, Practical Sourcing

The desktop interface, even when its use is persuasive to users, must be supported by strong supplier selection and management. The work "behind the scene" must deliver low-cost, high-service/high-quality vendors or the system will deliver only appearance without substance. Sourcing skills that leverage data cleansing, spend analysis, sourcing strategy, reverse auction/RFx, optimization, contract management, etc. produce valuable e-procurement results. Success also requires planning in two other important areas—adequate staffing and purchasing channel/tool matchups that drive usage.

Staffing

At a large manufacturing company, purchasing leaders convinced their CFO to mandate that all buying decisions had to be made by the purchasing organization, ending years of "legitimate" maverick indirect spend buying. Internal controls enforced the mandate. Viewed as an enormous victory, professional purchasing was finally in charge of almost 100% of the company's purchases—a victory, that is, until the orders started pouring into an organization that had not been staffed for the increase in work.

Deluged by "one-off" buys and people-consuming catalog maintenance issues, the program "fell beneath its own weight." After a 4-year struggle, the program was declared a failure and in need of a relaunch. Sourcing became slipshod, as overwhelmed staffers put having a supplier—almost any supplier—ahead of sourcing-for-value acquisitions. The professionals were buying like the maverick amateurs they had replaced because leadership had failed to anticipate the demands of "a new world." It was truly a Pyrrhic victory. (*Note*: Pyrrhus, king of Epirus, sustained heavy losses in a defeat of the Romans, losses that were costly to the point of negating the benefits of victory.)

Channel and Tool Choices

The second sourcing challenge is thinking through channel decisions. Purchases can be made via traditional purchase orders sourced by purchasing; by users placing orders with catalogs sourced by purchasing; and with P-Cards (procurement "credit cards") that let users source, order, and pay for goods. (*Note*: P-Cards can be limited to certain suppliers for certain classes of items, thus enabling sourcing "behind the card.") Channel strategy requires consideration of several things:

- Order size (dollars not volume) for control purposes
- Volume levels to determine the choice between catalog or formal sourcing
- Efficiency or staffing to deal with workload issues
- Spend documentation both for control and sourcing strategy reasons
- User support to push system utilization
- User compliance and budget control to deliver bottom-line results

Two examples illustrate channel choice:

- A major U.S. chemical company designed their e-procurement around monetary order size, with large orders (five figures) going through purchasing; routine families (e.g., office supplies) being handled by catalogs; spends between $15K and $1K using e-procurement POs; and unique item orders below $1K using P-Cards.
- A pharmaceutical company set up an e-procurement approach that stressed effectiveness for most spends (catalogs and electronic purchase orders placed by users from a preferred supplier list) and purchasing support for larger spends (over $100K) in their major facilities. In small satellite operations with small purchasing staffs (one or two people) and despite real concerns about P-Card sourcing

effectiveness, P-Cards were still implemented for efficiency reasons (the tradeoff with effectiveness being viewed as "good enough, but not ideal").

The P-Card debate continues, with proponents citing efficiency and "good-enough" documentation in strong compliance and internal controls cultures as reasons to put "more rather than less" through the cards. Detractors counter that documentation is not good enough. Although card providers say level 3 data (detailed spend data) can be captured, they also admit that very few suppliers provide the card company with level 3 data. Unless the buying company uses its leverage with suppliers to insist on level 3 data, obtaining deep spend data is an unlikely outcome. Detractors are also concerned about fraud, given the user's combined source/order/pay role and with controls being largely after the fact, rather than before.

Pareto analysis typically channels "nuisance spends" to P-Cards. Nuisance spends are often unique, low-dollar-volume items (not particularly catalog compatible) that represent over half of the transactions and less than 10% of the spend—the classic "non-critical" Kraljic spend quadrant strategy.

Is there one best way to do P-Cards? Probably not. The best approach, however, is "thinking the channel choices through" and driving the plan to its conclusion.

Leg 3—Policy Compliance

Policy compliance entails two kinds of policies—those that drive users to the company's channel of choice (use the tool or adoption) and those that ensure that the negotiated savings show up in the bottom line versus encouraging increased usage because budget is available to spend. For channel compliance, spend visibility, including assignment to the department or budget center where the spending resides, is critical. Too often, senior executives want to insulate their organization from the need to comply because "they are different" or "Procurement doesn't understand" and thus become the root cause behind e-procurement spend channel policies that do not work. Policy might be written by Procurement (unlikely to work), Human Resources (a little better) or Finance (much better), but at the end of the day, senior management must agree to comply and legitimize the policy by asking the managers of maverick buyers why their buyers are not using the proper channels.

Measurement of corporate losses when a local requirement is sourced off-contract is vital. Often the isolated local cost can be lower than the corporate deal (or it is perceived to be because the discount is not transparent to local people), but volume losses due to large local policy violations can undermine savings at other locations when a deal spans numerous sites. Without compelling data and management support, policy violations can be a major issue. Typically successful implementations bring variations to the attention of the local budget owner, which often solves the problem. In other cases, the "user friendly principle" is in place so compliance works because the overall system works. (*Comment:* The authors are aware of termination for multiple compliance violations at only one company and the information was from a second-hand conversation.)

Some savvy companies intentionally "under" contract the corporate volume, which allows local deals to be accepted without hurting compliant sites, but this requires leading-edge data systems to monitor total spend and user policy management to avoid willful user violation of a deal.

As budgetary policy, the best in class build purchasing savings into forecasted profit plans for the upcoming year, thus raising general manager (GM) questions during budget reviews when indirect spend usage levels along with supplier deal compliance are not delivering forecasted cost reductions in the financials. Another successful use of transparent cost and usage levels is the escalation of certain decisions to the GM or comptroller for a conscious choice about savings—to take savings to profit or to spend gains on other value opportunities (e.g., marketing spend savings can either go to the bottom line or to fund additional top-line growth plans—the key is rigorous financial success criteria for new projects audited by the comptroller's office to avoid wasteful spending to protect budgets for next year). (*Comment*: Without rigorous oversight by finance, many GMs will submit to the "siren's song" of marketing spend because that is the strongest cultural imperative and the cause of much wasted expenditure.)

Leg 4—Supplier Enablement

The first three legs look internally. The fourth leg looks externally. Supplier enablement, as defined in a 2004 benchmark study,[1] applies to the catalog process and deals with the enormous workload of managing supplier catalog content, data maintenance, and transactions.

Catalog Management

Early on, buyers chose catalog self-management only to discover that maintaining information, ensuring that price discounts were realized, and simply dealing with the large numbers of site arrangements and suppliers/catalogs drained their resources. The ideal solution seemed to be "punch-out" or "round-tripping"— transferring the responsibility for data maintenance to the supplier. Users would be routed to supplier catalog websites. Unfortunately all websites are different (users are not thrilled about this). Comparison shopping across more than one catalog for the same item is complex to impossible (requires more than one round-trip) or unlikely (a user just buys at the first punch-out location regardless of price). Inconsistent transaction management across supplier sites is another variable.

Software vendors are extremely helpful in supplier enablement. Software vendors provide supplier networks—a set of suppliers recruited by the software vendor (directly or from other customers) that uploads their catalog data into the software. The data can be augmented by buyer-specific suppliers. Buyers are "enabled" to check multiple catalogs for similar items and do not have unique buyer-specific maintenance tasks. These catalog hubs can tailor the buyer's view of specific deal information, plus add price check and discount verification services. However, the 2004 benchmark report notes that just over half of the catalogs in a 147-company survey use these networks or hubs, leaving many companies still internally handling catalogs, thus making catalog transaction management the top challenge cited.[1] A well-designed e-procurement success plan needs supplier enablement for efficient and effective catalog data housing for use and control purposes.

Real-World Application

Conceptually, expanding supplier enablement beyond catalogs opens a huge number of options though the use of tool suite supplier portals. Suppliers can access their own data—scorecards, buyer specification changes, shipping schedules, and invoice payment information.

Personal experience has brought this home to co-author Rogers. After 30 years with a large multinational corporation, he now works as an independent contractor in a small 30-person consulting consortium or singly as a supply management consultant. In a subcontract arrangement with another consultant to manage a supplier relationship project, the consulting firm was to manage client invoicing and reimburse Rogers.

Several weeks after an engagement, reimbursement had still not arrived. The consultant's administrative office said that the invoice had been sent and the payment issue was with the client. The client had supplier self-service invoice tracking in its SAP Accounts Payable supplier portal service. As a registered supplier, Rogers accessed his accounts payable data and found that no invoice had been received. Pressing the consultant's office manager revealed that the invoice had never been sent, triggering a call to the consultant's president. As a result, (1) the invoice was issued; (2) Rogers tracked the invoice until payment to the consulting firm; and (3) once funds had transferred, Rogers ensured his own next-day payment. This is supplier enablement (and the difference between a big company buyer and a tiny company seller)!

e-Procurement suites allow suppliers to use their own data to solve problems via portals and various modules in the toolset. In fact, these portals represent an SRM-enabler as well (see Chapter 6). Dan Kraus, head of Hallmark's global sourcing group, began managing long-distance relationships long before procurement and SRM software were available. He endorses the use of these portals as a strong enabler for relationships and e-procurement because strategic suppliers worldwide can access their data from the portal to manage ongoing business.[2]

The Table Top—Constancy of Purpose

What is constancy of purpose? Two examples will illustrate it.

The HP Experience

Technology leader Hewlett-Packard (HP) has had a major e-procurement effort underway for 6 years. Chris Connors, a 20-year HP veteran, spent 5 years leading indirect spend e-procurement solution implementation at HP and is now the Procurement Director of Strategy and Planning. The HP journey was described by Connors at the National Association of Purchasing and Payables (NAPP) conference in February 2006, illustrating the planning and ongoing drive necessary to get the most out of e-procurement.[3]

Over the 6-year effort, HP experienced enormous change—the Compaq acquisition/merger, expansion of HP IT services business, and a highly public CEO change, to name a few. Yet the program continued. With the focus of new CEO Mark Hurd on creating a competitive cost structure to battle the highly contested hardware and service businesses, importance of the program can only increase. Results to date are strong:

Category	Inception	Current	Projected
Indirect Procurement Operations Cost (% of Spend)	0.95	0.72	0.65
Tactical Headcount (% of Total)	60	40	30
Strategic Headcount (% of Total)	40	60	70
Number of Suppliers (Thousands)	125K	55K	<45K

Savings are up significantly and 95% of indirect spend goes through the HP Ariba Buyer system. The HP "headline" metric is indirect spend as a percentage of revenue and its "affordability" metric is procurement budget expense as a percent of spend. Additionally, effectiveness and efficiency are benchmarked against the

Hackett Company's value grid system, in which HP is in the "world class" quadrant, but still sees improvement opportunities.

More impressive is that HP started from a very challenging place— a strong, locally focused culture of fragmented organizations, local tools, locally focused internal metrics, numerous suppliers, and many legacy systems. The HP plan, which has four stages, has been comprehensive and sequenced for steady improvement and sustained results, while engaging budget owners in the business units. The first three stages are well underway and a fourth stage aligns with CEO Hurd's cost structure strategy:

Stage	Description	Process Leader
1. Supply Management	Focus supplier relationships on value for HP	Procurement
2. Compliance Management	Capture savings, by using preferred suppliers	Procurement + Business Units
3. Consumption Management	Reduce TCO by addressing usage drivers	Procurement + Business Units
4. Budget Compliance	Book savings into budgets	Business Units

A phased cost-reduction framework emerges from the table—negotiate better deals (savings and cost avoidance), increase spend compliance (use preferred supplier contracts), and tighten spend controls (control consumption, analyze spend trends, report to business unit budget owners).

A stepwise approach to user channel strategy helps manage the cultural challenge necessary for change:

Step 1. Use the tools (e.g., Ariba e-Procurement and P-Cards)

Step 2. Use the suppliers (buy from approved vendors)

Step 3. Get the right price (enforce contract pricing)

Step 4. Reduce spend (address consumption, deliver savings)

Step 5. Have spend controls (budgetary commitment)

Doing everything at once is like trying to jump over a canyon—the risk of failure is high. In a stepwise approach, each step delivers results that build on the others and over time a new culture emerges (Figure 7.1).

The Pfizer, Inc. Experience

Pharmaceutical giant Pfizer also relates a steady "constancy of purpose" story.[4] Pfizer's e-procurement system deals with enormous complexity and scope breadth—operations in 150 countries, as many as 60,000 users buying items on

Compliance Stages

1. Supply management:
   focus suppliers on value

2. Compliance management:
   focus users on right suppliers

3. Consumption management:
   reduce/change usage drivers

4. Budget management:
   build savings into profit plans

User Channel Evolution

1. Tools:
   e-procurement suite, P-Cards

2. Suppliers:
   preferred suppliers

3. Pricing:
   price enforcement with suppliers

4. Spend:
   reduce usage and lower prices

5. Budget:
   turn reductions into commitment

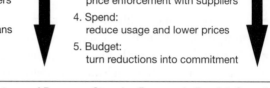

Figure 7.1. e-Procurement Constancy of Purpose—Stepwise Progress in Parallel: Compliance and Channels.

the system, and major acquisitions to be integrated. Pam Prince-Eason (senior director in Pfizer's Global Sourcing organization) has responsibility for the design and implementation of electronic P2P. She views P2P as an end-to-end process that requires close coordination between the upstream side (requisitioning, sourcing, ordering) and the downstream end (receiving, invoice processing, discrepancy intervention, and disbursement). In her words, "Purchasing and Accounts Payable belong together and should live happily ever after." The Ariba e-Procurement suite sitting atop Pfizer's Oracle ERP system seeks to accomplish this by including not only typical buying modules, but also electronic invoicing (e-invoicing).

Prince-Eason's plan used classic "as is" and "to be" gap analysis to create a blueprint for its e-procurement implementation. Given the variety of Pfizer's operations around the world, this blueprint has to be worked out with local organizations that have a key voice in both supplier and catalog selection. The plan has four dimensions over a 6-year horizon:

- Governance boards, including local users, procurement, and accounts payable
- Spend management guidelines that drive channel compliance (Ariba e-Procurement and P-Cards)
- A range of training formats (classroom, interactive Internet meetings, and e-training)
- Tools that encourage adoption and really work

The last dimension is the reason that Pfizer uses the Ariba tool, not just its ERP procurement modules. In the end, "It's about adoption," Prince-Eason said. User reaction ultimately drove the decision to have a procurement system atop the

ERP backbone. The justification can be challenging, but to get results, people must use the system.

As any global e-procurement rollout continues, perhaps the most important insight from the process is that the range of three e-procurement options that are available to any company can be blended to integrate location size and culture for success:

- High compliance, with robust supplier enablement (high use of an e-procurement system with heavy focus on catalogs)
- Basic compliance, with minimal supplier enablement (e-procurement and P-Cards with less reliance on catalogs)
- Optimizing existing systems (manual, P-Cards, local e-procurement tools, limited use of corporate software suite modules)

The first two options should represent the overwhelming majority of e-procurement, but all three are necessary to cover the full range of user capability. One "size" rarely fits all locations, despite the belief of IT management that it should (Figure 7.2).

Comment: Constancy of purpose is clear in both of these success stories—6-year journeys through major organizational and business changes along the way and attention to the four "table legs"—user friendliness, sourcing, policy, and supplier enablement.

CLOSING THOUGHTS—THE ACCOUNTS PAYABLE INTERFACE—DO NOT DROP THE BALL!

The National Association of Purchasing and Payables seeks to improve interaction and integration between the purchasing and payables disciplines. For P2P to work, purchasing and accounts payable must overcome differences to seamlessly create an efficient and effective process. Although some companies include purchasing and accounts payable in the same organization, most do not. Accounts payable often resides in finance or, as is the case in a growing number of companies, accounts payable is outsourced to low-cost countries for internal overhead savings via labor arbitrage and the specialized expertise of these outsourcing companies. Regardless of location, accounts payable and purchasing must work well together. When they do not, the organization will experience deterioration of payment-on-time (POT) metrics.

A major company experienced this the hard way. In the early 1990s, during a downsizing, accounts payable moved from purchasing into finance. Things were fine for the first 2 to 3 years—until existing accounts payable and procurement boundary staff began to retire, move to new assignments, or leave the company

	Type	Description	Benefit	Risk
1	Extensive catalog High automation	High supplier enablement Best-in-class implementation	Full e-buy usage SOX visibility	Up-front sourcing Long time line High investment
2	Minimum electronic compliance model	Focus on SOX compliance Partial use of front-end user interface	Lower SOX Cost Partial e-buy usage	May need future changes IT resource conflict
3	No or minimal e-buy suite	Improve business process Use legacy systems High site resourcing	Fast incremental improvement High site commitment	Little ERP or IT leverage Will need future changes High site resources

Figure 7.2. P2P Deployment Options.

for other opportunities. Gradually, so gradually as to be almost unnoticeable, mutual understanding of the sourcing and payment process intersection points drifted away. Then there was a series of major "initiatives"—an extremely difficult SAP implementation with its massive retraining to allow basic system use; an off-shoring project to move accounts payable to a low-cost country; and another reorganization including simultaneous procurement administrative staff reductions and outsourcing of much of the offshore accounts payable organization to an even lower-cost third party. Suddenly, almost 10 years later, the company began to encounter supplier refusals to ship to new locations and price increases to cover slow payments. The arrival of the Sarbanes-Oxley Act and its need for strong P2P processes to ensure financial reporting integrity added even more headaches. What was once a sourcing sales pitch—"We pay supplier bills on time!"—soon became embarrassing, as supplier management confided that on-time payment was a growing concern. A point of pride had become a "crisis of confidence" at the purchasing/accounts payable interface, which required a 2-year intensive effort to finally solve.

Part of the transactional functionality of user-friendly e-procurement tools can help avoid these types of situations, when connected to downstream process-efficient payables workflow-management tools such as paper invoice imaging and electronic funds transfer (EFT) e-tools. Whether managed internally or managed as part of an outsourcing agreement, the sourcing/accounts payable boundary must be rigorously handled.

The "downstream" receipt/post to ledger/payment process was vividly described in a 2005 *Business Week* article about India's IT and outsourcing companies.[5] The article pointed out that reapplication of Toyota's manufacturing

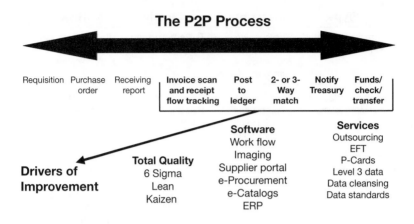

Figure 7.3. Back-Office P2P Improvement.

principles to paperwork flow is part of India's outsourcing success recipe—not just wage arbitrage, but also quality improvement. The *Business Week* article followed the path taken by an invoice through an accounts payable outsourcing operation in Bangalore. The description included passing a paper invoice through scanners to make electronic copies and the path of the work flow software that tracked its trip from accuracy verification to accounting entry to payment authorization and ultimately to payment itself.

Tight linkage between purchasing and payment is critical—regardless of whether the work is done internally or externally. The key to efficiency is minimizing the number of "touches" along the invoice journey—electronic invoices (e-invoices) instead of paper; pay-on-receipt approaches that eliminate invoicing altogether (the buyer creates e-invoices upon receipt of goods using e-procurement suite capabilities); vendor-prepared service receipts that users verify; e-invoice consolidation (combines multiple invoices into one periodic payment); etc. Essentially, procurement e-billing modules meet accounts payable workflow management software tools to image, post, track, check, and pay electronically (Figure 7.3).

The old AT&T (part of the reincarnated AT&T with SBC Communications, Inc. and BellSouth) stressed supplier e-invoicing for years, but by 2002 the effort had stalled at 87% until AT&T leveraged the Ariba e-Billing module to drive to e-invoicing to 97%—instrumental in reducing the accounts payable headcount by 56% between 2002 and 2005.[6]

This purchasing/payables connection is also a component of total cost of ownership (TCO) for materials and services, especially when the process goes electronic using e-procurement invoicing and ERP integration modules. Timken, a bearing manufacturer, dramatically increased use of purchased goods and services after a major 2003 acquisition significantly reduced its level of vertical integration.[7] TCO analysis was instituted as an integral part of a renewed Timken sourcing strategy process. TCO analysis identified transaction costs as one of the top five TCO components (others were price, quality, supplier reliability/capacity, and transportation/logistics). This analysis made supplier P2P invoicing capability an important part of sourcing evaluations, leading to supplier selection criteria:

- An ability to access the Timken Supplier Network (Timkin's enablement network)
- Supplier electronic data interchange/evaluated receipts settlement (EDI/ERS) capability
- A supplier back-office enterprise system (ERP development level)
- Ease of payment terms and currency requirements
- Quality assurance applied to the billing/collection process

Bottom line, purchasing recognized that the number five TCO cost contributor required sourcing to incorporate expectations that suppliers have effective e-procurement/supplier billing/accounts payable interaction.

LESSONS LEARNED

- The P2P aspects of e-procurement tools have improved steadily over time and are no longer largely hype.
- Procurement and accounts payable must work together.
- Organizational capabilities are extremely important to manage the cross-functional process of procurement and accounts payable collaboration.
- User-friendly interfaces are a must.
- "Do the sourcing" before the organization is "set loose" to desktop buy.
- Corporate buying policy development and enforcement are vital.
- Supplier enablement improves the efficiency of order/delivery/payment operations such that supplier P2P capability becomes an important component of a TCO analysis.
- Constancy of purpose is not a sprint, but rather a marathon. Constancy of purpose across organizational changes, business condition shifts, and buying tool/channel evolution facilitates ever-larger benefits.

Web
Added
Value™

This book has free material available for download from the
Web Added Value™ resource center at *www.jrosspub.com*

CONTRACT MANAGEMENT— DOCUMENTING AND USING THE DEAL

Many people regard execution as detail work that's beneath the dignity of a business leader. That's wrong. To the contrary, it's a leader's most important job.

— **Larry Bossidy,** CEO
Co-author of *Execution: The Discipline
of Getting Things Done*

One of the most chilling events in the life of a senior executive, whether a CPO or another corporate-level executive, is to hear these words: "Boss, somehow we lost sight of the expiration date on the Acme raw materials contract. It expires next week and the supplier is not returning our calls. What do you want us to do?"

If you think this does not happen in big or medium-size companies in the twenty-first century, think again. It happens all too often for a very simple reason—most companies do not have a central repository for contracts and contract information.

So what is at stake and why is it important? Contract management is more than just the tactical and administrative requirements of having an expiration date reflected on a calendar. With the advent of the Sarbanes-Oxley Act and other regulatory requirements, contract management is now at the core of corporate risk management.

Table 8.1. Reasons to Make Contract Management a Corporate Priority

Contract management can proactively:

- Shorten cycle time of new sourcing efforts through "standard clauses" and contract building capability
- Reduce maverick spending
- Preplan resourcing of a category or renegotiating the current agreement
- Pursue supplier-centric strategies
- Manage supplier relationship and contract terms

Contract management can better manage the risk of:

- Inconsistencies between contract terms and invoices from a supplier
- Automatic contract renewals/rollovers when not wanted
- Either party failing to live up to the terms and conditions of the contract
- Falling short of Sarbanes-Oxley Act requirements

In this chapter the reasons why contract management is important and where it adds value will be discussed. Then the technology tools that are available to support these important business objectives will be examined.

CONTRACT MANAGEMENT—A CORPORATE PRIORITY

Fundamental proactive reasons (Table 8.1), which make contract management a corporate priority, include:

- The cycle time needed to accomplish new sourcing efforts can be shortened considerably if there is a central repository of relevant contracts and if advantage is taken of the "contract building" capability that most contract management systems possess (more on that later).
- Preparation for upcoming strategic sourcing and contract negotiations can be better by having a definitive calendar of future expirations that can be used for planning *well in advance* of contract expirations.
- The value of contracts can be proactively optimized by communicating new contract features to internal stakeholders and by encouraging the use of those new contracts so that benefits are maximized. (In other words, a tool is available to minimize the amount of spend that should go through the new contract, but does not—the so-called "maverick spend.")

Shortly after the implementation of a spend analysis tool, the procurement council at a major company watched a live demonstration of how to use the new tool. After the basic "how-to's," a council member asked to see the spend analysis for the category "office supplies." His rationale for selecting that category was that office supplies had a corporate-wide contract which had been in place for several years, the benefits associated with that contract were compelling, and the spend analysis tool should readily show the extent to which that contract had been eagerly adopted by all locations.

The information that appeared on the projection screen caused everyone around the table to roar with laughter. Although the "corporate contract" vendor was in fact number 1 on the list of office supply vendors, *over 150 other vendors* regularly received office supply business from the company's locations. The total amount of business given to the "nonapproved" vendors was significant. Because of weak contract management, significant amounts of spend were not benefiting from the contract terms of the corporate contract. Additionally, the company actually risked being in violation of its commercial terms to award most of its business to the corporate contract vendor.[1]

- Good contract management allows going beyond commodity-focused strategic sourcing to the application of overarching "supplier-centric" strategies as well.

With supplier-centric strategies, a company seeks to add additional value to its supply management activities by optimizing the total relationship with key suppliers. Optimizing the total relationship adds value by shifting the focus from individual, category-specific contracts to a holistic view of the current relationship with that supplier, plus the areas in which the supplier might grow its involvement with the company.[1] Without good-quality contract management information that literally spans all relationships with the supply base, doing a good job with supplier-centric strategies is impossible.

In short, contract management allows proactive management of a company's suppliers and supply relationships to achieve the intended objectives that have been established during the sourcing and negotiations process. Furthermore, significant administrative efficiencies and benefits are possible when using a contract management system—literally helping to streamline processes and reducing cycle time for new sourcing efforts.

Additional benefits on the risk management side (Table 8.1) of the equation, which support contract management, include:

- Ensuring that negotiated contract terms "make it" to purchase orders and into the accounting system
- Ensuring that invoices received from a supplier are correct

- Ensuring that contracts do not automatically renew or rollover, which may delay the ability to re-source a contract
- Ensuring that both the company and the supplier live up to the terms and conditions of the contract
- Having confidence that the company is meeting its Sarbanes-Oxley Act requirements

The opportunity for both proactive and risk management benefits is significant and the performance impact of adopting contract management can be substantial:[2]

- Improves compliance by 55%
- Improves rebates/discount management by 25 to 30%
- Reduces contracting cycle time by half
- Reduces administrative costs 20 to 35%
- Mitigates risk and improves analysis capability

In the development of a business case, these benefits often play a key role in supporting the purchase and implementation of a contract management system.

CONTRACT MANAGEMENT—SYSTEMS

What are the basic building blocks of good contract management? Twenty years ago, the answer might have been as simple as a paper spreadsheet that listed the name of the supplier, the subject of the contract, and the expiration date (Figure 8.1). Migration of this information to an electronic spreadsheet may have been the next evolution—something companies did 10 to 15 years ago. Other companies with substantial IT budgets developed in-house homegrown systems of varying capabilities.

Today, contract management systems are standardized offerings that are Web-based, accessible, and strategic. Most sophisticated contract management systems track the basic information noted above, but they also make the entire contract available electronically, have contract authoring capabilities, track the revisions history of each contract, and capture details on pricing and other terms for analysis:

- Pricing matrices
- Service-level agreements
- Quality requirements
- Milestones and milestone-based payments
- Specifications
- Supplier key performance indicators (KPIs) and metrics

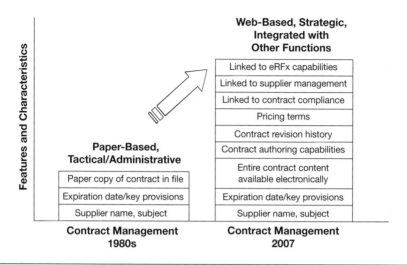

Figure 8.1. Evolution in Contract Management Practices.

- Insurance requirements
- Shipping and delivery requirements
- Reporting schedules and requirements
- Termination issues
- Disclosure requirements
- Safety, health, and environmental requirements

A few vendors (Emptoris, Inc., Ketera Technologies, Inc., I-many, Inc., Procuri Inc., etc.) offer contract management systems that span several functional areas such as supply management, sales, real estate, and intellectual property, to name a few. These comprehensive contract systems (Figure 8.2, lower right quadrant) seek to optimize the contract management process across all subjects, but are not connected to the sourcing process per se.

Some sourcing-focused contract management systems go the next step and are integrated with other critical functions of supply management such as contract compliance, supplier management, and eRFx capabilities. These integrated offerings are typically referred to as "closed-loop" systems (Figure 8.2, upper left-hand quadrant). In general, closed-loop systems offer a sourcing organization a best-of-breed opportunity to have contract management features within the broader offering of a complete sourcing suite. As an example of how dynamic this arena is, at the time this book was being prepared, at least one supply management solutions vendor (Emptoris, Inc.) had taken the next logical step. The Emptoris comprehensive closed-loop sourcing suite includes a contract management capability

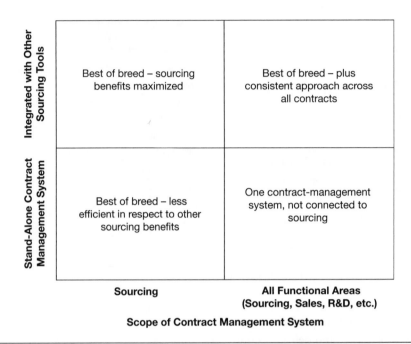

Figure 8.2. Contract Management in the Sourcing Suite.

that manages both sourcing as well as nonsourcing functional areas. To top it off, the the suite is NetWeaver certified for SAP ease of integration.

CLOSING THOUGHTS ABOUT CONTRACT MANAGEMENT

At a time when organizational politics can make centralizing the procurement organization difficult, utilizing common contract management tools can permit an organization to act as if it were centralized and to benefit from a central, visible repository of information that is critical to world-class supply management.

LESSONS LEARNED

Sometimes contract management software implementation assumes the basics—contract clauses and agreement from the legal department. Driving tool implementation before broadly agreed-upon contract templates are available can make success much more difficult. In the experience of several large global companies, the contract management effort has two parts—software and contract clause/template development. The lessons learned are that contract clause/template development must *precede* the software phase. Often, key success factors include:

- A workable contact template (relatively short and understandable)—For example, at one company, different contract templates have been developed for each major area of spend. The raw materials templates are different from MRO templates, which are different from the services templates, etc. Agreeing upon the templates for each area actually took considerable time because in the company's experience each contract reflected the personal style of the sourcing person and the assigned attorney. Thus, dozens (if not more) of contract examples existed in each area of spend. The process of reviewing the "best practice" clauses proved to be a valuable experience for the company.
- A formal training program plus a mechanism in the tool for instruction at time of use, including clause negotiation arguments, backup clauses when suppliers balk, and clear direction on inviolate clauses and those which could be modified for gain elsewhere
- An engaged, globally dispersed purchasing/legal team
- Inclusion of local enforcement differences and addendums to deal with them

The resulting process typically requires a multidimensional approach:

- Common goal—A commercially viable contract template, globally usable, with training to support it both in the tool and in the organization
- Geography—A purchasing team of thought leaders from across the world, under central leadership, to develop a global contract with any necessary local addendums
- Cross-functional—A parallel legal team with a central leader plus engagement with vital stakeholders such as finance, patent, insurance, etc.
- Spend—Contract templates for different spends on a common backbone (e.g., marketing contracts contain mandatory consumer privacy protection that others do not)
- Simplicity—Understandable negotiation limits, clause priorities, and language
- Controllable—Clear authority and commitment limits, documented and auditable

Web
Added
Value™

This book has free material available for download from the
Web Added Value™ resource center at *www.jrosspub.com*

PLM—EVERYONE GETS TOGETHER

The future does not belong to the big; it belongs to the agile.

— **Percy Barnevik**, former Chairman
Asea Brown Boveri

Lucent Technologies, the giant telecommunications equipment producer based in Murray Hill, NJ, earned $8.5 billion on revenues of $28.9 billion in 2000—at the height of the high-tech boom. The high-tech crash exposed a plethora of business process problems at Lucent, the proud parent company of the renowned technology organization Bell Labs. Lucent had a cumulative net loss of $29 billion during the next 3 years. Its once high-flying stock had fallen to a low of 58 cents a share—many wondered if Lucent, inventor of the transistor and the laser, could survive.

Out of necessity, innovation efforts at Lucent abruptly shifted from technology development to business processes. In early 2001, Lucent began a self-scripted transformation process that emphasized retrenchment, particularly in manufacturing assets, margin enhancement, and an entirely new approach to SCM. When Lucent was much larger, its operating margins were about 10%. By the end of 2005, they had risen to 46%.

Lucent estimates that about 60% of its cost improvement is from product redesign and product evolution. This chapter focuses on the 60% that is from savings that are achieved through improved designs and design processes. (*Note*: The product development makeover at IBM, another American icon, is discussed in Chapter 14, which centers on the complete supply chain overhaul at IBM.)

PLM—INTERNAL AND EXTERNAL COLLABORATION

The procedure for developing products that allows significant internal and external collaboration and the subsequent management of that process and all related information throughout a product's existence is often referred to as product life cycle management (PLM). PLM is used widely by software companies, but PLM is *not* software—it is a *business process*. The software is an enabler. (*Note*: The software that preceded PLM software is known as PDM or product data management software.) A core component of PLM is product data management—the creation of a centralized, usually Web-based, repository of all current technical information related to a given product. Increasingly, that repository follows a product through its life, monitoring any warranty, recycling, or disposal issues.

PLM has roots in computer-aided design and manufacturing (CAD/CAM). The trend toward manufacturing outsourcing "lit a fire" under PLM and motivated its further development. Not surprisingly some of the large players in the market such as Parametric Technology Corporation (Needham, MA) and Dassault Systèmes (Woodland Hills, CA) are leaders in engineering design software. (*Note*: Although not originally conceived as a supply management system, PLM has enormous ramifications for buyers—all of them good.)

PLM—THE LUCENT EXPERIENCE

The success achieved at Lucent is one of the most dramatic examples of how redesign of the product development process can yield tremendous benefits. The lessons learned can be applied almost anywhere, with results that include savings on initial development, spend visibility, improved quality, speed to market, better responsiveness to customer demands, and further savings through reduced warranty and other costs.

Consider two often-quoted opinions:

- About 80% of product cost is built in during the product development phase.
- As much as 90% of the time required to bring a new product to market is consumed in product planning and development. Engineers spend 15 to 40% of their product development time doing routine searches and retrieving information from disparate sources.[1]

PLM attacks these issues. At its most basic level, PLM creates a data management system for products, the engineering equivalent of a buyer's spend data warehouse. A PLM data system may include a "vault" that stores data, which has been created by CAD software. Companies that have multiple CAD systems can use a PLM tool as a data integrator.[2]

PLM implementation includes at least four critical requirements—an executive mandate, internal and external collaboration, cross-enterprise data standards, and excellent metrics.

The Transformation

A detailed look at the Lucent transformation illustrates how the process can work. How did design engineering at Lucent change from 2000 to 2005?

Consistency

"First of all, we have a lot more consistency in how design is done across the corporation," commented Dave Ayers, Lucent's vice president of Multimedia Network Solutions R&D, Platforms, and Quality Engineering. He continued, "There were multiple business units and design teams. The consistency in design starts with a couple things. We have really rationalized and brought together all of the sourcing strategies that define how technology choices are made. That is such a critical place to start because early on in design is where those key technology decisions are made that determine which design partners, which suppliers, you are using. That then defines so much of the follow-on architecture, price and cost. So we first start with a set of well-defined sourcing strategies in components and systems, in operating system software, in mechanical. That helps to define a set of guidelines which our design engineers would then leverage."[3]

A redesigned product introduction process was introduced at Lucent in 2001. In 2003, it was rolled out to all teams. Up until 2001, Lucent had multiple business units, multiple factories, and multiple design teams. There were 11 different business units, each with its own purchasing and design strategy. For example, six different contracts existed for the same memory chip. Lucent operated 29 manufacturing plants and nearly 600 warehouses. Lucent spun off its Avaya and Agere Systems businesses, outsourced 95% of its manufacturing, and focused on the service provider market, betting on a boom in broadband and mobile Internet products and services. (*Note:* This excellent bet was an important part of Lucent's improved financial fortunes.)

Leveraging

The second big change at Lucent was increased leverage of an extended supply chain. According to Ayers, "You win in this business now by building partnerships with a winning team of suppliers. And that really starts right at the beginning of design just when we are starting to develop the architecture of a project. We'll be deciding which suppliers and partners we'll be working with, sharing with them the goals of the project, the high-level architecture, and even some market imperatives, such as the pricing targets. We'll get them in on the game with us on how to come up with the right innovative solutions that hit cost and quality targets and get the right functionality. And so a core set of suppliers is really with us at the beginning."

Suppliers are organized into four groups: strategic, key preferred, preferred, and select:

- Strategic Supplier—Provides best-in-class price/performance, delivery, quality, and service and is a supplier to which Lucent has made a long-term commitment to achieve strategic alignment through the supplier's full participation in Lucent's Supplier Relationship Program

- Key Preferred Supplier—One with a long and successful history of working with Lucent, which is clearly differentiated as a leader in the marketplace and is actively engaged in the Lucent Supplier Relationship Program

- Preferred Supplier—A consistent performer for Lucent, generating a strong relationship without any major risks and involved in the Lucent Supplier Relationship Program to the extent deemed necessary to achieve business objectives

- Select Supplier—Minimally engaged in the Lucent Supplier Relationship Program and one with which Lucent primarily has a transactional relationship

At most companies, suppliers are evaluated based on standard performance metrics, such as cost, delivery, and quality. Lucent also has an automation tool that evaluates suppliers on collaboration, said Michael Massetti, senior director of supplier management at Lucent.[4] Representatives at the supplier and at Lucent are separately surveyed and asked to rate the quality of the relationship, which accounts for 50%. Another 30% focuses on collaboration, while technology and innovation account for another 20%.

In early 2002 the process began with a series of what Lucent termed supplier partnership workshops. The initial focus was on redesign, in what was a twist on a process termed "value engineering" or "value analysis" in the 1970s and 1980s. As the worth of the process became clear, it was used to develop new products from day one.

Outsourcing

A third major change was the outsourcing of some product design. "It's sometimes more efficient for a design partner to take on a particular technology building block area while we focus on other areas of our intellectual property," said Ayers. Lucent now has strong design and supply agreements with suppliers for certain subsystems, such as power amplifiers, RF (radio frequency) building blocks, certain wireless elements, and network process units. Ayers continued, "They are a critical part of our product, but we have a very strategic relationship with one or two suppliers who design them on our behalf while we focus on other areas. We will show those suppliers our design requirements, share some market factors, and have them tailor some of the silicon for us." Lucent may also invite one of those suppliers to bring in one of their embedded software partners to develop the core reference design that would form an integral part of one of its products. Part of the strategy is to really "push the envelope" on hardware/software code design.

Software Utilization

Not surprisingly, on the software side there is significant momentum toward open systems, represented most famously by Linux. Lucent is also using more third-party software, which is merged with its own. Pretransformation, all of the software would have been custom developed by Lucent engineers. The same logic applies to outsourced software as it does to outsourced manufacturing—the third party is an expert in that specific area and can do the work more efficiently and expertly, based on the third party's previous experience, than Lucent.

Network Architecture

The new strategy also plays into telecom network architecture technology trends. For example, before 2000 networks were more monolithic, characterized by high-end switching systems. The trend in 2005 was toward a more distributed architecture, in which applications more frequently operate on third-party servers. Increasingly those servers are being operated by Lucent's key supplier partners, which are providing the engines that run the applications in telecom networks. For Lucent, external collaboration runs the gamut from amplifiers to reference design in silicon to servers. Ayers calls it a new "design ecosystem," which fosters innovative integration.

Simplification and standardization of components also became a baseline strategy. Component and software reuse is imbedded into the thinking of engineers at the earliest stage of product development and becomes a key aspect of product specifications and sourcing strategy. "In most areas, we drive to make sure we leverage a platform strategy as well as open industry standards," says Ayers. A key metric now tracked by Lucent is adherence to sourcing strategy. In 2005, the company was 95% ± 1% in adherence to sourcing strategy, which is high enough because Lucent wants engineers to integrate new technology as it emerges. Often valid reasons exist for using unique components to solve a particular problem.

The Results

Supply Base

One result was a dramatic reduction in the size of the supply base—from about 3000 to 1500. An even more significant development is that Lucent is directly managing only a relatively small group of strategic suppliers. According to Joe Carson, Lucent's Chief Procurement executive, in 2005 Lucent consolidated its supplier base even further, relying on just two EMS (electronics manufacturing services) providers—Celestica and Solectron. Simple, commodity-type parts are managed through third-party manufacturers, such as Celestica, which manage those products groups for much of the industry. Some 50 to 100 suppliers are closely managed and are critical partners in the design and development of new products.

The result is that the design chain has been dramatically simplified. A small number of key suppliers are supplying products that map to industry standards. Lucent can now manage demand much more effectively and respond much more rapidly to changes in customer requirements, either in functionality or in volume. Lucent is less susceptible to component outages that can slow production so much that margin targets are missed.

Inventory

Inventory costs have also been reduced. Pretransformation, Lucent carried an inventory of $8 billion (for a much larger business). Inventory turned once per year. Inventory levels as of September 31, 2005, the close of fiscal 2005 at Lucent, were reported at $731 million. According to Jose Mejia, president of Supply Chain Networks at Lucent, inventory turns in 2005 were more than seven times yearly. (*Note:* Mejia left Lucent in 2006.)

Mejia noted that in spite of the success Lucent has already seen, improving inventory turns remains an important goal and is another important metric used to measure supply chain effectiveness. He said, "We continue to look for ways to leverage strategic buffering while still keeping inventory low so that we are always confident that we will be able to meet the needs of our customers and support Lucent's ability to grow revenue." He added that Lucent's more effective management of inventory will help the company better weather a downturn because the company will be much less susceptible to the losses associated with liquidated inventory. The costs required to dramatically reduce the inventory in its overstocked warehouses were among the major problems Lucent faced in 2001.

Pricing

According to Ayers, a significant benefit of the new approach is improved product pricing. He commented, "Suppliers are much more motivated to give you better pricing if they know they are one of two driving for your business instead of one of ten. They have become much more aggressive with us, giving us a lot of price reductions, and now they are increasingly helping us with our design work." Estimates from Lucent are that cost-reduction efforts drove eight points of gross operating margin improvement in the year 2004 alone. A little less than half of that was derived from benefits of supplier consolidation. Ayers said, "That was primarily from materials' cost savings, which is easier to measure. We're also trying to get some of those less tangible benefits that are so important to the business."

For example, on-time delivery rose to the mid-90% range. On-time delivery was probably in the mid-80% range pretransformation—but it was not measured as a meaningful metric with the same diligence.

Quality

Quality levels are higher. Ayers estimates that about half of product defects derive from internal errors and half derive from defects shipped in from suppliers. Now quality management with suppliers is much tighter. Fewer internal areas exist because designs are less complex. All potential problems are considered collaboratively before designs advance. One confirmation is a dramatic reduction in warranty costs—another important metric. Warranty costs have dropped by half at Lucent.

The Pros and Cons

Is there a downside? Have Lucent's technical gurus lost some ability to innovate? The debate is ongoing and healthy at Lucent. According to Ayers, "I'm of the opinion that a majority of the time, it's better to standardize and then innovate around standard building blocks. You can do that far more than you might expect." Lucent design teams can almost always achieve a 5% cost advantage through optimization of a product beyond a standards-based design, but that would cancel out all of the supply chain benefits that accrue from sticking to a common standards approach, including the ongoing price benefits over the life of the product, the inventory advantage, and the demand planning. The trend in technology products also allows more flexibility. The basic building block was a custom ASIC (application-specific integrated circuit) pretransformation. New choices in programmable logic now play into Lucent's strategy.

Better responsiveness to customer needs is one of the biggest payoffs at Lucent. When results were announced by Lucent at the end of fiscal year 2005, financial analysts were told that the company had achieved its highest-ever customer loyalty scores, exceeding its own targets.

President Mejia said, "Clearly, having an efficient, cost-effective approach to product development and management is critical to the financial success of any company, and an efficient supply chain that leverages the talent within the company and the talent of its key suppliers is a valuable asset. But that financial success is further bolstered by the impact this has on the service we can provide our customers. Lucent is a leader in a very sophisticated, high-tech market. We have many smart people working on phenomenal new technologies. The challenge is getting those products ready for customers who require 100% reliability and quality before they deploy them into their networks. Our customers' industry is in transition as new capabilities are being built into the networks. If we can continue to offer them new technology that helps them run their networks more efficiently and enables them to generate more revenue, then their appreciation for what Lucent can do for them will naturally continue to grow."

The Metrics

Key metrics tracked by Lucent to monitor success of the program include product development time, warranty costs, development expense as a percentage of revenue, and on-time delivery (Table 9.1). Other benefits, not necessarily tracked, have been noted. For example, Lucent has fewer abandoned product expenses. Introduction of a tightly gated review approval process ejects certain projects before substantial funds are invested. According to Ayers, "The process forces the question early on about whether or not a project is go or no go. We do most of the pruning at a gate right at the end of the concept phase."

Enabling Software

Software is an enabler of the improved product development process at Lucent, which uses Agile Software Corporation (San Jose, CA) software for product data

Table 9.1. Lucent Supply Chain Transformation

	2001–2002	2005
Inventory	$8 billion/1.3 turns	$892 million/6.1 turns
Factories	29 (10 million square feet)	3 systems integration centers
Manufacturing Budget	$1.9 billion	Less than $150 million
Lucent Repair Centers	16	4
Managed Warehouses	500+	0 (+50 logistics providers)
Supply Base	40% of the spend with 1000+ suppliers	86% of the spend with 90 supplier partners
Gross Margin	13%	45%
Delivery Performance	80% for systems 50% for materials	+90% systems and materials
Customer Satisfaction	6.78	8.02 (3QFY05)

Source: Data from Lucent Technologies.

management, design file transfer to its contract manufacturing partners, and design changes with its design partners. Noted Ayers, "The catalyst was originally just to allow us to move efficiently to a contract manufacturing model because you need to be able to move design files very efficiently to any EMS (electronics manufacturing services) provider you might be working with."

Ayers continued, "That's how we started, but it was how we built on it that gave us discipline. For example, we have implemented enhanced capabilities to make sure that component selection by design engineers is tied into the previously developed sourcing strategies. Taking that to the next step, we have leveraged the increased visibility to BOMs (bill of materials) and parts, such that we have a real-time view of the prices being quoted to the EMS providers." Ayers added, "So the really interesting aspect is that you can get a connection between cost impact and the margin impact as engineers are selecting the components they are using in designs. It's a really neat advantage that came in secondarily. Our first priority was to manage the manufacturing outsourcing transformation. Lucent is now expanding on this for design collaboration activities."

PLM—THE J&J EXPERIENCE

In some companies, PLM software is used more intrinsically. In 2005, Johnson & Johnson (J&J) deployed a product specification system from MatrixOne (now part of Dassault Systèmes) that is intended to manage the creation, approval, and distribution of all technical specifications related to all raw materials packaging and standards used for its products. At launch, the J&J system contained in excess of 250,000 specifications. The new system replaces 25 data vaults serving some 4000 users.

Santosh Jiwrajka, vice president of Quality Assurance, J&J Consumer and Personal Products group, commented, "We wanted to develop faster product development worldwide."[5] The benefits are the same as those cited by Lucent: more standardization of specifications, rapid communication of changes, and overall better visibility of information.

Procter & Gamble (P&G) developed a program in 2003 to manage its internal specifications of more than 700,000 standards, using a combination of its own tools as well as a software platform, also from MatrixOne. One benefit, says Dan Blair, director of Worldwide Technology Standards and Systems, is to facilitate new product introductions. A country-of-sale feature allows P&G to better mate packaging and art for the right country.[6]

PLM—INTERNAL DATA MANAGEMENT

The software industry is becoming a driver of PLM. According to a report from consulting and research firm CIMdata, Inc., the world PLM market reached $16.9 billion in 2005 and is expected to reach $25 billion by 2009, achieving a compound growth rate of 8%. CIMdata has a broad view of the PLM market, including software such as CAD/CAM. The part of PLM which is focused on collaboration, management, and sharing of product-related information is the fastest-growing segment and represented about $6 billion in 2005.

Ed Miller, president of CIMdata, comments, "Senior-level executives now recognize that PLM is critical to business success." Companies in the automotive and high-tech industries are the fastest adaptors of collaborative product management software tools. Comprehensive technology suppliers include Agile, IBM/Dassault Systèmes, Parametric Technology Corporation, SAP AG, and UGS Corporation. According to CIMdata, those providers are increasingly rolling out packaged solutions that focus on specific industry segments. Sales growth is strong for companies with less than $1 billion in annual sales. Systems integrators, resellers, and value-added resellers such as Accenture, Deloitte Consulting,

INCAT, and T-Systems also play an important role in developing the market. Additionally, there are niche players such as RuleSteam Corporation and Product Sight Corporation that add additional capabilities and value to PLM.

Unquestionably the journey to PLM for the great majority of users begins with an effort to understand internal product data. Examples of the types of information that might be viewed in a PLM system include:

- What is the current status of drawings for a particular project (e.g., not started, drafted, waiting for approval, approved, released, or inactive)?
- Who made changes to the document? When? Why? (The system also establishes permission levels for changes.)
- What are all of the approved items in a certain category (e.g., natural copolymer polypropylene resin with melt flow of 8 to 12 with particular impact and weathering properties)?
- Who are the approved suppliers for those products globally?

Bills of Materials

Without the use of organized product management, very commonly data in BOMs and CAD models can be in sharp disagreement. Sales personnel with access to faulty data may sell products that cannot be manufactured. Procurement teams in companies in which purchasing and engineering processes remain disconnected may put out bids for materials that do not reflect design changes or which contain out-of-date part numbers. The most significant problem was probably the random assignment of different product numbers to the same exact item—one of the biggest banes of buyers trying to assemble a spend data warehouse. Horror stories abound. When companies manufactured internally, conflicting product data on BOMs was a nuisance, which led to heightened tension between engineering and manufacturing departments. When high-tech companies outsourced manufacturing, as Lucent did starting in 2000, errors in BOMs led to an invoice.

BOMs are often used as a kind of shorthand when referring to benefits of PLM. It should be clear, however, that a BOM is strictly a single-level, flat, manufacturing parts list, while a PLM data structure is hierarchical, showing the relationship of different items to each other. The difference is important for a myriad of reasons, including the ability to see how one change will impact other items. In most PLM systems, product structure can be filtered to allow examination of larger, more complex product structures. Examination of the product structure also facilitates after-sales management.

Product Records

PLM at its most basic level is a data management system that creates a complete, centralized product record for everyone to see. The initial focus was on the requirements of engineers and PLM systems that evolved from CAD such as the PLM offering from provider Parametric Technology Corporation (Needham, MA) that is derived from Pro/Engineer. Creation of a standard technical data repository greatly enhanced efforts to use common parts. For the first time, engineers had visibility into what parts were already being used by the company. The repository also made it possible for buyers to access inventory from a different plant or division, rather than ordering the same item (which previously had a different part number) from a supplier.

Bidding

The entire bidding process is also greatly simplified with PLM software. Buyers no longer have to include all technical data with a request for quote (RFQ) or electronic reverse auction. RFQs simply list part numbers and provide links to the repository where suppliers can access technical data as needed. Another big "plus" is that the PLM software ensures that suppliers are getting the right terms and conditions (T&Cs). Also at its simplest level, PLM represents an enormous improvement in communications over constant telephone calls, faxes, overnight deliveries, meetings, and e-mails. All data is up to date and in one place, which is particularly important for tier 5 of the supply chain, such as the manufacturer of an injection mold who often fails to have proper communication about design requirements and changes.

Collaboration

As stated earlier, a criteria for the implementation of an effective PLM system is senior executive support because one of the biggest obstacles to PLM is failure to properly define who has ownership for data (which assumes that the chief operating officer of the company even wants an enterprise system, another requirement). Obviously, commitment to a common business process for new product development is required as well as a commitment to a collaborative work environment—a "design ecosystem" as Ayers from Lucent terms it. IT can also be a stumbling block. A corporation with a number of disparate systems that do not "communicate" easily must untangle that mess first.

The business process of PLM takes on its biggest role when companies such as Lucent move to a more-collaborative style of product development, incorporating internal stakeholders such as purchasing as well as key supplier partners.

The concept of PLM applies equally well to large and small companies. Benefits are greatest when applied to a highly fragmented design chain with a number of participants. Development of a plastics product is a good example. The diagram in the top part of Figure 9.1 shows the traditional serial model in which different companies are involved in a "hand-off" process. In this diagram, the amount of supplier input into the design process is often limited, even though significant product enhancement, such as part's integration, can be achieved through knowledge of the manufacturing processes. Molders perform a "shoot-and-ship" function when press time is purchased on an "hourly rates" basis. (*Comment*: The trend of moving to electronic reverse auctions, which began in 1999, has exacerbated the emphasis on piece part costs, not total value, in some supply management organizations.)

As another example, many medical OEMs (original equipment manufacturers) have made strategic decisions to focus on product development, R&D, and marketing and have begun to outsource more and more responsibility to manufacturing partners, who have developed greater expertise in assembly, packaging, sterilization, and even SCM of a fully produced medical device. Increasingly, molders have become involved in the design process, either through in-house programs or through third parties. At the same time, best-in-class companies such as Phillips Plastics Corporation (Hudson, WI) have fine-tuned a more collaborative approach. The diagram in the lower part of Figure 9.1 shows the more collaborative approach used by Phillips Plastics, in which even tooling options are considered in the design phase. The impact of a more integrated approach has been significant:

- Major medical programs can go from concept stage to commercial stage in a few months, rather than in years.
- Costly revisions are greatly reduced. In the 1990s, engineering change orders (ECOs) could add 50% to the cost of a project and increase time to market significantly. In the experience of Tim Reis, vice president of Healthcare Markets for GW Plastics (Bethel, VT), an OEM that spent $500,000 to fix a million-dollar tooling program in the mid 1990s because of manufacturability issues typically spent $50,000 to $100,000 for tweaks 10 years later.[7]
- Products are improved. Phillips Plastics saved an OEM customer a quarter of a million dollars by redesigning an existing part and using a two-shot process with a secondary operation, according to Dave

TRADITIONAL TIME LINE
(Outsourcing activities)

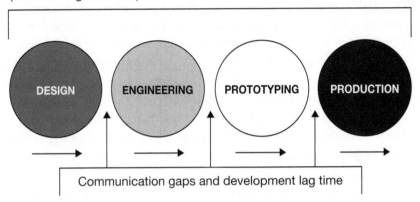

PHILLIPS PLASTICS CORPORATION TIME LINE
(In-house capabilities)

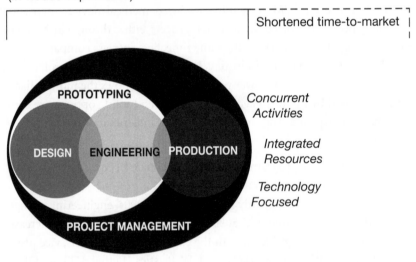

Figure 9.1. Traditional Time Line versus New Approach. (Source: From *A Serial Approach to Product Development: An Integrated, Collaborative Approach to Product Development*. With permission from Phillips Plastics Corporation.)

Thoreson, Medical Molding and Assembly plant manager.[8] Widespread adaptation of new technologies, such as overmolding of elastomeric materials to rigid plastics, created even more reason for supplier involvement in design.

- Abandoned project expenses are hugely reduced through early insight into manufacturing problems. (According to one estimate, only 2% of proposed projects in the medical field ever reach the commercial stage.)

PLM Software—An Added Bonus

PLM software becomes "icing on the cake." In 2005 Phillips Plastics was one of five companies pilot testing the Windchill ProjectLink product from Parametric Technology Corporation. Kelly Stichter, who at the time was vice president of Design Development at Phillips Plastics commented, "This software provides a way for our customers to go to the Internet and see all project details. So instead of a push system, in which we send e-mails, customers can go to a website and see exactly what's happening and what the open issues are on their own time. They can have access to everything that relates to the project. As the project manager, I can see a red, yellow and orange alert system. I can dig down and see all of the details of why an item has a certain level of alert."[9]

CLOSING THOUGHTS—WHAT IS NEXT IN PLM?

What will/should the next big wave of PLM bring? Users such as Kelly Stichter would like to see PLM improvements that make communication easier between customers and engineers.[9]

Early iterations were at times too cumbersome. The authors agree. We would like for PLM to be used more often to make supply chains even more responsive to customer demand (Table 9.2). Obviously the improvements to date already permit companies to be much more responsive to market demands. Supply chains can be mobilized to produce a new product in weeks or months instead of years, even for complex medical devices. New software features will enhance the capability. Product structures contained in PLM systems can greatly facilitate production of customer-specific product configurations. The PLM system can be used "configurationally" as a device that is used by the sales office (or the sales website) to determine the available features. Products could also be changed more quickly as market needs shift.

Table 9.2 What to Shoot For

- Establish an on-line, up-to-date repository that contains all technical information for a given product and that is accessible by all stakeholders, internal and external.
- Leverage corporate capabilities and data across the global enterprise.
- Create a capability to design and manufacture the product anywhere in the world with any partners.
- Enable complete synergy between the product development and sourcing processes.
- Make the supply chain more responsive to customer demand.
- Monitor performance throughout a product's life and create post-use opportunities through recycling (when possible).

LESSONS LEARNED

- Product life-cycle management creates a centralized, common data repository for engineering data, which ensures accurate bills of materials.
- Product data management is an important first step toward reduction of supply chain complexity through elimination of duplicate part numbering for the same items and creating visibility for buyers on total use of an item.
- PLM creates a system that allows greatly increased product development collaboration with internal stakeholders such as purchasing and key suppliers/partners.
- RFQ and engineering change order processes are greatly expedited because suppliers can access the most up-to-technical data for a given product via the Web.

Web
Added
Value™

10

SHOULD COST—FROM SPREADSHEETS TO SCIENCE

Knowing what you should be paying when you go into a negotiation gives you a lot of strength. Also, any understanding you have of how to optimize and reduce costs goes right to the bottom line. It's pure profit.

— **John Kagan**
Lenovo

Solving the simpler problems in supply management pays enormous benefits. For example, in the 1990s Thomas T. Stallkamp, a pioneer of modern supply management, was "flabbergasted" when he discovered that the use of two part numbers for the same fastener in a Chrysler data system had created $40,000 in administrative costs.[1] Efforts toward parts standardization and sophisticated spend analysis systems have resulted in massive savings for many companies. The next step is tougher—analysis of the attributes of products in the system to determine what they really *should* cost.

Should costing (also called reverse price analysis by Monczka, Trent, and Hanfield in *Purchasing and Supply Chain Management*, a well-known supply management textbook[2]) is a huge potential weapon in the supply management arsenal. Often many big suppliers will not provide cost data because the data is proprietary. Many small manufacturers do not understand their cost structures. They make sales to utilize machine time and hope that all of the numbers "add up" at the end of the fiscal year. It is a small wonder that 35 of the largest 100 injection molders in the United States went out of business from 2000 to 2005. The mad rush to electronic reverse auctions that started in 1999 accelerated this crisis.

In reverse price analysis, very rough cuts of suppler costs are made based on publicly available data, such as average profit and selling, general, and administrative (SGA) expense by industry group, labor costs as a percentage of a product's cost (from the U.S. Department of Commerce), or producer prices (from the U.S. Department of Labor's Bureau of Labor Statistics). When using publicly available data, proceed with great caution. U.S. government-generated statistics range from OK to extremely poor. Broad-brush industry estimates from various sources are also perilous. Using these types of data may give a supplier a much larger profit margin than he had ever hoped for. For example, profit margins for American injection molders, a significant part of the manufacturing supply base, are close to 1 or 2%, even for above-average performers.

COST ACCOUNTING SYSTEMS

Sophisticated costing departments are not unusual in very large manufacturing companies. Large manufacturing companies typically use spreadsheets or some other type of database to allocate costs based on traditional cost accounting or activity-based costing (ABC) principles.

Traditional Accounting Systems—The Challenges

In traditional cost accounting, overhead costs are arbitrarily allocated to product costs. In ABC, each overhead expense category is traced for each product, e.g., how much engineering time is consumed? How long does the setup take? How much of what type of machining takes place?

Commercial systems that use ABC principles include Starn Job Shop Manager (Starn Technical Services, Inc.), Acorn Systems Profit & Cost Analyzer (Acorn Systems, Inc.), Goldenseal Business Software (Turtle Creek Software), and Lead Software Activity Analyzer (Lead Software, Inc.). Capturing cost information is a time-consuming process, particularly if senior management wants a quick review of how well a major project is conforming to target costs.

Commercial systems are also often not particularly accurate. For example, a major manufacturing company that launched a $1 billion product quickly realized that costs were far beyond target levels, which resulted in losses on the product line. Engineering and purchasing subsequently launched a major cost reduction effort. After 3 years, this effort resulted in $17 million in cost reductions. Total losses on the product in that time period were $31 million.[3]

Important: The point of new should-costing efforts and approaches is to *do it right the first time*.

Table 10.1. Should Costing and On Demand

Hostile Supplier Relationships	On-Demand Relationships
• Electronic reverse auctions—preferred sourcing strategy	• Long-term partnerships are established with critical suppliers
• Large supply base—for most important purchases	• Relationships are virtually "open book"
• Mandated across-the-board cost reductions	• Costs are scientifically analyzed and then optimized through mutual effort and gain
• No design collaboration; no reward for supplier innovation	

Another major failure of most efforts at cost estimating has been a general failure to leverage those systems as supply management tools. Most supply management departments "wing it" without access to costing system professionals and without the tools that allow them to analyze the true cost basis of many of the manufactured products they buy. Best-in-breed supply management departments try to develop meaningful costs through detailed supplier questionnaires and spread sheets. Purchasing guru R. David Nelson has famously pursued this path during stints with Honda, John Deere, and Delphi Automotive. In the best-case scenario, buying companies can then help suppliers develop more cost-effective designs or manufacturing processes through supplier development engineers.

In an on-demand, technology-driven world, old paradigms fail (Table 10.1). A scientific and rapid system is needed for determining product cost. The system should be a "sword that cuts two ways"—one that is inward looking and one that is outward looking. A company's SCM must ensure that product development teams are meeting target costs and that suppliers are providing the most-efficient costs. Additionally, in an on-demand world, there is an even loftier goal—one that is truly rare in today's world. *Important*: No longer should it be a company's goal to seek the best deal with no concern for the impact on suppliers' profit and loss (P&L) statements, particularly if suppliers are—or could be—technology partners. On-demand relations require having a new, much-higher level of partnership with suppliers that in effect necessitates a full understanding of costs. Both companies then share the risks and reach optimum performance levels.

Software Solutions

Technology solutions have stepped into this breech. Should-cost software dates back to the 1980s. Two engineers in Rhode Island, Peter Dewhurst and Geoffrey

Boothroyd, developed a system in 1980 that predicted manufacturing costs during the product design stage with a software analytic system they called design for manufacture and assembly (DFMA). A library in the software allows product developers to investigate alternative materials and processes for producing parts and helps them select the most cost-efficient design. In the first 4 years of using the tool, Ford Motor Company stated that it had saved $1 billion. Increasingly, the Boothroyd-Dewhurst tool is being used for supply chain analysis, particularly for determining whether to source a product in the United States or in China.

In another development, Thomas Charkiewicz, a former machinist and manufacturing manager who had studied computer-aided manufacturing at the University of Massachusetts, launched MTI Systems, Inc. in 1982. His software, known as Costimator, models manufacturing costs. Many other companies have subsequently entered the cost-estimating business. Charkiewicz commented, "Out in the front office is a four-drawer file cabinet full of all of my competitors who are not here today."[4]

More recently, should-cost software development has taken a more scientific, and parametric, turn. Caterpillar developed an internal, engineering-driven system that estimated part costs and optimization opportunities for castings, forgings, and other manufactured products and spun out the technology into Akoya (Peoria, IL), a venture capital-backed firm.

Meanwhile an "incubator" of technology solutions for cost estimating at the University of Illinois, headed by Michael Philpott, was approached by John Deere, which was in search of a better approach to target costing. Philpott and graduate student Eric Hiller, among others, worked with professional managers to launch another venture capital-backed entry, aPriori (Concord, MA). The aPriori model is unique in its efforts to model costs of specific suppliers into a library used with the tool.

Contemporary software tools allow sourcing professionals to receive alternate price quotes almost immediately through "what if" scenarios. What if we made a specific component from polypropylene instead of high-density polyethylene? What if we machined a core pin using high-speed or high-feed techniques versus electric discharge machining? What if we changed a draft angle 1%? What if we replaced four fasteners with a snap-fit? What if we replaced a 21-part front module with a 1-piece metal molding?

UNDERSTANDING COSTS

Cost analysis is the investigation of what something should cost based on a construction of its cost elements or the use of a features-based analytics tool or both.

An understanding of actual costs is most important when dealing with subcontractors. Underlying cost factors include materials' costs, labor costs, equipment, overhead, and margin.

Even if an organization has no interest or need to become an on-demand organization, there are many powerful reasons why an understanding of cost is required.

Supplier Pricing Verification

The first and most obvious reason to understand cost is to ensure that suppliers' pricing is in line with reasonable economic and performance requirements. (*Note:* For this discussion, we are differentiating between price and cost analysis.) Probably more than 99% of all procurement investigation is done strictly by using price analysis. Price analysis primarily involves a comparison with the previous price paid. Some organizations may also compare the price with a previously developed in-house estimate or use a comparison with third-party sources of pricing information. Some procurement managers use carefully constructed requests for information to investigate the pricing structure of suppliers. In 2002–2003, some buyers used electronic reverse auctions at the depth of the economic recession on an almost weekly basis to "plumb the depths" of prices for electronic and other components.

An Inward View

Another good reason involves inward looking. When developing a new product in discrete manufacturing industries, the new analytical tools are powerful ways to ensure operations are within cost targets. At least 70% of costs typically are built-in through product design (Table 10.2).

New product design analysis reveals features that are particularly expensive. Are they really needed? Designers can also determine if alternate designs could make products more easily manufactured. Such issues are particularly important when designing tooling. Few product design engineers understand well how certain features, or a lack of features, can significantly increase tooling cost. Complicated tooling (usually with several internal movements) incurs significant capital expense, but there are hidden costs as well, e.g., maintenance or lack of full tool functionality when several cavities fail to function or make repeatable parts. The inward-looking process, of course, is not new. Since at least the 1960s, it has been widely practiced as value analysis or value engineering (VA/VE). (*Comment:* The authors sense that VA/VE was a more-valued process in the 1970s and 1980s than it is today. VA/VE should move back to the forefront.)

Table 10.2. Product Candidates for Costing Models

Ideal Should-Cost Candidates
Injection-molded parts
Machining services
Forgings
Castings

Better for Reverse Auctions
Polyethylene and other commodity resins
Memory
Caustic soda and other commodity chemicals
Fasteners
Hot-rolled steel sheets

Good Fit for Should Cost Combined with Design for Manufacturing
Any complex assembly

Cost Modeling

In process industries, cost modeling takes a different form, but is equally important. When Bethlehem Steel was preparing for negotiations with industrial gas suppliers, co-author Rudzki would engage a senior member of the company's research department to build a process economics model, based on that individual's intimate knowledge of the air liquefaction process. That model was then "field tested" on individual suppliers in a carefully planned manner, which permitted buyers to obtain the verification needed to have confidence in the economic curve. That curve played a critical role in negotiations planning and execution. *Comment*: This approach is best suited for large spends, due to the professional time required.

Some research firms have developed commercially available models of chemical processes for supply management departments that cannot afford to undertake a process modeling project. Data Resources, Inc. (DRI) famously developed a model of the entire U.S. economy in the 1970s under economist Otto Eckstein (a veteran of the administration of President Lyndon Baines Johnson) and then hired industry experts to build cost models of specific processes, such as sulfur production, to model and predict costs. In 2002 DRI merged with Wharton Economic Forecasting Associates (WEFA) to create Global Insight, a major player in this area. Global Insight offers a "purchasing and pricing" service that combines models of manufacturing costs of a wide variety of industrial products, which are tied into its database of materials prices, micro forecasts, and macro forecasts. The Global Insight's service is widely used by the U.S. Department of Defense to monitor contractor costs and by purchasing executives of many Fortune 1000 companies. According to Franz Price, managing director of Industry Practice at Global Insight (Philadelphia), "We provide forecasts of prices of products they buy as well as forecasts of the cost structures of those products so purchasing managers can see what is really driving the prices of those products." This type of modeling was particularly effective in coping with the "roller coaster" steel and plastics prices in 2003–2004.

Comment: However costs are modeled, business process is at the heart of a recommended approach. First of all, you must decide you want to do it. And then you must move forward using a cross-functional team approach—design engineering, manufacturing engineering, procurement, and finance, at the least.

USING SHOULD-COST SYSTEMS

Lenovo, a Chinese company, which is one of the three largest manufacturers of personal computers (including the ThinkPad developed by IBM) in the world, is an advanced user of should-cost systems. When Lenovo bought the IBM PC business in 2005, it also acquired one of most sophisticated should-cost operations in the world.

In the 1970s and 1980s, industrial engineers had studied costs associated with IBM operations to manufacture monitors, terminals, keyboards, typewriters, and mainframe computers. Processes studied included captive injection molding, die casting, cable and card assembly, and some tool manufacturing. IBM software engineers developed a tool called Pisces, which became the repository for all of the standard time, labor rates, machine time, and other data. Data was recorded based on geography, and Pisces became a tool that could be used to study manufacturing economics in different parts of the world.

John Kagan, the former manager of PC Cost Management at IBM and Lenovo, said the system had two uses—to estimate internal manufacturing costs and to compare internal costs to suppliers' costs for potential outsourcing—which set the stage for a massive move to outsourced manufacturing by IBM in the late 1980s and early 1990s. IBM and other high-tech electronics manufacturers jettisoned much of their own manufacturing capacity to contract manufacturers, such as Celestica. This was not an arbitrary move—it was based on a very scientific calculation of costs. Third-party manufacturers that specialized in certain manufacturing operations achieved enormous economies of scale and allowed optimal equipment investment and process optimization.

The role of should costing at IBM continued to evolve—first into a process for improving internal designs and then to a comparison of competitors' designs with IBM internal designs. Kagan said, "We started looking at our competitors' designs, tearing them down, and estimating what their costs were. We then compared them to our own designs. We began to develop a lessons-learned approach which could then be applied to our next generation of designs."[5] IBM also applied rigorous cost-estimating to various design iterations, using the tool to determine the best-possible approaches.

Costimator—The IBM Experience

About 2000, IBM decided its Pisces tool should move to a higher level. Kagan commented, "It took a lot of time to train on and it wasn't very user-friendly. IBM considered development of its own software and also studied commercial offerings. In 2002 IBM bought Costimator OEM from MTI Systems, Inc. (West Springfield, MA), the firm started by Tom Charkiewicz. Many of the products on the market focused on machine shop operations. Costimator had its roots in the machining industry, but had branched out to several other manufacturing processes.

Kagan continued, "The main purpose is to understand what your costs are and what they should be. Once you understand that, you are in a good position to achieve those costs. Knowing what you should be paying when you go into a negotiation gives you a lot of strength. Also your understanding of how to optimize your designs produces savings that go right to the bottom line."

Kagan was manager of PC Cost Management when Lenovo acquired the personal computer business from IBM in 2005 and is now manager of Global Desktop Manufacturing Engineering at Lenovo. Kagan estimates that in 2003 and 2004 IBM saved more than $10 million using Costimator. Kagan commented, "We used Costimator on a plastic part where we developed the optimal cycle times and materials usage. Costimator provided rates for the optimal injection molding machine and showed the estimated should costs. We use aggressive assumptions, which we should for high-volume manufacturing and the types of suppliers we are using. We input the tooling cavitation, part yields, and cycle times, and we believe the resulting cost estimate is what we should be paying for the part. Negotiations require detailed discussion on the variables used in the assumptions. Injection molding times have been modeled within Costimator for about the past 2 years."

Costimator also includes a function known as IQ Builder in which customers can model almost any manufacturing process, using their own historical data. The manufacturing data that resides within Costimator was derived from the company's 900-plus customers in addition to various independent industry sources. Labor costs come from the U.S. Bureau of Labor Statistics (data collected from W-2 forms).

Thomas Charkiewicz (MTI Systems, Inc.) estimates that use of Costimator can save 10 to 30% as a should-cost tool.[4] If companies use Costimator as a "could-cost" tool, savings potentially rocket to 70%. Charkiewicz said, "Could cost is where purchasing has done a better-than-average job fitting the part to the right-sized shop. Generally a purchasing person will request a quote from a supplier he/she trusts and is comfortable with. That supplier may use a 90-hp machine to make that part when only a 5-hp machine is required."

Charkiewicz also says that buyers who use could-cost analysis should also "wise up" to the fact that suppliers use operators to run more than one machine and group jobs for various customers in a single work table. A machine shop may charge a customer $X for a part made on a given machine, which is actually making parts for four customers on a given cycle. The supplier pockets four times $X for the cycle of the machine.

An example of a new, improved manufacturing model is Mar-Lee Industries (Fitchburg, MA), which has dramatically improved its efficiency to remain competitive. In 1990, typically two operators manned one molding machine with an annual output of 10 million units. In 2006, one operator typically ran three machines with an annual output of 55 million units.

Another area for improvement using costing strategy is how a company pays for set-up time on a machine. According to Charkiewicz, "One customer was paying $65 for a part that should have cost only $3.50 at the most. The first time a buyer ordered the part, he only ordered six and that price went in the books. The next buyer was a recent college graduate who looked up the price and ordered 10,000 for $65 a piece. The supplier laughed all the way to the bank."

The Costimator system is based on a detailed step-by-step analysis of the costs to manufacture a part or assembly. The data includes optimal times for each step and the amount of labor input required. At Lenovo, internal data for materials costs based on negotiated contracts are then plugged in. IBM had also conducted significant research on manufacturing costs in various geographies around the world—costs can be estimated for China versus Mexico, for example.

The Lenovo tool operates on a stand-alone basis, i.e., it has not been tied into the company's spend data warehouse or product life-cycle management tools. Charkiewicz says that is generally the case because of the high costs involved in integration. Interestingly, the cost management team at IBM was part of the finance department, not purchasing or the supply chain. At Lenovo, the cost management group moved into the procurement department.

Cost Estimating—The Challenges of Functional Isolation

According to executives at aPriori Technologies, one of the failings of cost estimating in general is that it is generally a highly specialized function that is not well integrated into the rest of the company. Frank Azzolino, President and CEO of aPriori commented, "Say, if a company has 40,000 employees, 4000 design engineers, and 1000 people in purchasing, there may be 21 people in the cost estimating department. Most cost estimating tools focus on those 21 people. There are many different communities of people engaged in determining cost. They are not integrated well in the process. The people who know the most about cost often have the least ability to impact it in a significant way."[6]

The functional groups with the most ability to impact costs are design engineers, manufacturing engineers, and procurement professionals. That is why companies with sophisticated cost estimating departments can experience significant problems in achieving cost targets, e.g., as in the earlier-cited $1-billion product example that lost $31 million over 3 years. This is a niche that aPriori wants to mine with its Cost Management Platform, which in early 2006 was being used by six customers.

At the heart of the system architecture is a Cost Model Engine. As a design engineer creates a geometric engine with his CAD software, the Cost Model Engine automatically derives geometric cost drivers and interrogates the Cost Management database to obtain information about the planned manufacturing facility, either internally or externally; nongeometric cost drivers; and Process Cost Scripts. The Cost Model Engine returns a manufacturing cost estimate to the user automatically. As the product is designed, other functions (e.g., procurement, manufacturing, and cost management) can view the process through a Web client. Co-founder of aPriori Eric Hiller explains that cost structures of planned manufacturing facilities are developed through a question-and-answer process by individuals who run those plants. Although other systems would use a "best-case" model, the aPriori engine is based on actual costs at potentially a very wide variety of manufacturing sites, possibly around the world. The Process Cost Scripts calculate manufacturing process time and convert that time to cost.

Important: The "Holy Grail" would be integration of the "cost record" into other enterprise software, such as the "product record" created by the product lifecycle management or product data management systems, the "production record" maintained by the manufacturing resource planning system, the "supplier record" managed by SCM systems, or the financial "accounting record" of the ERP system.

Azzolini said that aPriori's Cost Management Platform became Netweaver compliant in 2006, which is an important first step for integration with the SAP ERP system.

CAD—The Akoya Experience

Another new CAD approach is being undertaken by Akoya (Peoria, IL), whose core technology was developed at Caterpillar, Inc. CAD serves as the foundation for its primary product, an on-demand Web-based cost-estimating tool for highly engineered products known as CostPoint. Users put CAD files and purchasing data into the system and receive should-cost analyses of the parts. Besides providing costing benchmarks, the system is also useful for showing cost impacts of proposed engineering changes or the cost impact of material substitutions. Careful study of the data can allow 10 to 15% cost reduction through design optimization. Initial focus was on castings, while forgings and stampings were added in 2006. There are also plans to introduce a module for injection molded parts.

Akoya is targeting the technology at purchasing and engineering. According to Brett Holland, COO at Akoya, and Nelson Jones, a technology guru at Caterpillar, who developed the software, "If a cooperative product modeling effort were to take place early in the process, accompanied by knowledgeable input of material and supply costs, there could be proactive collaboration to create the same products, but at a lower cost."

Holland also said that the Akoya tool can also be used to perform cost analyses of suppliers' parts. According to Holland, "The limitation on supplier-generated designs would be access to them. However, we anticipate engagements in which we would start working with OEMs and then push the tool upstream. Suppliers could use the models for quoting and to determine their relative competitiveness."[7]

As of early 2006, Caterpillar and Textron, Inc. were using the Akoya service. Each company has unlimited usage because Akoya is not based on a seat license fee model. Subscribers pay a fee based on the size of their spend. Implementation costs as well as hosting and data updates are priced based on time and materials' expenses. New versions feature plug-in integration with other electronic systems.

BDI Software—Current versus New Design Analysis

Boothroyd and Dewhurst, Inc. (BDI) software allows users to analyze current and new designs to quickly determine how to simplify the design for significant cost savings. Various manufacturing processes and materials can be studied while a concurrent costing module instantly shows the cost ramifications of alternate designs. BDI played a role in the turnaround of Harley-Davidson, the iconic

American motorcycle manufacturer, through redesign of various bike compo-nents. Product cost is now a bedrock approach at Harley-Davidson. BDI also helped Dell redesign the chassis for its desktop computers. (*Note*: Peter Dewhurst has turned over active management of the consulting company to Nick, his son, and co-owner John Gilligan.)

Nick Dewhurst commented, "If you have a project already in production and you do what we do—apply design for manufacturability and assembly (DFMA) techniques and take parts out and look at different materials and processes—you get about a 50% reduction in product cost. That same thing is achievable if you do these things early."[8] In his estimation that happens less than 20% of the time in the American new production development process.

If many OEMs paid better attention to costs, they would probably send less manufacturing business to China. In a paper, Nick Dewhurst and David G. Meeker state, "Outsourcing overseas is often being done with little or no under-standing of what the true costs really are." At least 24% must be added to an Asian price quote to account for shipping and logistics expenses, supplier selection costs, quality issues, and travel and communications, among other factors in the total cost equation. BDI says savings on a DFMA cost study yield on average 50% savings. If companies do a thorough cost analysis on the product, and add in the extra costs of Asian manufacturing, then a 60 to 70% savings would be required to justify the outsourcing. Dewhurst said, "Interestingly enough, I've run into two companies in the last 2 months that have products in China that they are re-designing and bringing back to the United States for a percentage cost savings."[9]

CLOSING THOUGHTS ABOUT SHOULD COST

Some final points about should cost include:
- Focus where pay-off is greatest. According to Monczka, Trent, and Handfeld (2001), 20% of purchased items typically account for 80% of total costs.[2] Within that 20%, certain items are highly engineered and are particularly outstanding candidates for should-cost tools—castings, forgings, injection-molded parts, and complex assemblies.
- Get involved early—very early. At least 70% of a product's cost is com-mitted during the first part of the design phase.
- Keep your eye squarely on the big prize—total cost of ownership. Suppliers' sales officials love to say that purchasing people pay no attention to total cost of ownership. Translation—purchasing people will not buy the suppliers' products because doing so is too expensive. In the narrower sense, total cost means how long the product will last,

maintenance costs, and the impact of the quality of the part on every-thing around it. In a broader sense, total cost of ownership includes inventory-carrying costs, delivery-related issues, life-cycle costs (end-of-life recycling opportunities or disposal costs), packaging issues, administrative costs, etc. Figuring out how important each issue is in the total scheme of things, including a company's financial goals (such as cost of capital), is the really tough part.

- Ensure that the company's approach is totally cross-functional with plenty of visibility from key supplier partners.

LESSONS LEARNED

- Use should/could costing for internal and external cost analysis.
- Apply should costing at the earliest possible stage of the design process.
- Focus on products that yield the biggest payoffs—highly complex, engineered assemblies that represent a significant percentage of spend.
- Include life-cycle costs that represent total cost of ownership.
- Electronically integrate cost records into other appropriate data.

Web
Added
Value™

SERVICES—THE HIDDEN GEM

It's important not to ignore indirect spend because the total amount spent throughout the company on indirect can be very large, especially for non-manufacturing companies.

— **Roger Whittier,** former Director of
Corporate Purchasing
Intel

The services arena is often overlooked when executives talk about what they want procurement and supply management to achieve for their companies. Classic reasons for this oversight include:

- Services spend often is viewed as "less strategic" than raw materials spend.
- Some areas of services spend are often viewed as "unique" and therefore unable to benefit from modern supply management tools and best practices (e.g., legal services, travel spend, workforce management, and printing).
- The tools and best practices which direct spend has enjoyed in the last 10 to 20 years have been slow to migrate to the services spend arena.

All of these classic reasons for overlooking services spend have effectively faded away in recent years. Tools and best practices have evolved to support virtually all areas of services spend. Many examples of applying supply management tools to services and achieving great results exist. The sheer impact on the bottom line, and on corporate competitiveness, of focusing on services has elevated the services arena to an area that deserves strategic attention. Add to this the growing trend of many companies to adopt a "services model" to complement the traditional manufacturing "hard product" model and there is a growing mandate to focus on doing services strategically, creatively, and well.

SOFTWARE PRODUCTS AND SOLUTIONS—SERVICES MANAGEMENT

Travel and Entertainment Expense

A wide variety of software products cater to the complex services segment and range across several service categories. One of the first was travel and entertainment expense management, in which early systems combined outsourcing of the travel buy to major players (such as American Express) with workflow software to enable reservation placement, expense report filing, and departmental budget accounting reports. The tools continue to evolve as described in *Business Week*[1]— use of an approved credit card is tied into the system to alert cost auditors before the fact rather than after. The article quotes Rajeev Singh, president of Concur Technologies, a travel and entertainment service company: "The key is to control the expenses at the front end and constantly monitor them so you know what you are going to pay for." The combination of credit card/travel procurement/cost accounting enables numerous analytical reports on price gaps, unauthorized upgrades, and cash versus credit payments.

The travel arena has continued to evolve in recent years with the advent of easy-to-use "online booking" systems, in which the client's travel policy guidelines work hand in hand with a Web-based online booking system for both airfare and hotels. This helps to highlight travel options that are consistent with the client company's travel policy or, if they are not, it advises the individual traveler of the potential variance to policy (and the amount of that variance). Because a business traveler is in the best position to judge the tradeoffs between costs and time/convenience, online booking provides an ideal marriage of efficient transaction processing, policy guidelines, and human judgment. Online booking systems have become increasingly popular in companies with large travel budgets due to the significant documented savings which have occurred, plus the ability to receive variance reports on specific travelers who selected less-than-lowest-cost options.

Many companies embarking on such programs target achieving 75% compliance within 9 to 12 months—and they achieve it. Compliance reports, by traveler, showing variances on airfare and hotel bookings, create credible and actionable data for improving compliance in future months. Of course, improving compliance requires that management use the data to have meaningful discussions with an individual traveler.

Complex services tools typically combine a measure of procurement outsourcing, complex workflow, and multistep costing and internal reporting, either to budget owners directly or as an extension of the procurement organization under supply manager oversight. Examples include spends such as printing (NewlineNoosh, Inc., Printcafe, covering the print buy, including sourcing, specification management, artwork management, and scheduling) and temporary labor (Workbrain, Viewsuite, Workforce HR, managing the hiring manager's requisitioning, temp sourcing, time card tracking, attendance, and the invoice/payment process plus reports). The value of each specialized spend tool is driven by the complexity of the material/service supply chain that the tool oversees. These are typically multistep processes, often with high user initiative and complicated pricing and supply options.

Telecommunications Expense

An interesting example is telecommunications, combining wireless, land line, local, and long distance services with equipment from major office systems to mobile phones, smart phones, and personal data assistants, etc. and with a range of "phone plans"—minutes, unlimited, domestic, and roaming—you name it. Anyone who has seen a corporate telephone bill that is presented as a CD gets the picture. Cost control is difficult and value leakage is insidious.

A buyer at a major power and controls equipment company has related an interesting experience. A full-time staff managed the telecommunications area, including one individual who monitored company telephone policy (type of telephone, unauthorized use, turning off the telephones of people who leave the company, etc.). The individual's job included reviewing the telephone bill line by line each month for a major office complex and sales organization (1500 users). In a cost-savings move, policy administration was outsourced, but the ancillary bill checking was really not part of the work process—just an "extra" that the employee performed—before the employee was let go, that is. Six months later the telecommunications costs had increased to $600,000 over budget, far outweighing the $35,000 wage savings.

The resulting crisis entailed several experienced people reviewing the telephone bills—and finding clear reasons for only $250,000 of the overage. The rest were billing errors, inappropriate user plans, and the constant personnel turmoil of shifting job travel requirements that did not match operational budget expectations.

Part of the monitoring issue is that most corporate users never even see their bills. This is an area in which telecommunication consultants and their software tools offer a services product that can keep up with all the moving parts by using consultant/software products with telecommunications sourcing, policy, and plan expertise, plus invoice accuracy and reporting capabilities. Several companies offer this service—TRAQ Wireless, Profitline, and Control Point—to name only three.

The situation just described in the telecommunications experience repeats itself in other service categories such as freight and transportation, waste management, and HVAC services.

Whether ongoing use of these tools makes sense depends on the using company's situation. Staying with the telecommunication example, after engaging these tools for a couple years, if a company can establish strong policy with top-down enforcement, internal telecommunication industry expertise (supplier consolidation tracking/global geographical knowledge, technology/features, billing plans, etc.), billing accuracy audit processes, timely key performance indicator (KPI) reporting (cost/minute, cost/user, roaming/user, etc.), and user behavioral modification (e-mails to the top 200 premium cost users and their managers, telephone use guideline training for heavy users, etc.), in-sourcing the effort might be cost effective. Without these elements, ongoing internal control of the spend carries risk. As an experienced telecommunications sourcing expert has said, "Cell phones are like the ocean, never turn your back on it."

The Workforce

Much like the comprehensive telecommunication management platforms, workforce management systems (WFM) are a growing, hot topic. As noted in an AMR Research report, "This means more than just finding, acquiring, assimilating, and retaining workers. It also means optimizing the workforce once you have it in place."[2] As also noted in the report, WFM software acquisition has been growing much faster than core HR information systems spending. WFM solutions are available directly or through managed service providers (MSPs) such as Ensemble Workforce Solutions that provide a wide variety of human resources-related services and systems.

Nontraditional Spend

Beyond unique, service-specific applications such as those noted above, modern supply management tools are increasingly being used to identify, negotiate, and select service providers in so-called "nontraditional" areas of spend in which procurement has historically had no role. For example, strategic sourcing and reverse auctions have been successfully applied to such challenging spends as outside legal services, automobile fleets, marketing and media spend, accounting services, real estate services, and employee relocation services. The bottom line is that advanced supply management tools can add value in virtually any area of external spend, if allowed to do so.

With regard to future trends, world-class companies are showing increasing interest in bundling multiple services and service providers to take advantage of low-cost labor and the efficiencies that are derived by using one supplier's labor for multiple services. Certain categories of spend lend themselves to bundling, in which qualified suppliers can proactively leverage related services. Figure 11.1 is an example of services capable of bundling in the facilities services arena.

ADOPTING A SERVICES MODEL—THE JCI EXPERIENCE

Johnson Controls, Inc. (JCI) is a global leader in interior experience, building efficiency, and power solutions. The company provides innovative automotive interiors that help make driving more comfortable, safe, and enjoyable. JCI offers products and services for buildings that optimize energy use and improve comfort and security. JCI also provides batteries for automobiles and hybrid electric vehicles, along with systems engineering and service expertise."[3]

JCI provides an interesting case study for companies contemplating making services a part of their core business strategy. JCI's extensive building management services require it to be on the leading edge of services management best practices—both internally and in conjunction with its sizeable supplier base of contracted service providers.

Mike Patton, former director of Supply Chain Management for the JCI facilities management business, notes that key market drivers and trends are at work in the service industry:[4]

- Customer focus on their core business
- Pressure for continual cost reductions and innovations
- Changing demographics (including labor shortages)
- The need for flexible business models and staffing flexibility
- Customer demand for improved safety, service quality, and standards

As a result, service providers are being differentiated based on several key dimensions:

- The ability to understand the customer's business and goals
- The ability to work within the customer's culture
- A commitment to customer satisfaction, including quick response time
- Strategic insights and innovation
- The ability to keep mission-critical equipment running
- Quality and safety
- The effective use of technology

- Doors and lock services
- Windows and siding
- Interior lighting
- Minor electrical services
- General repairs and cleaning
- Flooring repairs
- HVAC maintenance
- Minor plumbing repairs

- Striping and parking lots
- Wall repairs
- Roof patching and repairs
- Fences and gates
- Interior and exterior painting
- Landscaping
- Ceiling repairs
- Overhead door maintenance

Figure 11.1. Services—Ready for Bundling. (Source: Adapted from a presentation by Mike Patton. With permission.)

With a geographically diverse group of customer facilities under management, and a large and diverse group of suppliers supporting JCI's facilities management delivery capability, effective use of technology is a fundamental requirement for success.

JCI heavily uses classic supply management tools such as RFIs, RFPs , strategic sourcing, and reverse auctions (where appropriate) to provide discipline and rigor to supplier selection and negotiation. Furthermore, and this is part of what distinguishes JCI, JCI automates virtually every part of the daily and ongoing services management process—a process that includes activities such as accepting customer calls for service, dispatching, monitoring the response of the dispatched service technician, automatically redispatching an alternate if the first dispatched party does not respond within "X" minutes, online metrics about the work done, invoicing, and inventory management. This comprehensive approach to services management technology enables JCI to confirm its performance compared to customer KPIs and to measure the compliance of JCI and its service providers.

CLOSING THOUGHTS ABOUT JCI

Performing compliance measurement and reporting well can be an important differentiator from the competition. However, for services businesses, compliance measurement and reporting are typically a major challenge, partly because data is incomplete or unavailable. At JCI the facilities management business contributes significantly to the overall growth of the company, and leading-edge management of services at JCI has been, and will likely continue to be, a major contributor to that success.

Web Added Value™

This book has free material available for download from the Web Added Value™ resource center at *www.jrosspub.com*

GOVERNANCE AND RISK— LIVING IN A REGULATED AND DANGEROUS WORLD

In these matters the only certainty is that nothing is certain.

— **Pliny the Elder**
Roman scholar and scientist

In 2002 Sarbanes-Oxley (SOX) legislation changed the intersection of purchasing and corporate governance for companies operating in the United States. Similarly, in 2001, the 9/11 World Trade Center attack and the dot.com bust dramatically raised the profile of physical and financial risk. Although these events reoriented thinking on supply risk, simply attributing the need for governance to them is a mistake. To become and stay leading edge, avoiding regulatory and reputation pitfalls, knowing where the money goes, and assuring purchased goods and services will arrive in good shape all are prerequisites. SOX and 9/11 only increased the urgency and raised the bar to higher levels.

Books have been written on governance so the goal of this chapter is to briefly highlight two major risk areas—financial reporting and operational supply— starting with the SOX controls and then focusing on the discipline that is necessary to avoid reputation and financial damage and supply outages.

SOX spawned its own set of e-tools, yet utilization of systems *already in place* is usually the most cost-effective management approach. Compliance people worry less about user friendliness and more about the rigor, accuracy, and timeliness of information—the perceived user drawbacks of ERP solutions elsewhere are huge advantages here.

SOX—WHAT DOES IT MEAN ON THE SUPPLY SIDE?

Driven by accounting excesses that brought down Enron and WorldCom, compliance with SOX concerns accurate and prompt financial reporting. Purchased goods and services, often 50% or more of revenues, caused SOX to "land in the lap" of supply management. Section 302, CEO/CFO certification of financial reports; Section 401(a), reporting aggregate contractual arrangements; Section 404, management and external auditor assessment of internal controls and work process adequacy; and Section 409, timely disclosure, impact procurement specifically:

- Accurate cost of goods sold (COGS) and sales, research, and administration (SR&A) tracking (see Chapter 2, *Spend Management—Start Your Engines*, and Chapter 7, *P2P—Where e-Procurement Meets Accounts Payable*, which describe tools that help avoid excessive spending, unknown commitments, inaccurate tax reporting, and fraud)
- Contractual commitments, both typical "on balance sheet" and more unique "off balance sheet" (e.g., volume shortfall penalties)(see Chapter 8, *Contract Management—Documenting and Using the Deal*)
- Documentation and approval processes (e.g., delegation of authority for making supplier commitments and spending approvals)
- Supply chain control skills so that organizations knowledgeably operate under financial controls, write effective contracts, and effectively oversee work processes (e.g., separation of duties, signed contracts on file, etc.)

The combination contains accurate financial (spend) reporting, strong purchasing controls processes, and a clear audit trail. Section 404, in particular, has come under much criticism because interpretations of the work process assessment and certification that is necessary to meet its intent have been quite stringently applied. At the time of this writing, the Securities and Exchange Commission has announced, but not clearly defined, an intent to modify Section 404 in response to these complaints to make it less costly for big business to enforce and simply more manageable for small business in total. Like most regulations, SOX will evolve over time. However, the point remains that being "top notch" in supply management requires knowledge of money flows and implementation of processes to control those flows.

Accuracy and Timeliness

The first aspect—accurate and timely numbers—leverages the full range of cross-functional e-procurement system activities—procurement, vendor data maintenance, goods/services receipt, invoice processing/check requests, disbursements, accounting application, and budget/expense reporting, which makes a single contract repository a huge advantage for combining accurate contract price/quantity access with workable productivity. (*Comment*: Without a central contracting system, searching multiple departments for contract copies and aggregating that information are enormously inefficient and expensive.)

Accurate and timely numbers are balance-sheet and income-statement requirements, but as the Enron disaster has shown, off-balance-sheet liabilities can be missed in the process. SOX compliance requires documentation of potential liabilities that are not part of COGS or balance-sheet credit/debit accounts. These off-balance-sheet potential liabilities occur when contract provisions allow material cost structure changes when contracted volumes are missed or when complex pricing formulas trigger contingent supplier payment liabilities not built into financial forecasts.

One major manufacturer incorporates off-balance-sheet commitments into their contract management solution. They use a contract coversheet in the electronic repository that details commitments or clauses with potential off-balance-sheet implications that must be tracked. Close cooperation between accounting, purchasing, and internal controls help ensure that these items are routinely reported and auditable. Examples from the coversheet check list include:

- Price change formulas
- Cash advance requirements (up-front funding of customer-specific supplier investments)
- Supplier loan guarantees or supplier use of the contract as loan collateral to implement the agreement
- Capital guarantees for dedicated capacity purchased by the supplier
- Volume commitment shortfall penalties
- Contract cancellation lead times and penalties
- Progress payments for capital equipment not yet installed or commissioned/qualified
- Any other unique financial obligations triggered by unplanned contingencies

Process and Organizational Requirements

Although reporting is obviously important, the work process and organizational development requirements of SOX are far more difficult tasks, and vital, to embed compliance into daily behaviors and organizational activities. In addition to high e-tool adoption (see Chapter 18, *Adoption—the Real Measure of Success*), doing so requires two elements—organizational controls training (see Chapter 19, *Education—Training the Tools and Tools for Training*) and maintaining separation of duties.

The "off-balance-sheet cover-note company" also requires all sourcing and supply personnel to successfully complete a controls assessment training course as part of a three-tier governance approach—self-audit, audit by internal controls, and SOX-mandated external auditor assessment. This training is key to effective self-audits that find problems and maintain organizational awareness and skill levels. The training spans more than a narrow SOX agenda to include other areas that are important to effective supply management. The self-assessment control areas in the e-training are:

- Management communication of purchasing policy and standards
- Adequate separation of duties
- Requisitions, contracts, purchase orders, and commitments executed by authorized personnel
- Effective sourcing processes in place and utilized
- Accurate, documented, up-to-date, controlled master data, including both supplier and material master data
- Purchasing commitments in accordance with legal/corporate requirements and communicated to users, including P-Cards
- Purchase orders and contracts monitored to ensure effective execution and renewal/closure
- Invoice discrepancies identified and resolved in a timely manner
- Claims against suppliers issued, recorded, followed for settlement, and cancelled only with proper authorization or receipt of credit
- Company assets controlled by or provided to suppliers tracked, protected, maintained, and accounted for
- Supplier electronic catalogs properly controlled and documented with completed periodic price audits

Electronic Access and Separation of Duties

According to Tom Poe, practice director at Hudson (a managed services consultancy), over 14% of the 10,000 reports filed in the first year of SOX had adverse opinions filed by outside auditors. The convenience and productivity of e-tools can compromise separation of duties requirements that were more obvious in the pre-electronic era. Good controls rely on maintaining separation between order placement, receipt verification, and invoice payment approval duties (Figure 12.1).

Potential P2P Fraud Pitfalls

Modify Vendor Master to:
1. Enter PO for personal use and accept receipt
2. Modify PA for automatic delivery of goods and receipt of goods
3. Enter PO and render payment to false vendor
4. Release goods requisition and render payment to false vendor

Modify Item Master to:
1. Add material not ordered and change automatic delivery to receive goods
2. Add material not ordered and change PO and then accept goods
3. Add material not ordered and release material for receipt

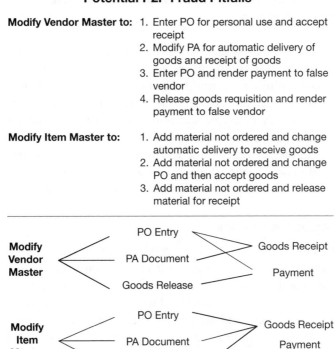

Figure 12.1. Separation of Duties—P2P Fraud Risk. PO, purchase order; PA, purchase agreement.

Yet, in an e-tool environment, the same person can often have authorized access to all three areas of the software. Poe identifies this as a top reason behind material weakness audit findings. The interaction between ERP- or SOX-specific electronic systems and manual control processes requires high levels of careful coordination that are difficult to create and maintain.[1] Although companies skilled in manipulating and using ERP system data can, with considerable effort, maintain separation of duty controls, even Forrester Research expressed reservations in fundamental software capability to do so. A 2005 *Forrester Wave* assessment of nine SOX compliance software offerings (including ERP vendors) revealed only one (Oracle) in its challenger quadrant and none in the leader quadrant—the reason?—"ability to execute" challenges.[2] New versions and releases are undoubtedly making improvements, but the risk still exists and with it the need for blending electronic- and people-skills development.

OPERATIONAL RISK—THE SECOND HALF OF THE GOVERNANCE ISSUE

Although SOX receives coverage from the media, the rest of the supply governance story still revolves around operational and supply assurance. All of the internal financial controls in the world will not help when physical or virtual supply chains break down, creating public issues that hurt a company's reputation or physical/virtual delivery problems that undermine customer relationships. The advent of global supply networks, social-responsibility issues, terrorism and war, fast-moving technology, frequent product change, rapid financial deterioration of companies, and major functional/process outsourcing or off-shoring have made business continuity planning and operational governance crucial.

Savings versus Disruptions

Ironically, as pointed out in a September 2005 benchmark report on supply chain risk,[3] many sourcing best practices that deliver cost, cash flow, and supplier linkage benefits also add significant increased risk of supply disruption. Low-cost-country sourcing, supplier rationalization, business process outsourcing, and lean and Just-in-Time production all make any supply chain "hiccup" more apt to create problems. When natural or man-made disruptions occur (e.g., Hurricane Katrina, the Asian tsunami, the 9/11, London, and Madrid terrorist attacks, or the 2002 West Coast dock strike), the resulting small margin for error makes occurrence of outages/premium costs more likely.

The benchmark report determined that 82% of the 180 companies surveyed had a supply disruption over the previous 24 months, with the average having 12.9 outages per year.[3] Traditional supplier quality and delivery problems are most common, each one affecting about 50% of the companies. Worse, 65% of respondents were completely reactive with no formal metrics or assessment procedures to anticipate these types of risks. Operational risk boils down to six basic areas—operational, physical, trade, logistics, financial, and social (Table 12.1).

Planning

Developing physical supply assurance plans is important—business continuity plans for all critical suppliers, prudent sourcing strategies that balance supplier rationalization with multiple supply sources, supplier scorecards that track performance trends (see Chapter 6, *Supplier Relationship Management—Bringing Home the Value*), and even plans for engaging outside experts in areas such as trade management. Effectively using e-tools to manage risk can elevate performance to a new level. Social responsibility adds yet another dimension to that risk.

Table 12.1. Physical Supply Chain Risk Factors

1. Supplier operational risk (quality, late shipments, capacity shortage)

2. Physical disruption risk (terrorist attacks, labor actions, weather, etc.)

3. Trade management compliance risk (tariffs, duty classification, import/export procedures, etc.)

4. Supply chain logistics risk (transportation delays, delivery capacity, long pipelines and product handling damage)

5. Supplier financial risk (bankruptcy, liens, legal judgments, supplier performance strains caused by inadequate funds)

6. Supply base social responsibility and reputation risk (human rights, environmental, animal rights, etc.)

Nike, Inc., which underwent major disruption due to supplier working conditions in the early wave of global manufacturing outsourcing, has become a model today—in 2005 even going as far as to post all its suppliers and an assessment of their strengths and weaknesses for public information—unheard of openness at the time.

e-Tools and Risk Assessment

e-Tools have long been seen as a promising means for supplier risk assessment. In 2001, Dave Nelson, Patricia E. Moody, and Jonathan Stegner (2001) mentioned a small software company, Intellimet International, Inc., in their book.[4] Dave Nelson even went so far as to help organize a half-day meeting for leading procurement companies at a Chicago O'Hare Airport hotel to highlight the potential of that software tool to do "virtual supplier risk assessment." One of the speakers at the event was then CPO of United Technology (UT), Kent Brittan, who was working on a pilot project with the technology.

Five years later Intellimet International is just a reference in a book and no longer a company. Meanwhile, UT remains a leader, using Open Ratings, Inc. software. UT leverages pattern recognition technology to monitor supply bases several tiers deep by searching third-party information (court filings, EPA, OSHA, consumer complaints, etc.) and comparing specific suppliers to peer groups. If a pattern is of concern, UT is alerted; a more-detailed specific assessment survey is sent to the supplier; and UT can take proactive action rather than just reacting to a crisis after the fact. For example, UT "smelled out" a 22% sales drop at a castings supplier and sent its lean manufacturing experts to help the supplier turn around.[5] Leadership by the $4.5-million revenue Open Ratings in this area resulted in its acquisition in March 2006 by financial risk assessment company

Dun and Bradstreet (D&B) for $8 million cash, which highlights what D&B believes supplier risk e-tools can add to its software product portfolio.

At one time, an Intellimet competitor was Valuedge, Inc., a company led by founder and CEO, Sherry Gordon, previously head of the New England Supplier's Institute. In late 2004, after reselling the tool for 2 years, Emptoris, Inc. acquired the company (and Gordon's deep expertise), giving its suite a supplier assessment module. Assessing suppliers is a vital, yet often inconsistently performed task. Why?

- Questionnaires (paper- and Web-based) are often poorly constructed, too long, and reliant on buzz words, which lead to supplier resistance.
- Supplier system data extracts require a significant IT effort for data cleansing and a management effort for data access/dispute resolution.
- Site visits (the gold standard) are a high-cost, high-resource, difficult-to-scale option.
- Third-party certifications (e.g., ISO 9001) often measure procedural documentation, not results.

Supplier assessment software, using simple, focused questions applied across supply chain tiers, provides real intelligence, especially when the buying company requires suppliers to have front-line employees in multiple functions fill out the assessment. Gordon's approach goes beyond scorecards to understand supplier practices and processes and requires fewer resources than visits. A simple example—a supplier's acceptable quality scores that are delivered via inspection rather than by statistical process controls will inevitably have cost and repeatability issues. Process questions answered by multiple people (checked for consistency by the software) catch this and focus the improvement efforts. Gordon's Valuedge continues as part of a broader tool suite.[6]

e-Tools and Import/Export Management

Long, complex global supply lines snaking between continents and across borders have spawned another risk. Steve Johnsen, book co-author and manager of International Trade Compliance in Bayer Corporation's Business Services group, is a trade compliance expert. Johnsen identified two areas in which e-tools make a difference in the global, post 9/11 era.[7] The first area is global trade management (ensuring that tariff classifications, duties, taxes, and import/export paperwork all come together). The second area is the documentation requirements of U.S. Customs' C-PTAT anti-terrorism program.

Global trade management software covers a range of functions, often supplied by different software vendors, including duty and tax management, inventory control, international logistics design, logistics outsource management, and transportation spend management. For import/export management, three options are available:

- Compliance modules from specialist software companies such as Management Dynamics (formerly Nextlinx), GT Nexus, Inc., or TradeBeam, Inc. that seek smooth material flow by avoiding costly customs violation penalties and inspection delays
- Use of ERP system data to manage the trade process—SAP, in particular, has focused on trade management and has launched a module for that purpose. Companies such as Bayer, skilled at using SAP functionality, are able to link tariff classifications to material masters and then input taxes and duties to calculate delivered costs, avoid penalties, and delays. This takes real skill, which can lead to the third option.
- Third-party logistics providers

According to a March 2005 trade management study,[8] most companies outsource import/export management to their 3PL (third-party logistics provider) or freight forwarder's information systems—61% of U.S. companies use third-party systems (only 38% of non-U.S. companies do—perhaps due to more familiarity with cross-border trade in general). Ultimately, the drawbacks of this outsourcing approach to import/export management are that it raises exit barriers to changing freight forwarders and/or requires multiple systems, one for each broker's subcontractor network. Integrating the data and matching it up with the buying company's internal, customer service, and supply management information systems are daunting tasks. As trade management tools develop, they may become tools for either importers/exporters or a potent tool for expert third parties to overcome the data integration challenges.

Supply Chain Security

Shifting to supply chain security, the U.S. Custom's C-TPAT (Customs-Trade Partnership Against Terrorism) program requires substantial documentation. C-TPAT is a voluntary program that includes the use of a secure Internet portal for communications and certification that a company's supply chain partners are secure and that they use security best practices for shipments into the U.S. In return, certified participants enjoy priority entry status, fewer inspections, and a streamlined flow of their goods across U.S. borders. As of April 2006, 40% of U.S. companies handling 80% of incoming cargo have already been certified.

The management challenge is that as supply chains evolve, companies must constantly send and maintain questionnaires and send security practice documentation back and forth with suppliers of goods, warehousing, and transportation. Tools such as Integration Point's hosted compliance software help to simplify the effort. This relatively inexpensive Web-based product is highly customizable and provides good metrics to statistically analyze supplier risk criteria, security profiles, and best practices. Accessing a company's entire global supply base through a common tool is immeasurably better than having multiple spread sheets and databases scattered across internal servers.

Compliance software products represent a leading edge of tools needed to connect complex multitiered supply chains including outsourced material, manufacturing, distribution, and delivery suppliers—each with its own IT system. Limited visibility across independent systems is a recipe for supply flow risk.

RFID

Looking forward, the "Holy Grail" will probably be RFID (radio frequency identification) tags and readers to track goods throughout the various steps of the supply chain. The retail trade, led by Wal-Mart, is pushing hard to implement RFID technology (as is the U.S. Department of Defense for military supply and security reasons). The promise is enormous—on-demand goods tracking across the nodes in complex chains from deep into supplier tiers to manufacturers and through the distribution system to store shelves and consumer shopping carts. Ultimately, RFID is likely to redefine chain visibility, but challenges remain.

Retailer interest (which as of this writing is lagging actual execution) is not surprising. Many benefits—lower inventory, less warehouse labor, and reduced out-of-stocks—occur at the retailer, while the overwhelming share of the not-insignificant cost and management complexity of RFID is borne by their supply chain partners. It is an easy retailer ROI proposition—that is the rub.

Until chip, capital, and data analysis software costs become affordable, manufacturers will struggle to find a similar ROI, especially given retailer power to resist product price increases covering the investments. Ironically, manufacturers with the highest retailer savings potential—those making frequent shipments of inexpensive consumer nondurable goods—have the biggest economic challenge. Meanwhile, for manufacturers with higher-value, lower-volume products, the relative cost of RFID is more affordable. Pharmaceutical distributors can, when unit value is high and regulatory controls are vital, make sense of RFID now. For Schedule II drugs (e.g., morphine and codeine), RFID tags help distributors such as H. D. Smith track each bottle throughout its system with expansion to retail customers being the next step.[9]

For less-expensive goods, RFID technology will begin at the pallet and case level, but until technology and cost structures improve, financial returns will remain elusive. The level of attention on the incredible promise for supply chain visibility and risk management from RFID will drive some solutions, although others will require negotiation and public policy acceptance. Like many revolutionary ideas, the learning curve will be steep across multiple areas:

- Chip, tag, barcode, and reader technology advances to enable lower costs, capital investment, and improved readability—Dual (RFID/non-RFID) systems will be needed for years to come, which will take time to occur—nothing like a pit stop changeover for a race car.

- Data sifting and sieving technology and development of corresponding analytical people skills to collect, analyze, and use massive amounts of RFID information to get economic value

- Clear data ownership agreements that define who "owns" the data and who has access to it for what purposes—What details will flow along the chain? (Remember that Wal-Mart withdrew its scanner data from industry share measurement systems a few years ago. Will RFID intelligence become a retailer revenue flow even though supply partners are shouldering much of the hardware cost?)

- Mutual agreement between retailers and manufacturers about use of this supply chain data—Will manufacturers obtain visibility into retailer stores? Will retailers obtain access to manufacturer supply chain intelligence for their competing private labels? Will that access allow house brands to access manufacturers' suppliers and perhaps "disintermediate" the relationships?

- Well-defined consumer privacy regulations to preclude gathering consumer data without permission or to preclude actions by third-party criminals to use chip readers to track valuable consumer purchases as they leave the store—Privacy questions often have different answers in different parts of the world, which leads to more complexity.

- Worldwide RFID data standards to reduce complexity (not there yet)

Manufacturers such as Procter and Gamble (P&G) still continue to work on the RFID value proposition and find ways to deliver returns. Prior to coming together, both P&G and Gillette were RFID pioneers. Dick Cantwell, now vice president and RFID leader at P&G, described the use of RFID on promotional display cases during the Gillette Fusion razor expansion in early 2006. P&G tracked the cases through 2 retailers, 4 distribution centers, and 400 stores. The transparency into customer stores allowed P&G to monitor whether the individual store displays were on the floor and restocked. When displays were missing, P&G either contacted the store or sent staff members to ensure compliance with its promotional plan. Cantwell said, "We achieved 92% availability by day three of the launch. In my industry the average is 60 to 80%. We know we get a 20% sales lift, on average, by being in stock and on time—a huge business benefit."[10]

SUPPLIER FINANCIAL RISK

The first type of supplier risk that often comes to mind for procurement people is supplier financial risk—the implications of supplier financial instability and bankruptcy on supply. The impact of the Delphi 2005 bankruptcy on General Motors and the United Auto Workers made news for literally months.

Financial data supplier D&B offers its supply management e-tools directly or as integrated offerings into ERP solutions. Integration with other tool platforms lets supply management professionals leverage their spend management, contract management, SRM, and e-procurement/accounts payable solutions into the supplier financial risk assessment. (With its acquisition of Open Ratings, Inc. and its ownership of Hoovers, D&B spans the full financial and operational risk space.)

Assessing Risk

The banking and financial services industry is the leading-edge industry in assessing supplier financial risk. Therefore, it is no surprise that Bank of America's Supply Chain CIO Andy Gomez used D&B factoids to highlight how fast financial situations can change when speaking at the Procuri 2005 user conference:[11]

- A new supplier begins operations every minute.
- A supplier files bankruptcy every 8 minutes.
- A supplier ceases operations every 3 minutes.
- A judgment is filed against a supplier every 14 seconds.
- A supplier's risk profile changes every minute.
- A supplier changes its CEO every minute.
- A supplier's name changes every 2 minutes.
- A supplier's ownership changes every 4 hours.

In 2001, as the IT industry "depression" hit, banks and financial services companies "woke up" to grave risk. They had outsourced IT services and had invested in software solutions that suddenly *were the problem, not the solution*. IT service relationships can also have high exit barriers. Dot.com bankruptcies, mergers, restructured business models, and opaque IT supplier networks all raised the risk of serious banking customer outages and cost surprises across the banking industry. Worse, many of these failing businesses were privately held, so financial information was much harder to access, even with the help of sophisticated tools.

Banking—Federal and Industry Regulation

In November 2001, regulatory pressures from the U.S. Office of the Comptroller of the Currency (OCC) led to a set of risk-management principles for financial services industry third-party relationships. The resulting "deep dive" into IT supplier viability created leading-edge techniques to assess and manage supply base financial risk. Industry regulatory councils (the Federal Financial Institutions Examination Council, or FFIEC, includes the Federal Reserve Board, or FDIC, the OCC, etc.) and industry councils (e.g., the Financial Services Roundtable, which includes CEOs from leading financial institutions) were galvanized to create vendor management guidelines and a series of risk assessment templates, workflows, and questionnaires. The Information Technology working group (BITS) of the Financial Services Roundtable, which includes the 100 largest U.S. financial institutions, has created a due diligence framework (in 2003); expectations defining key questions to ask IT suppliers to monitor relationships (in 2004); and contractual exit strategies (in 2005). BITS has also identified two important aspects of the "IT as problem more than solution" dilemma:

- Work processes and skilled people must be part of the solution.
- Suppliers must be responsible for their suppliers and report their findings back (no "black box" supply chains).

CLOSING THOUGHTS ABOUT RISK ASSESSMENT

Simply automating risk assessment is not enough. Banking industry work processes and asking probing supplier risk questions are leading-edge tools. Other industries would do well to study, tailor, and reapply the supplier financial risk management programs of the financial institution industry. The BITS website (www.bitsinfo.org) has several documents that provide valuable references for this type of due diligence.[12]

LESSONS LEARNED

Governance and Risk Lessons Learned

Financial Reporting

1. SOX forced more discipline on companies.
2. Rigorous use of existing systems, ERP, and e-procurement/AP modules provides significant benefit.
3. Balance sheet commitments and off-balance sheet potential commitments must both be tracked.
4. Separation of duties can be more difficult in an electronic environment and represents a frequent controls issue.
5. Organizational expertise on reporting requirements and e-system use is essential to manage this risk area.

Supply Chain Reliability

1. Both physical and financial aspects of the supply base must be monitored several tiers deep.
2. e-Tools are available to help monitor the physical and financial elements of the supply base, including specialized tools for security and trade compliance.
3. People skills are vital. Software cannot do it alone, despite alert and data-mining capabilities.
4. The Holy Grail of physical chain transparency is RFID, but much development still remains to be done.
5. Financial risk includes the IT supply chain. The financial services industry is a model for assessing that risk.

Web Added Value™

This book has free material available for download from the
Web Added Value™ resource center at *www.jrosspub.com*

THE ON-DEMAND SUPPLY CHAIN—WHAT IS IT?

There is only one boss. The customer. And he can fire everybody in the company from the chairman on down, simply by spending his money somewhere else.

— Sam Walton

In 2005 Chinese manufacturers exported 13.12 million cell phones to the United States from the Port of Tianjin. Exports of cell phones from the major Port of Tianjin rose 19% in units and 24% in U.S. dollars compared to 2004, as the movement of cell phone manufacturing from Western countries to China went from a "migration" to a "tsunami." The size of the cell phone business was only one facet of importance. Cell phone manufacturing became the "touchstone" of the emerging on-demand business culture. Big-box retailers gave cell phone manufacturers such as Nokia and Motorola aggressive requirements to meet significant, specific requirements on shorter and shorter notice. These supply chains became nimble, using increasingly flexible supply chain systems and technology to respond "on demand."

For example, Nypro, Inc., a custom molder which is based in a sleepy Massachusetts mill town and subsequently grew into a Chinese manufacturing powerhouse, developed a new modular tooling system known as Maxis, which cuts the amount of time required to build a mold to an unheard of 2 weeks. Design and manufacture of a mold is usually the biggest barrier to rapid manufacturing because of the time involved in the craft.

According to Gordon Langton, chairman of Nypro and a global manufacturing visionary, "When we started making molds in China the lead times were 16 to 18 weeks. They gradually went down to 12 to 8 and then to 6 weeks. And now my guys say they can do it in 2 weeks. We are soliciting business from people who need that kind of speed." In the Maxis system, all components except the actual core and cavity are "off the shelf."

ON DEMAND—SUPPLY CHAIN VERSUS SOFTWARE

What is the definition of on demand in a supply chain sense (not a software sense)? The definition begins with consistently having the right product at the right place at the right time. In 2007, on demand in a supply chain means having the capacity to fulfill that commitment on a huge scale, without exposing the company to massive liability in the event of a sudden economic downturn. AMR Research, Inc., a crusader for supply chains that are responsive to demand uses this definition—"a system of technologies and processes that senses and reacts to real-time demand across a network of customers, suppliers, and employees."

The first requirements in becoming on demand begin with establishing the right internal business processes:

- Optimizing basic processes wherever possible—spend, going to market, and contract management
- Tackling complexity (as described in Chapter 9, *PLM—Everyone Gets Together*)—For example, when Theresa Metty was CPO for Motorola, the cell phone producer had in excess of 100 hardware configurations, 4 housing colors, and at least 30 different software versions. There was significant additional complexity for local customization. Motorola designed a cell phone with a snap-off cover. In a few days, a customer could have a phone with a unique cover. If the design requires installation of the cover at the factory, on-demand supply would be impossible.
- Making the company's supply chain as lean and efficient as possible through implementation of advanced supplier relationship management systems (see Chapter 6, *Supplier Relationship Management—Bringing Home the Value*)
- Planning and forecasting collaboratively with customers and supplier partners to the greatest extent possible—What will customers be promoting at what time? How long do customers want to carry the product? Advanced companies use customer scorecards to evaluate the

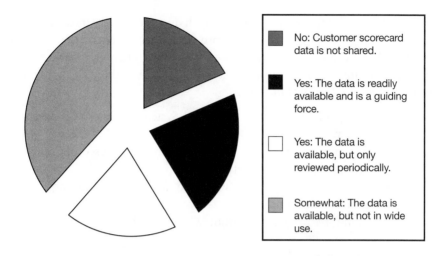

No: Customer scorecard data is not shared.

Yes: The data is readily available and is a guiding force.

Yes: The data is available, but only reviewed periodically.

Somewhat: The data is available, but not in wide use.

Figure 13.1. Use of Customer Scorecards—Do You Use Customer Scorecards? (Source: Adapted from AMR Research.)

performance of their supply chains (Figure 13.1). Eventually highly automated systems will replace manual activities.

- Implementing technology slowly and appropriately—Avoid the "bleeding edge" in technology implementation.

The Whirlpool Corporation Experience

An interesting example is from Whirlpool Corporation, the world's leading home appliance manufacturer. Whirlpool lost business to competitors because the company was not consistently providing the right products at the right time to its customers. Whirlpool product availability was only about 90%. Part of the problem was the complexity of the Whirlpool supply chain. Whirlpool had 8 factory distribution centers, 11 regional distribution centers, 60 local distribution centers, 450 tractors, and 1200 trailers. Whirlpool had needed to improve its systems to better cope with the volume and complexity of its business, partly because of acquisitions and internal growth. Manual processes and spreadsheets were "mishmashes." Another issue was poor internal process integration such as lack of collaboration on IT implementations.

Whirlpool installed an SAP system in 1999, but the system was not well integrated with a legacy production scheduling system and other legacy systems. The supply chain systems lacked granularity and did not integrate with retail customers' or major suppliers' systems. Critical forecast planning with customers was done via e-mail. Nikhil Sagar, a supply chain project manager for Whirlpool, commented, "This led to confusion about which documents were most current."[1] Monthly meetings were held to discuss production, shipments, and inventory (PSI) and handwritten notes were used to assure alignment. Sagar said, "Unfortunately, this alignment would last only the week of the PSI." Technology in place at Whirlpool in 1999 included:

- The Whirlpool Manufacturing Control System, an internally developed system
- A homegrown system for distribution planning that used optimization software from a third party
- An SAP ERP system, which was used for order processing and accounting applications
- A demand forecasting system from i2 Technologies, Inc.

Customer Requirements

Formulation of a battle plan to tackle the crisis began with a focus on customer requirements. According to Reuben E. Slone, former vice president of Global Supply Chain, "Our approach to developing our supply chain strategy would be to start with the last link—the consumer—and proceed backward."[2] Extensive customer meetings pointed out the most critical needs from the customer's perspective. Whirlpool's performance was evaluated in 27 different ways by its retail customers.

Following the surveys, several steps were taken. One was outsourcing of transportation. The Whirlpool private fleet was sold to Penske Logistics of Green Hills, PA, which contributed significant logistics IT. Penske determined that the number of local distribution centers should be reduced to 54. Regional distribution centers were designed to hold inventory of approximately 59,000 units per month with more than 3,000 different product types. No inventory would be carried in local distribution centers, which would function as cross-docking facilities. IT systems that were implemented to improve the order-to-delivery process included:

- The SAP enterprise-wide system was expanded to manage and track orders throughout the supply chain.
- A warehouse management system was installed.
- A damage claim system allows creation, reporting, and resolution of all claims.
- The Penske proprietary Logistics Management System manages operational functions, including resource optimization.
- The StreetView routing and scheduling tool optimizes performance at the distribution centers.

- The i2 Technologies Transportation Optimizer manages the shipping process by automating carrier and service selection and customer service inquiries, as well as accounting functions.

In the Penske system, orders are captured by the SAP system and transmitted to the Logistics Management System and then sent to the regional distribution centers for routing. The results of all of these improvements were that on-time delivery rose to 99% and point-of-delivery damages dropped by 40%. According to Penske, in the new system, orders were handled and routed within 72 hours. Inventories contracted by 90% in 2003. Third-party collaboration agreements dramatically reduced supply chain costs at Whirlpool.

Comment: In 2007, Whirlpool expects to roll out an improved logistics system. According to Kevin O'Meara, director of Supply Chain Operations at Whirlpool, "We are going to an inventory stratification system where we have low-volume centers in about four or five locations. The rest will be higher-volume centers. The Whirlpool supply chain will guarantee a delivery time of 48 to 72 hours. Whereas prior to this (especially on low-volume stock keeping units maintained at the factory), it could be a week or two to get that product to the customer."[3]

Sales and Operations Planning

Another innovation was an improved sales and operation planning process that expanded forecasting capability with improved CPFR (collaborative planning, forecasting, and replenishment). A Web-based tool enabled Whirlpool and its retail customers to collaboratively develop better forecasts in real time. Nikhil Sagar wrote in a review of the i2 Supply Chain Collaborator (SCC), "The most current version of any file is now located in the secure, shared files section of SCC, easily accessible by any planner from the viewpoint of either Whirlpool or the partner. SCC has allowed us to migrate from a monthly alignment of forecasts to a weekly alignment, improving overall accuracy levels."[1] The number of forecast errors was reduced by 50% within 30 days of launch. Error rates dropped from almost 100% to about 45%.

Whirlpool also developed a single, unified system that integrates from master scheduling to deployment and inventory planning. i2 Technologies tools were implemented, including Supply Chain Planner for Master Scheduling, Deployment Planning, and Inventory Planning. Whirlpool was delivering close to its target of 93% availability and rose to 97% in 2005.[4] At the same time the number of days of finished goods in inventory dropped from 32.8 to 26 days. Working capital and supply chain costs were lowered by substantial amounts.

Not surprisingly, suppliers are playing a big role in the on-demand transformation at Whirlpool in an innovation-focused approach that goes well beyond the automation of relationships and the development of customized inventory solutions, which range from Just in Time to consignment. Steve Rush, vice president of North American Procurement at Whirlpool, said, "Introduction of innovation into the corporation through suppliers is a major cornerstone of our strategy."[5]

Rush continued, "A supplier may come in and say, "I can make those screws out of plastic instead of metal.' That may be an innovation in their minds, and it might cut costs. But that's not how we're defining innovation. We want consumer-relevant innovation. If the consumer can't see real differentiated value, then it probably will not be meaningful to them." Another example was a supplier who suggested that refrigerator liners be compounded with antimicrobial agents that kill germs on contact.

Whirlpool has conducted several training sessions on innovation with suppliers. Rush said, "We tell them that not only are you supplying us with motors or compressors, but you are also consumers. In many cases you are thousands of consumers." Whirlpool's procurement team solicited nearly 300 ideas from suppliers in a recent 2-year span. Rush ensures that ideas receive serious consideration and at times cuts through red tape to make sure ideas receive a hearing relatively quickly from key decision makers. All of this is part of an overall approach, still in development, to foster more collaborative relationships with key suppliers.

Challenges

Bumps are still in the road to on demand. Skyrocketing commodity prices (e.g., steel, resins, copper, nickel, zinc, and aluminum) in recent years have been a challenge to partnering. Lack of enterprise-wide transparency to sales data and good forecasts is a challenge for almost all organizations.

Another challenge Whirlpool is successfully tackling is the $1.7-billion acquisition of Maytag Corporation, which was completed in 2006. Creating efficiencies in manufacturing and distribution are major goals. A tool Whirlpool will be using to optimize spend is combinatorial bidding from CombineNet, Inc. Upcoming are bidding events for ocean freight and North American truckload shipping.

CLOSING THOUGHTS—THE BENEFITS OF BEING DEMAND DRIVEN

A study by AMR Research shows that companies that lead in the area of demand forecasting have 15% less inventory, 17% stronger order fulfillment, and 35% shorter cash-to-cash cycle times than other companies.[6] AMR calls the practice "demand-driven supply network." According to Lora Cecere, Research Director for AMR Research, "Being demand driven is a fundamental shift in how business is done. It involves redefining the work of marketing and sales, integrating the processes for product life-cycle management, and leaning-out supply processes."

LESSONS LEARNED

- Start with the customer and work backward.
- Implementation of technology is the last step in supply chain transformation. All other phases of supply transformation must be in reasonably good shape first.
- The chief information officer and chief procurement officer must be "on the same page" about major technology issues. Is the emphasis on cost, specific functionality, integration to other systems, or something else?
- Develop clear, written goals and obtain up-front buy-in from all other major internal players.
- Involve suppliers early in network design.

Part III

BUSINESS DARWINISM
AT WORK

ON-DEMAND
TRANSFORMATION—IBM

We need to become even more of an on-demand business ourselves. It means shifting resources closer to the point of contact with the client, creating enterprise-wide processes that are commonly shared and establishing truly global operations that capitalize on the talent and scale now available in every part of the world.

— **Samuel J. Palmisano,** CEO
IBM

Soon after Bob Moffat became the first-ever IBM senior vice president for Integrated Supply Chain in 2002, he summoned a leadership meeting. From the podium, he saw manufacturing people at one table, logistics people at another, and procurement people at a third. Site personnel were similarly gathered—a table with IBM people from Raleigh, NC, Glasgow, Scotland, and Singapore. This view embodied the single biggest problem that Moffat encountered in trying to deliver the goal of CEO Sam Palmisano—an integrated, on-demand supply chain that would be more responsive to customer requirements, dramatically improve cash performance, simplify logistics, reduce engineering costs, and achieve a multitude of other goals.

The problem at IBM was corporate culture—the purchasing guy would blame the engineering guy if a specification was too tight. The manufacturing guy would blame the logistics guy if a part failed to arrive on time. The engineering guy would blame the purchasing people for picking the wrong supplier. Everyone was mad at sales for accepting customer orders that the company could not deliver. It was a vicious circle, and it was no one's fault at IBM—instead they all blamed the customer who had placed the original order.

IBM began a massive effort to reengineer its supply chain. The primary focus was on the business process—getting people to work more collaboratively in everything that they did. Then the IT people kicked in to make all of the communications electronic and real time so that the company's massive global supply chain (not *chains*) could move in a more unified manner *on demand*. The new mandate occurred while IBM was "morphing" from a manufacturing company into a services company. The emphasis was shifting from hardware to people. In 2006, considerably more than two-thirds of IBM's business was in software and services and less than one-third was in hardware. Those numbers represented a complete reversal in 12 years.

IBM HISTORY

In IBM's history, there have been four phases—launch under Tom Watson; "fat and happy" as Big Blue; the downfall; and the turnaround under Lou Gerstner and then Sam Palmisano.

Big Blue was a symbol of American business dominance and even arrogance in the 1950-to-1990 time frame. Many American icons of that era (e.g., Xerox, Polaroid, and Harley-Davidson) had near-death experiences in the late twentieth century as foreign competition exposed poor business processes. Gerstner remembers: "Gross profit margin was sinking like a stone because we had to reduce mainframe prices in order to compete. The only way to stabilize the ship was to ensure that expenses were going down faster than the decline in gross profit."[1] New CFO Jerry York reported that IBM spent 42 cents to produce $1 of revenue versus the 31 cents spent by its competitors. Almost overnight IBM eliminated half of its workforce—a sum of people equal to the population of Providence, RI. Hard decisions were made to exit legacy businesses such as hard disk drives and memory chips called DRAMS—two hardware technologies which had been invented by IBM. In 2005 IBM sold its personal computing division to Lenovo, a Chinese company.

According to Palmisano, "If you lived through this as I did, it was easy to see how the company's values had become part of the problem. But I believe values can once again help guide us through major change and meet some of the formidable challenges we face."[2] What the new IBM had learned from the Big Blue era was that a top-down, smothering bureaucracy was not compatible with the flexibility, speed, and innovation that global clients demand in the twenty-first century.

THE IBM TRANSFORMATION

Palmisano began the new transformation of IBM on several levels. Changes that emerged were:

- IBM began pricing cross-enterprise software and services as part of a corporate package. Prior to the change, putting together a simple package at a single all-inclusive price was nearly impossible because all pricing had been set by brand-specific finance officials.
- Palmisano allocated $5000 to managers who could spend the money internally to avoid the lengthy delays, which were caused by several layers of executive permissions across business units. For example, a sales engineer executing a major software package in Shanghai could assign code-writing work to a software engineer in Texas without obtaining five layers of sign-offs.

The supply chain was a more intractable "lion" to tame:

- In 2001, IBM operated 30 separate supply chains organized by profit and loss (P&L) unit. Redundant or excess physical inventory cost $4 billion.
- Collaboration between supply managers and demand managers was very weak. For example, a shortage of ceramics that were used in chips hurt sales of mid-range Internet servers in 2002. Stock prices "tanked" following a report of lower server sales. The irony was that IBM actually made the components, but had overpromised shipments.[3]
- Even though purchasing had been centralized by Lou Gerstner in the 1990s, business units were not totally aligned with sourcing strategies. Many had favorite suppliers that they were determined to keep and they fought purchasing on leverage issues.
- Poor governance on IT implementations resulted in a highly layered and balkanized IT structure throughout the supply chain. IT protocols were particularly lacking in the rapidly growing services sector, where flow processes remained manual.[4]

Palmisano centralized all of IBM's $39-billion supply chain backbone from product development to customer service in 2002. Gerstner had taken the first step by centralizing procurement and improving supplier relations in the 1990s under the leadership of R. Gene Richter. The supply base was streamlined, yet in 2002 there were still 33,000 suppliers. IBM's product slate included 78,000 items with millions of configurations. In North America alone there were 6.5 million customer records.

The new integrated supply chain organization includes manufacturing, logistics, procurement, customer fulfillment, operations and strategy, import compliance, and business growth initiatives. The group has its own finance, communications, and human resources executives.

Purchasing and Product Development Processes

The transformation also began with a thorough reengineering of the purchasing and product development processes within IBM, which had started in the 1990s. However, the reengineering effort was complicated by multiple IT systems that greatly slowed electronic, real-time information hand-offs. Henry Pruitt, who has procurement IT responsibility, commented: "One of the challenges we had is that we began transformation before there were suppliers in the market that had good packaged (software) products."[5]

For example, significant custom work was done at IBM to develop a single, global business data warehouse. Today IBM examines off-the-shelf software for supply chain applications and adapts the software as necessary. Complete electronic integration into other business processes at IBM such as accounts payable can be a challenge because integration at IBM usually means tying into an SAP backbone. Even that was not always easy because IBM has several SAP software systems. Another issue, adds Pruitt: "You really don't want to go to a vendor and say I want that product, but change it in these 50 ways. Then we spend more money than we want." One overarching goal is that IBM wants all business to be able to connect electronically. *Note*: In general, IBM connects electronically via the Internet through a portal that requires registration and establishes entitlement. Creation of the electronic framework is the "icing on the cake" in the transformation process.

The Dysfunctional Phase of the 1990s

The first step was acknowledgement at the highest level of the company that *there is a problem*. Walking through the IBM corporate campus in Westchester County, NY, and meeting various levels of managers involved in the supply chain transformation process was a bit like meeting with members of some type of recovery group: "I had a terrible problem … I had to admit that I had the problem … Then I started toward the road to recovery."

For IBM earnings and stock prices crashed in the early 1990s and many questioned if IBM could survive (Figure 14.1). New CEO Lou Gerstner (former McKinsey consultant and CEO at American Express and RJR Nabisco) said, "We needed fundamental change in the way we carried out almost every process at IBM. All of our business processes were cumbersome and highly expensive."[1]

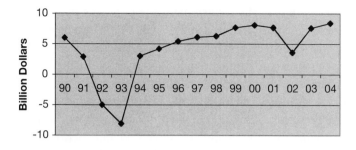

Figure 14.1. IBM Annual Earnings.

When interviewed in 2005, "IBMers" who worked through the experience were much more blunt. John M. Paterson said, "We were dysfunctional in the early 1990s. We were decentralized with around 100 discrete purchasing departments. The role of purchasing was largely administrative, processing purchase orders. We had many different processes because we were a decentralized company. And we had lots of technology because we were a technology company. As a result, there was a large gap in results."[6]

Jim Dickerson, who had worked for 28 years as a design engineer for systems and microprocessors at IBM, had his own take. Dickerson said, "Development expense as a percent of revenue at IBM was more than 10%, which was well over double best-in-class performance. We had similar metrics in time to market, where we were also running poorly. The majority of our business metrics were all going in the wrong direction. We had a call to arms."

IBM began the process of redesigning its product development process in the 1990s and gave Dickerson the job of developing integrated solutions. In 2003, Dickerson made the decision to move his group into the Integrated Supply Chain (ISC) organization under Bob Moffat.

The Internal Supply Chain

Product development is the area in which the internal supply chain process begins. Pretransformation, each of the 20 business units made their own design and procurement decisions. Dickerson said, "As you can well imagine, engineers want to do their own thing, add their own twist. Designs were handed "over the wall" to purchasing departments, who all independently made their own deals with suppliers. What we really wanted to do was centralize the decision-making, starting with the design itself. We needed to common-up all of our requirements."

One of the first steps was to create development councils, which had responsibility for creating a product roadmap and a strategy. One of the first councils was for memory products. The council mapped out functional requirements for current-generation memory products and then developed a time line for the next generation, as well as the requirements for the next generation. Key technical leaders from core design teams throughout IBM were asked to align to a common strategy, which became enterprise policy. Technical roadmaps were developed for eight categories, including memory, cable, connectors, and power supplies. Procurement engineers at IBM participated, indicating how the internal plan aligned with supplier capabilities and cost targets. Requirements were passed on to sourcing councils who would determine which suppliers had the best supply pipeline, financial makeup, most favorable terms and conditions, and the best track records in areas such as quality.

As engineers generated bills of materials, the BOMs were scoured to ensure that parts were in conformance with reuse strategies developed by the councils. Dickerson commented: "Before the new process was developed, most decisions had been made by the engineering community without a lot of business insight into the rest of the company."

A critical step in the transformation process was the creation of a strong cross-functional team for new product development. At its helm would be a leader who drove the project from conception to launch and to end of life. This individual would have worldwide P&L responsibility for the product throughout its life. The team would include marketing, procurement, manufacturing, and finance. The approach would have four other aspects:

- New metrics would be applied.
- Product development and market planning processes would be tightly integrated.
- Decisions would be reviewed at key points in a stage-gated manner.
- Suppliers would play a much more important role in the product development process, which would provide an important innovation engine.

With implementation of the cross-functional aspects from the start of a project to its completion, the "over-the-wall," serial approach to product development would be eliminated.

Above the product development team was an integrated portfolio management team, which was made up of executive-level participants from the business units, as well as from manufacturing, marketing, and procurement units. Dickerson said, "They will be the people who take all of the input and make the business decisions on how we manage the portfolio." This group commissioned the product development teams to work on specific projects.

Procurement and Design Processes

A big change and innovation at IBM is the very significant involvement of procurement with core design teams. The role of purchasing engineers in the design process in general is to ensure balance between technology and cost, to alert design teams to potential supply or supplier issues, and to push reuse of products from enterprise-approved lists. As an illustration, purchasing engineers at IBM urged designers to move away from tantalum capacitors and toward alternates such as electrolytic capacitors whenever possible because of global supply problems with tantalum. Purchasing engineers also pushed design teams toward one or two suppliers with whom IBM has global contracts. Who has the best quality and delivery record? Who has the best terms and conditions? In the on-demand era, there is new focus on what the capabilities of these elite suppliers should be. IBM also employs procurement engineers who work with suppliers to ensure that they are moving in the same technology directions as IBM. Increasingly, OEMs such as IBM and Lucent are technology partners with their suppliers in determining the future direction of products.

Standardization

The move toward a standard parts list is one of the most important drivers toward a less-complex supply chain and is one of the key metrics applied to the IBM integrated product teams. *Important:* Centralized procurement is fine, but it cannot accomplish as much without centralized engineering specifications. Without centralized specifications, only a fraction of the total buy of products such as polypropylene or cable can be leveraged because the specifications are so fragmented.

Pretransformation, design teams in each business unit and plant established a discrete specification without regard to overall corporate needs. The new development councils take ownership of the technology strategy for major product groups such as memory, connectors, power supplies, and cable. They develop functional requirements for current-generation products and also develop the evolution roadmap, e.g., which new chip will replace the current chip and at what time. The key players on the development teams are technology leaders from the core design engineering teams.

Proposed BOMs for new products are then scrutinized to ensure there is maximum use of preferred parts. Before the transformation process, the percentage of parts that were common across the enterprise was 1 to 2%. Dickerson says, "I like to joke that this is a kind of an error. How do you have 1% of parts reused? It was more haphazard than by plan." Since 2005 , about two-thirds of parts specified are used across business units and design teams. The remainder includes customization items for the most part. A simple example of standardization was the decision to use a standard power cable on the ThinkPad (pre-Lenovo). Previously there were several power cables. IBM participates in industry groups to promote even broader standards development such as the International Electronics Industry Manufacturing Initiative (iNEMI), an industry-led consortium that "can collectively anticipate future technology and business needs and effectively develop collaborative courses of action to meet those needs."

Other metrics used to measure product development effectiveness include development expenses as a percentage of revenue (now 50% lower), hardware development time (now 67% faster), abandoned project expenses (more than a 90% improvement), and warranty expense as a percentage of total revenues (a 25% improvement). Those metrics are made available to analysts who follow IBM and are discussed during earnings conference calls.

The integrated process presents significant, new opportunities and challenges to purchasing. First and foremost, integration presents an opportunity to raise the bar on what a highly organized centralized procurement department can deliver in cost and supplier performance. On demand raises the bar yet again, with emphasis moved from conventional financial metrics to improved customer satisfaction.

Governance

IBM moved aggressively to gain total control over the buy. Paterson's procurement group arguably has more power than any other big-company procurement group in the world. The supply transformation began in the 1990s as IBM changed its organization, its governance model, and then its leadership and culture. At IBM in 2006, more than 5000 procurement employees, including 600 procurement engineers, report to one financial division. They operate in more than 400 locations in over 80 countries. The buy at IBM is overseen by 31 category groups who control 100% of every penny spent. The CFO established the office of Chief Procurement Officer, giving the position executive standing. At the behest of former CPO R. Gene Richter, the board of directors passed a resolution vesting all power to buy into the hands of the central procurement group. Maverick spending was controlled by establishing linkages to accounts payable. Ian J. Crawford, vice president of Strategic Sourcing at IBM and a protégé of John Paterson, said, "People get fired at IBM if they try to go outside procurement to place an order with a supplier."[7] Most importantly, managers create clarity on what is expected. According to Paterson, communication from the entire senior leadership team was "clear, consistent and relentless."[8] A "baker's dozen" of key performance indicators (KPIs) were established and regularly measured—sourcing expertise, cost savings contribution, supplier quality, maverick spending, business controls, client satisfaction, e-catalogs, e-enabled supplier connections, e-purchases, buyer-less transactions, purchase order processing time, contract closure cycle time, and contract length.

The governance model at IBM has evolved since the board of directors first passed their resolution. Paterson commented: "Trying to get control of buying throughout the organization on the basis of fear is not really sustainable. It helped the first year. But if the processes that the people are being asked to use do not really work or produce results, then the organization is going to revolt. And they have every right to do so. I think our view of the governance model today is a bit more of a 'carrot and a stick,' with much more carrot than stick."[8]

Supply Metrics

The first supply metric established at the new IBM was "sourcing expertise in place" (Table 14.1). In 1993, less than one sourcing professional in ten was estimated to have adequate expertise. Today, Paterson says the sourcing expertise of professionals is at 100%. IBM has invested more than $50 million in skills development for supply professionals. Training starts with core skills in negotiating, finance, supplier diversity, workstation essentials, strategic outsourcing, and contract statements of work. At the highest level, courses cover strategic cost management, advanced intellectual property law, strategic supplier relationship management, and managing the cost of the supply chain. Instruction includes on-site as well as Web-based training.

How people spend their time has also changed. About 50% of the procurement focus is now on suppliers and markets versus 10% in 1995. Procurement focus on clients now takes up 8% of their time versus 0% in 1995, when 70% of their time was spent on back-office duties ("place and chase").

At the core of the procurement organization are global sourcing councils, which develop 3-year strategies and supplier relationships for specific categories of spend. From 2002 to 2005, the number of categories exploded to 53, with all of the growth being in indirect categories as IBM "morphed" from a manufacturing organization to a services organization. As of 2006, there were 11 categories within facilities, 9 categories within human resources, 4 categories within marketing and advertising, and 5 categories for IT. The sourcing teams are run by Ian Crawford, who began his career as an accountant and after 5 years moved into various supply chain roles at IBM, including production control and fulfillment. Crawford then took charge of all direct procurement at the IBM PC Division in Raleigh, NC. In August 2004, Paterson put Crawford in command of all procurement within the ISC. In 2005 the office was relocated to the Glasgow, Scotland area.

Table 14.1. Key Procurement Metrics at IBM

Metric	1993	2004
Sourcing expertise in place	<10%	100%
Cost savings contribution	?	$6.5 billion
Supplier quality level (shipped product)	85%	99%
Escapes/bypasses (maverick spending)	>35%	<0.2%
Acceptable business controls (audits)	55%	100%
Client satisfaction	40%	84%
e-Catalogs	0	1,000+
e-Enabled supplier connections	<500	33,000
e-Purchases	<20%	98%
Buyer-less transactions (hands-free)	0	98%
Purchase order processing time	30 days	<1 day
Contract closure cycle time	6–12 months	<30 days
Contract length	40+ pages	6–8 pages

Source: Adapted from IBM data.

Supplier Relations

Building supplier relations was "job one" when the sourcing transformation began at IBM. Emphasis moved to global, long-term relationships with suppliers who could provide IBM with a competitive advantage. In 2005, 85% of IBM's $19-billion direct spend was with 20 suppliers. Its $24-billion spend on services and general procurement was less concentrated, in part because suppliers are less global in nature. About 600 suppliers represented 85% of spend.

Supplier evaluation moved into a higher gear as on-demand goals were created. Crawford said, "For a certain segment of suppliers, we are much more collaborative. The level of integration of processes, ideas, and culture is so much more advanced. The relationship with suppliers is very different. We have tended to move toward those suppliers where there is more of a commonality in beliefs between the companies."

Top-level suppliers at IBM previously had the designation of "core" or "enterprise." In the on-demand world, the highest level is "premier," which requires a great deal of flexibility and a new, higher level of innovation and cost-sharing.

IBM wants an open-book relationship, in which each side shares all cost data and determines the relative value due to each. Much of the work is being done on the indirect side, where suppliers tend to be more regional and less sophisticated. One of the first breakthroughs was with a global supplier of temporary labor, in which customer requirements were built into an electronic database and shared with the supplier, allowing rapid response to staffing needs. According to Paterson, "In an on-demand world, you want to have truly interdependent relationships with a core supplier set, but not to the point where you put yourself at risk. Sole sourcing, for example, would not be part of the strategy. We are hugely dependent on our supply base for the success of IBM. These core suppliers become a virtual extension of us."

Core Suppliers

A first step that procurement must take in on-demand transformation is identification of the core supplier set. Those discussions have occurred throughout 2004 and 2005 and have not been a rapid process. Paterson said, "Procurement organizations have been talking for decades about developing better relationships with suppliers. Suppliers naturally are gun-shy."

Rapid roll-outs of electronic reverse auctions from 1999 to 2003 had created new skepticism with many suppliers. IBM did not adopt the reverse auction sourcing model. Instead, increasingly core suppliers have been located offshore. In 2006 IBM CPO Paterson moved his office from Somers, NY to Shenzhen, China, a huge manufacturing center just north of Hong Kong. The reasons were simple—IBM is transforming itself yet again to become a globally integrated enterprise.

A Virtual Network

The second major step is development of a set of processes and technologies that create a virtual network with core suppliers. The processes require significant investment on the part of core suppliers. According to Paterson, "Suppliers say they will not make that investment if you are the type of sourcing organization that bids every piece of business and the only guarantee they have is the last purchase order. We are not philanthropists here, but we have to convince them that we will be with them for a long time subject to their achieving what the model is for that category."

Sophisticated arrangements were in place in 2004–2005 for critical direct categories such as DRAM memory chips. Paterson commented: "These market arrangements say that you'll get X percent of my business if you have the right technology and the right costs and all of the other things that are needed"—a relationship level that has protected IBM during periods of supply constraint. Crawford said, "The way that we feel we protect ourselves is to have strong, fundamental relationships with suppliers. Then when things start to get tough, they give you preference over everyone else. We believe that we do better in periods of constraint than anyone else. In general, other than a few 'hiccups' which you will always have, we have had 3 years of excellent supply performance. One good example is disc drives for servers. There was a serious shortage when a supplier dropped the ball in bringing in a new product. We avoided the worst of the constraints."

Thinking about depth of supplier relationships over time has led to internal "soul searching" at IBM over its relationship with contract manufacturers, who took over most of the production of IBM products in the 1990s. Many OEMs originally delegated purchasing to the contract manufacturers, but IBM did not. Paterson said, "There is the whole issue of supply continuity in a constrained market. Do you want your revenues to be determined by a contract manufacturer who is also working for your competitors? Probably not. This type of ecosystem we need goes way beyond the first tier of the supply chain." For that reason, in the 1990s, IBM established its own private marketplace, the Singapore Trading Center, where it buys components and then resells them to its contract manufacturers, with actual costs disguised.

Relationship Challenges

The challenge now is to replicate close relationships with services providers, who are increasingly important. In 2004 IBM spent $9 billion on contract labor—its biggest spend category. Paterson said, "We have historically operated in that area on almost a transaction basis. Again, you are not going to get those suppliers, whose margins are much smaller than hardware manufacturers, to make the necessary investments in processes and information technology unless you make them some longer-term commitments in business. And that's the model we're pushing toward."

Besides cost sharing, another major requirement of on demand for the supply base is responsiveness. Paterson said, "It's not enough to be able to respond on just the up side. You also have to be very good at responding very quickly on the down side. We don't need a year's worth of combined liability in the supply chain. When the market is operating at a different cadence, it is very important that we share all of the information that we have." (*Comment*: Being able to condition demand more effectively is also important. If a big box orders a million green cell phones and only red and white phones are available, the company must figure out a way to "make it work.")

Paterson continued, "There's a lot of responsibility on all elements of the supply chain to make this model work effectively. If I tell a storage supplier I need a

million drives next quarter with specific types of configurations, and then suddenly decide I don't need them, the onus is on me to sell them. It's unreasonable
to expect the supplier to react to that level of change. The on-demand model
requires you to constantly bridge the gap between forecast and reality."

When Paterson first joined IBM in the United Kingdom, lead times were 4 to
6 months for a large desk-top terminal that contained only a cathode ray tube and
a few components. Today customers want almost instant delivery. Many companies have responded by building inventories of components and subassemblies in
the supply chain. That is *no longer* affordable. *Important*: The on-demand solution
requires more responsiveness by the supplier, more seamless communications,
and a tight partnership—and more accountability by the customer.

A small army of IT architects at IBM are working to make the connections
faster—and electronic. IBM is adapting a large number of commercial packages
as well as crafting some of their own solutions when needed.

Comment: As stated in Chapter 2 (*Spend Analysis—Start Your Engines*), the
co-authors believe that the logical starting point for technology in a supply transformation is spend analysis. You must understand what you spend before you can
develop meaningful strategies—or at least you should.

Data Management

In the 1998–2000 time frame, IBM had a "garbled" view of its spend. Multiple IT
solutions did not provide a consistent and logical view of general and production
procurement transaction data. There was no global view of total procurement
data. Significant delays occurred in obtaining the data that was available.
Operations were inefficient and maintenance costs were high. James W. Nugent,
IBM IT, who was responsible for core procurement systems and data management
applications, recalls that the commodity councils had a pretty good grasp on
direct spend—better than 95%.[9] Nugent said, "We knew how much money was
spent, but we didn't know how much was spent in the level of detail we needed."
At best the data was also a month old. Commodity leaders had to assemble data
from a variety of sources in a manual process, in part because each IBM division
had its own data warehouse—a total of 24 data warehouses.

In 1999 IBM launched a program to build a single data warehouse designed
around the common elements that procurement needed to drive its business
improvement processes. According to Nugent, "Our goals were to reduce the
amount of time spent looking for information, to allow more time for analyzing
the information, and to reduce the costs." The first specific activity in 2000 was
development of a set of "golden bridges," which allowed information to be pulled
from SAP software systems in a common format and which provided easy migration to the next application. Implementation was expanded in 2001 to include

general procurement (indirect) SAP systems, accounts payable data, and legacy systems from Japan and Latin America. In 2002 data from contract manufacturers was added to the business data warehouse. Spend summary data was added for non-purchase order data.

Nugent said, "It took us 3 years to get to the point where we had 99% coverage." An upgraded tool was rolled out in 2006, which gave new detail about IBM's biggest spend—temporary labor. Nugent said, "It will allow high-level people in human resources and elsewhere to see what we are spending on temporary labor and how that matches up with where IBMers are." The new Contractors Sourcing Application (CSA) will let managers choose the individual who is best suited for a particular job, whether internal or external, anywhere in the world. The application builds in the arrangements brokered by the procurement department. A manager selects a worker and then the tool issues a requisition, which leads to a purchase order being sent electronically to a supplier.

IBM moved to Emptoris, Inc., an outside supplier (which is now an IBM business partner), for its new sourcing tool, which replaces a homegrown application, the Internet Quoting Tool (IQT), which was developed in 1999. IQT provides a standard platform for all electronic requisitions and allows creation of templates usable by all IBM buyers. The new Emptoris tool, which IBM calls GAPS, provides all of the benefits of IQT and allows much more collaboration on a superior and expandable technology platform that links to other IBM systems (such as a contract tool known as COLT). The GAPS tool also allows real-time communications with the supply base during the RFx process (Table 14.2).

A new feature "sticks out" as an oddity—when legally possible, *eliminate* paper-based activity from the sourcing process. However, some countries require that a reconciliation report be printed out on a monthly basis. Pruitt added, "You also have to consider value-added tax and how it gets computed."

CLOSING THOUGHTS ABOUT IBM

The descriptions of work on spend analysis and sourcing tools that have been presented in this chapter are examples of the extensive work that is underway in applying technology tools to supply transformation at IBM. IBM has also developed a state-of-the-art tool for contract management, which is known as COLT. The company is leading the way in electronic integration of customer demand signals to multiple layers of the IBM supply chain.

IBM, which has impressive resources to tackle its on-demand transformation, might have more motivation than most because it wants to convert its supply chain services into a business. There is much to be learned from IBM—but the basics still apply—learn from your customers and lead from the top.

Table 14.2. What GAPS Does for IBM

- Global sourcing solution
- Enables information sharing with similar commodities to maximize saving opportunities
- Enables sharing of best practices in quoting activity through the use of templates
- Enables use of past sourcing information and the latest market intelligence information to find the optimal solution for IBM and influence customer decisions
- Provides productivity gains through elimination of double keying of data, linkage with E2E systems, and templates to minimize set-up time of quoting activity
- Aligns the contract management sourcing process, supplier management, marketing intelligence and procurement policy, and practice processes to fully realize the synergy
- Provides the ability to expand hands-free purchase orders
- When legally possible, eliminates paper-based activity from the sourcing process
- Provides the ability to support remote auditing of the sourcing process by enabling the centralization of all sourcing documentation, including communication between the requester, procurement, and the supplier
- Enables standardization of the process and drives adherence to process and policy worldwide
- Supports the diversity supplier process and provides a global tool and database
- Supports the supplier performance evaluation process and provides a global tool and database

Source: Adapted from IBM data.

LESSONS LEARNED

- Transformations must be customer driven.
- Transformations must be led from the top.
- Supplier relationships are the key enabler to achieving higher levels of cost competitiveness, quality, innovation, and responsiveness.
- Procurement can be a competitive differentiator.
- All elements of an enterprise must be "on the same page" and mobilized to achieve a transformation.
- World-class operational efficiency is a requisite.

This book has free material available for download from the
Web Added Value™ resource center at *www.jrosspub.com*

TOOL AND DIE—THE TORTOISE OR THE HARE?

How do you expect to win this race when you are walking along at your slow, slow pace?

— Aesop's Fables

The North American tool and die industry was one of the most notable industrial "graveyards" resulting from the huge global economic shift of 1996 to 2006. Across the United States, there was 30 to 50% overcapacity in this vital core of the manufacturing process. The devastation was even worse in areas close to the old "Big Three" of U.S. automobile manufacturing, notably Michigan.

The tool and die industry in the United States is the quintessential test of an on-demand supply chain. It is the weak link because of its history, the very small size of most tool and die shops, the lack of management expertise, and its pivotal role in the new product introduction process. Shaping a manufactured product requires that a tool be made first. Production time in the 1970s and 1980s for a tool such as an injection mold was often 4 months or more. The industry was also not well equipped to handle changes "on the fly." It was a craft industry run by skilled workers with little understanding of management disciplines.

THE DIE MAKER WAS KING

John Gravelle, president of Mar-Lee Industries in Leominster, MA, explained: "I was brought into the mold-making industry in the 1970s and 1980s. Everything then was about compartmentalizing everything you did. There was the artistic mold maker who built the entire mold. A mold would be assigned to a mold maker and he would have two or three helpers and they would focus on all aspects of that mold. And the mold was the direct result of their individual capabilities."[1]

The U.S. tool and die industry business model was poorly suited to compete with Asian tool builders who offered discounts of 40 or 50% or more. The U.S. industry was also not well prepared to deal with the rise of huge OEMs such as Samsung and Nokia, which had to meet the mandates of big-box giants such as Wal-Mart for huge orders of custom products almost on the fly. Nor was the U.S. industry ready to meet the demands of "transplant" automobile manufacturers that looked at tool shops as collaborative, long-term business partners and not job shops.

In Michigan, the tool and die industry had been shaped by U.S.-based automobile manufacturers, which had responded to financial problems by dictating across-the-board price reductions to vendors such as tool builders—which were also subjected to difficult financing requirements.[2] As a result, when Detroit automobile producers began losing market share, the local tool and die industry languished. The rapid trend to reverse auctions through Covisint accelerated the focus on price—and the demise of much of the U.S. tool and die industry.

A few tool builders, however, had studied the changing business climate and had then reinvested in new business practices (including supply chain strategy) and in new equipment to make their enterprises leaner, more profitable, and better able to respond to changes in customer demand. These companies included elite tool builders and molders such as Phillips Plastics in Hudson, WI; Mar-Lee Industries in Fitchburg, MA; and Nypro in Clinton, MA. They also de-emphasized the automotive business and looked for more profitable opportunities (Table 15.1).

A STATE OF CHANGE

In Michigan, the story developed a little differently. The Michigan Economic Development Corporation launched a large-scale retraining program for tool and die builders in an effort to create collaborative organizations that could be more competitive against global competition and respond more rapidly to developing customer requirements for responsiveness in terms of time, customization, and size of deliverables—in two words—"on demand."

Dave Martin, president and owner of Accu-Mold, Inc. in Portage, MI, recalled: "Around 2000, the State of Michigan realized two things. One was that our industry was being pummeled by global free enterprise. The other was that we were 7% of their manufacturing base. The 1100 tool and die shops in Michigan were not very important individually, but collectively we were a big number."[3]

Table 15.1. Reborn American Molders/Mold Makers

Nypro, Incorporated

Led by Chairman Gordon Lankton, Nypro has focused on automation, quality, global coverage, and key accounts and has risen from a $2-million company in the 1960s to a $1-billion employee-owned contract manufacturer in 2006. Nypro is based in Clinton, MA, operates 13 plants in China, and employs 7500 people in China. Lankton recalls, "When we first went to Hong Kong, we put robots on the injection molding machines. No one could believe it. The local television stations even came." Nypro operates three mold-making plants in the United States and three plants in China.

Phillips Plastics Corporation

In 1964 Phillips Plastics was started by Bob Cervenka and a childhood friend in Phillips, WI. Cervenka commented, "We made a commitment to never get caught with old technology and to always be looking ahead at the latest thing in the injection molding processes and new materials." All factories are located in the United States. Phillips Plastics focuses on specific markets and technologies, including multimaterial molding, micro-molding, magnesium molding, and metal-injection molding. Growth has been 20% yearly for 40 years, with a return on equity of 19% annually. Tooling capabilities are integrated into design, prototyping, and full manufacturing services. One new initiative is SCM for medical and other customers.

Mar-Lee Industries

Early in its early history in the 1970s, Mar-Lee built tools for giant consumer goods makers. That business and other less-sophisticated tooling subsequently moved to offshore sources. Owner John Gravelle expanded to injection molding in the 1990s and developed a focus on large customers in the medical and packaging areas that would make long-term commitments. Mar-Lee bought the latest equipment and systems for specific, sophisticated jobs. A more-recent specialty has been development of tooling and manufacturing systems for bioabsorbable compounds that are used in medical implants.

Representatives of 600 of the shops were invited by the Center of Automotive Research (CAR) to a presentation about a new way of doing business. Based on their location and business specialty, another 10 shops of the 600 were chosen to go through a 2-year program to completely reengineer their business models.

Martin said, "We were craftsmen who had become businessmen and we lacked the ability to deal with economic downturns and global competition. We needed some help and we got it." The shops also lacked economy of scale. More than 80% of the tooling companies in Michigan had fewer than 50 employees.

CAR, the Michigan Manufacturing Technology Center, and regional economic development groups helped small tooling firms to build collaborative business models through coalitions. The groups bid collectively for new business, with each company agreeing to a specialized role that would speed up development and leverage expertise and equipment capabilities. Three collectives emerged—one working on large sheet metal dies for automotive manufacturing purposes, another working on progressive dies, and a third working on plastic molds.

One of the new collaborative groups is the United Tooling Coalition (UTC), which was formed from 11 shops in Michigan. Each shop has a distinct specialty—prototyping, machining, engineering services, mold production, or die production. Martin said, "The key point to our tooling collaboration is aligning our core competencies and specialties to customers' needs. By having a group of diverse shops, we can work collectively on multifaceted projects. A classic example is an instrument panel cluster assembly. You can find a shop in UTC that specializes in every part of that assembly." The view of UTC is that costs of tools will drop as a result of the increased efficiencies. Additionally, the customer only deals with one point of contact for billing and other purposes.

Other aspects of the collaborative business model program are development of common mold-building practices and standards and purchasing alignment within the coalition. Once standards take effect, centralizing purchasing and gaining economy of scale becomes easier.

Rethinking Quality Requirements

Learning new business skills such as lean and functional build are at the heart of the effort. Jay S. Baron, CEO of CAR, is "preaching" an almost heretical doctrine—pay less attention to component quality and more attention to system quality.[4] That, says Baron, is the Japanese way, and the reason the Japanese have been outscoring American manufacturers on quality surveys. Baron calls that idea "functional build."

Baron said, "There's a misperception about Japanese quality. People believe that Japanese automakers build all their parts very precisely, and it just isn't true. We found that they don't care about making each part to a precise spec. They just want the assembly to be 'in spec.'"

Comment: Oddly, one of the lessons learned involves moving away from those amazing capability requirements as seen in the ubiquitous P_pk and C_pk indexes. Instead, the emphasis is on customer-perceived quality of the final product. Is this inconsistent with all of the reports on application of Six Sigma as exemplified in the Toyota Production System? The answer may be that the Japanese pay attention to quality, but they define quality differently when developing a system such as an automotive body. As Baron and co-authors state in a report which included significant research at Japanese car makers: "North

American automotive manufacturers traditionally have utilized a sequential process validation approach for the automotive body."[5] This sequential process validation approach starts with detailed quality assessments of a component and assumes that each successive level of assembly is dependent on the quality of the preceding work.

In the functional build approach, however, "Required changes are identified based upon lowest-cost solutions that might involve modifications to a product design, a stamping die or an assembly process," states Barron and co-authors.[5]

The magic is in the words "integrates product, process, and manufacturing." Partners working together decide where to make changes for the optimal result, as opposed to contentious relationships between an OEM and vendor in which "pass-go" gateways are controlled by a multitude of painstaking, often close-to-impossible, measurements. Another credo of this movement is that robust, repeatable processes produce consistent results—focus on the process, not the measurement.

Moving to Functional Build

For American mold builders and molders who have been hammered with quality specifications for the past 25 years, using the new approach is a leap of faith. "In the new approach, OEMs tell us what requirements are critical," says Dave Martin. "We go back, make the tool, shoot it, and then try the parts for fit and function. And then we'll go back and make the final adjustments. After that the drawing is changed. It's a much more efficient way of getting from A to Z."[3]

Moving to functional build may be one of the toughest issues for the rebuilding Michigan tool industry because the move requires U.S. OEMs to think differently. It does, however, position them to develop more business with transplant OEMs such as Honda, Toyota, and Nissan, which are expected to build more tools in the United States long term. Functional build is an interesting example of how engineering is becoming part of the supply chain solution as the United States morphs to an on-demand economy.

Comment: Another way to think about this—let the experts in tool design and construction figure out how to solve critical manufacturing problems based on their understanding of the processes rather than telling them to stretch their equipment to meet demands that at times may have been developed with little understanding of the manufacturing processes involved.

Measuring Repeatability

This type of thinking is happening by necessity in a rapidly growing area of the plastics and metal fabrication industries: micro molding, or the production of parts whose features can only be seen with magnification. There is no reliable way to measure such minuscule parts. So the emphasis is on development of very proprietary technologies, entirely owned by the mold builders, which are so robust they produce repeatable parts. Donna Bibber, a plastics engineer at Miniature Tool & Die in Charlton, MA, one of the pioneers in micro tooling, commented: "The mold is very repeatable, but what's not repeatable when you get down to less than a tenth of a thousandth of an inch is measurement. We talk to clients in proposal stage to determine how they will measure and how we will measure because gage R&R can be as long as the mold development and molding development."[6] (*Note:* Gage R&R, or gage repeatability and reproducibility, is a Six Sigma term. Gage R&R measures the amount of variation in a measurement system that arises from the measurement device and the people who are taking the measurement.)

Look at Dave Martin's bottom-up view of how the purchasing process for tools works in the United States: "The way the domestic OEMs do it, they put out bids and the guy who knows the least amount about how to build that tool had the highest probability of getting the job. The Japanese stay loyal to their suppliers. They get them in a niche and then let them do it over and over. That's a major learning-curve advantage for a given technology."[3]

Gaining Efficiency and Competitiveness

Another major aspect of the new approach is efficiency. Bruce Knapp of the Michigan Manufacturing Technology Center commented: "There is a huge opportunity to reduce tooling costs through the implementation of lean methods."[7] What does it mean to the United Tooling Coalition? Dave Martin explained: "We are reformatting our entire process from the front door to the back door."[3] (*Note*: Instruction in lean is by Jeffrey Liker, author of *The Toyota Way* and professor of industrial and operations engineering at the University of Michigan.)

Switching to the East Coast, John Gravelle at Mar-Lee Industries explained how implementation of lean is reshaping his shop. In the 1970s and 1980s, craftsman dominated the shop, but by the 1990s, shops were populated with specialized machines, such as computer numerically controlled (CNC) equipment or electrical discharge machining (EDM) equipment. "We had people working in a department and running two or three machines," Gravelle commented. "But that's all they did and their skills were limited. Everything was batch and queue. They were waiting for the next batch of parts, their programs, and their instructions. A 16-cavity tool would pass from department to department. The tool could be in a queue for 4 days to get through a given department. There was a 20% gain in efficiency from the craftsman days, but it didn't help that much because of the batch-and-queue issues." Gravelle continued: "In lean, we're creating work cells and teams that are trained in multiple skills. Instead of having an EDM department, we're breaking up the equipment into several cells. If a guy running the EDM machine is finished with one part of a job and the next requirement is wire, then he'll move over to the wire machine and start running that part of the job. Also, a guy who finds a problem fixes the problem, including engineering. We are finding that the employees have much broader skills than we ever imagined they had."

Changes such as lean which have been implemented at Mar-Lee Industries have had a profound effect on the company's competitiveness. The company had sales of $3 million in 1990 and $17 million in 2005. Gravelle expects to reach $25 million by the end of 2007. The focus at Mar-Lee now is on medical and packaging. Gravelle also wants partnerships. Customers are required to sign 3-year, or longer, agreements. Gravelle said, "We tell our customers that we will make a commitment to their products and develop a very high-quality process that will make products at a very competitive cost."

In the Mar-Lee business model, the focus is no longer on the purchase price of the tool as determined in a global electronic bidding event. Increased costs of the tool to improve reliability or efficiency are amortized over the life the agreement and are recovered many-fold times. This is a concept that the Japanese automotive OEMs understand well. Like functional build, it is a concept that is part of the new approach to business that allows more speed and faster reaction to customer demand.

CLOSING THOUGHTS—THE FUTURE

Companies such as the Michigan tool and die industry hope the future will include increased business with the Japanese OEMs. Dave Martin said, "They want to grow their tooling base in the United States. They recognize the importance of having an integrated supply base in North America. And they are working diligently and intelligently to select those suppliers."[3]

Meanwhile the signals from Detroit are more ominous. In 2006 both Ford and General Motors became much smaller companies that put pressure on their supply base to reduce costs. Ford and General Motors have not been telling suppliers to relocate to China, as some of the big-box retailers have done, but increased low-cost country sourcing appears to be a likely outcome of Detroit's growing economic plight.

The American tool and die industry certainly started the race like the tortoise did in the well-known fable. Like the tortoise, U.S. tool and die suppliers may well cross the finish line in good shape if they can continue to adapt to an emerging on-demand economy.

LESSONS LEARNED

- Rules of on-demand transformation apply to all companies or organizations, regardless of size or position in the supply chain.
- Focus on customer perception of final quality, not self-defined manufacturing or assembly minutia.
- Customers and markets are always changing and so must companies.
- Become long-term partners with your customers.
- Base pricing on long-term value, not unit price.

This book has free material available for download from the
Web Added Value™ resource center at *www.jrosspub.com*

Part IV

NOW DO IT!

MONEY—MAKING THE BUSINESS CASE

In the modern world of business, it is useless to be a creative original thinker unless you can also sell what you create. Management cannot be expected to recognize a good idea unless it is presented to them by a good salesman.

— **David M. Ogilvy**
Advertising expert

"It's all about leadership." That is the answer that co-author Robert Rudzki gave to a technology vendor, who was expressing frustration and puzzlement with the pace of technology adoption by big business. Success stories well document the various tools outlined in this book. So, why does it seem to take forever for some firms to make the decision to proceed?

In any supply management technology evaluation, the starting point should be the overall business strategy and the objectives for supply management at that company. For example, if a company has relegated supply management to a very tactical role, this decision will have a fundamental impact on the technology debate. In this case, you might be encouraged to think principally of tools that support the efficient processing of purchase orders and not much else.

On the other hand, if the company's senior management understands the value of supply management and has given supply management the strategic role that it deserves, the technology agenda will be much different. In this case, you will have the opportunity for a wide-ranging evaluation of all of the tools that can help you achieve your strategic objectives (Figure 16.1).

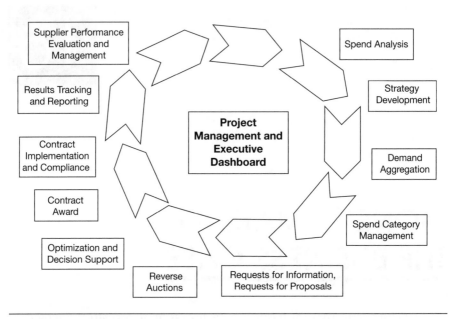

Figure 16.1. Integrated Supply Management Tools. (Source: From *Straight to the Bottom Line™: An Executive's Roadmap to World Class Supply Management.*)

This is another reason why we say, "It's all about leadership." Have you created an awareness among the executive team and among your internal clients about the opportunities for top- and bottom-line improvement through world-class supply management? That is step one.

STRATEGY

Once a sense of awareness has been created, then step two, the vision, the strategic objectives, and the transformation roadmap to get there, can be outlined. What are we trying to achieve in new, genuine, cost reductions during the next 3 to 5 years? What revenue growth are we trying to support? What are we striving to achieve in working capital improvements? How do we plan to get there?

All of these are strategic objectives. Developed properly, and with appropriate "stretch," strategic objectives will generate significant executive support and interest in your efforts—and that is the first step toward being able to evaluate and select the *right* supply management technology and tools.

Said another way, technology is an enabler. Enabling *what* is the key question. If strategic stretch objectives relate directly to overarching corporate objectives (such as improving return on invested capital), consideration of a certain type of

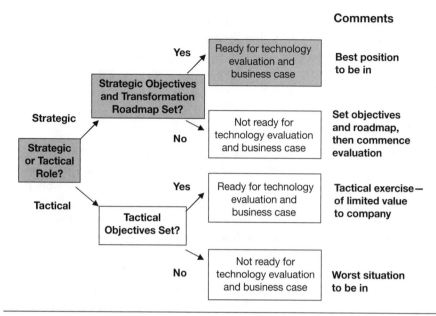

Figure 16.2. Which Path Are You On?

enabling toolset will be necessary. If objectives are ill-defined, or tactical, do not expect to have much support for spending money on new technology from anyone (executives, finance, or IT).

So, let us assume a good job has been done on step one and a sense of executive awareness has been created and there is interest and buy-in for your strategic role. Let us also assume appropriate strategic objectives and a transformation roadmap that relates to achieving the strategic objectives have been established (step two). If both of those steps have been done (Figure 16.2), you are in the best position possible to conduct a technology evaluation and build a business case. Anything short of that and you will be facing an uphill battle and risk looking at the technology options from a too-narrow perspective.

Participants

Inviting key stakeholders to participate on a cross-functional team that describes the "as-is" and "to-be" states contributes to the development of the business case and helps evaluate the vendor finalists. Finance and IT are natural candidates to invite to join this effort.

Finance is a valuable participant because of its role in encouraging better corporate performance, its credibility as a neutral, fact-based partner, and its interest in compliance with the Sarbanes-Oxley Act. Finance involvement can also help avoid the pitfall of letting the "financing" of a project unduly affect the strategic choice of technology and the vendor (more on that potential pitfall later). IT is a valuable participant because of its understanding of the corporation's current technology infrastructure and its ability to assist in quantifying integration costs, benefits, and time lines.

Technology Evaluation

Any technology evaluation must relate to the strategic objectives and the transformation roadmap that have been established for supply management activities. Do not become sidetracked by the "integration issues" that IT will inevitably point out. Integration issues are important topics, and they have a place in the business case economics, but they should *not* be used to limit the options that are to be evaluated. If options are approached from an IT cost-of-implementation perspective, the option selected might very well be the *wrong* one in terms of meeting the corporation's strategic growth, cost, and working capital objectives.

Similarly, do not let the various pricing approaches cause elimination of one vendor or another. The question of economic evaluation comes *after* the homework has been done on the objectives and a conclusion has been made about which approach can help achieve the objectives. An all-too-common error is to look at constraints (e.g., IT costs or the procurement systems budget) and let those constraints preselect the strategic path. If that is done, the company has been rendered a huge disservice. *Remember:* The point of a business case is to determine which path will enable you to achieve your strategic objectives most effectively and then to consider which alternative (of those that meet the strategic objectives) is the most attractive economically. To say it another way, a 500% ROI from a "cheap" software implementation that does not fully address your strategic objectives is not a good project.

Situation Analysis

An important early step, after the strategic groundwork has been established, is to analyze the current situation. A situation analysis describes the "as is" of an organization and is the baseline against which the "to be" will be compared. The "as is" should be described across all relevant dimensions and include as much quantification as possible. For example, the "as is" for a large company might look like this:

As-Is Company X

- Over $20 billion of external spend, involving five procurement organizations
- Inconsistent procurement tools and processes across five organizations
- 70% of spend is through basic sourcing processes; 30% has never been through a sourcing process
- Of the 70% that has been through basic sourcing, most was not done for spend pools across the entire enterprise (i.e., volume leverage was not maximized)
- Considerable debate about which categories should be selected for the next wave of sourcing efforts (not a fact-driven process)
- Spend compliance with new contracts ranging from 20% to 70% (maverick spend of 30% to 80%)
- Contract rebates and discounts frequently not optimized
- Contract authoring is a significant part of the cycle time for new sourcing efforts
- e-RFx infrequently used
- Reverse auctions infrequently used, as are optimizations
- Sourcing project management is informal and often not done
- Reporting of negotiated savings lacks credibility
- Supplier performance management is manual, ad hoc, or entirely lacking (As a result, business is probably not being awarded to the best supplier(s).)

To-Be Company X

- Consistent processes and tools across the entire enterprise
- 100% of spend through a consistent sourcing process, with all enterprise spend leveraged
- Use of spend data, compliance, and supplier performance information as inputs to decide on which sourcing categories to kick-off in the next wave
- Compliance with new contracts improves to minimum of 50% within 6 months, 75% within 9 months, and 90% within 12 months
- Contract rebates and discounts optimized
- Contract authoring cycle time reduced by 50%, with greater consistency of terms and conditions
- e-RFIs and e-RFXs used regularly and correctly
- Reverse auctions and optimizations used appropriately
- Project management tools used for all sourcing efforts, reducing cycle times by 25% and improving team results and productivity
- Credibility of reported savings higher
- Supplier performance management is a natural part of the sourcing management process, using the same metrics that are being factored into business decisions (sourcing and award) on a daily basis

If a cross-functional team is able to describe the "as is" and also envision the desired "to be," the team is well on its way to having what is needed for identifying relevant technology vendors and for developing the business case.

Vendor Selection

With regard to identifying relevant technology vendors, do not hesitate to use a request for information (RFI) as part of the early-stage process for gathering information (see the *Appendix* for an example). The field of players is changing and evolving and offerings are advancing so quickly that the landscape must be promptly surveyed in an effective manner before developing a request for proposal (RFP).

Once the RFI information has been assimilated and background conversations with vendors have been accomplished, prepare the RFP. At this stage doing due diligence on each of the candidate software vendors is also appropriate. Are software vendors in good financial condition? Are they growing or shrinking? Are they having personnel layoffs? Are they continuing to invest in product R&D? Are they likely to be in existence in 3 to 5 years?

All of these are critical questions that need answers before making a decision. Obviously, publicly held companies can be examined quickly. Public companies typically have Moody's or Standard & Poor's ratings that can be used to determine their current financial condition and near-term prospects. Many of the more exciting technology vendors, however, are not publicly traded companies. In the case of privately held vendors, a confidentiality agreement may need to be signed in order to gain access to summary financials for finance people to assess. If the vendor balks at signing a confidentiality agreement, indirect information must be relied upon, including bank and trade references, news releases about recent successes gaining additional financing from private investors, independent analyst assessments, and interviews with the vendor's senior management.

Comment: In a private-company assessment, you are looking for an understanding of whether a vendor is currently profitable and growing. If it is not, is the vendor adequately funded so that it will last until the breakeven point is passed?

THE BUSINESS CASE

At this stage reviewing the gap between "as is" and "to be" is also useful. Why? This gap is the basis for the economics of the business case. The value of addressing the gap can be quantified with your own estimates, with benchmarks available from numerous studies, or with estimates from experiences shared by benchmarking partners. At the most fundamental level, a picture is being built of:

- Quantifiable benefits, expressed in dollars per year or if applicable as one-time benefits (sometimes referred to as "hard" savings)

- Nonquantifiable benefits, expressed in words or as a range of dollar values (sometimes referred to as "soft" savings)
- Costs, principally involving license costs, implementation costs, and annual maintenance costs

For example, having a contract management capability can offer numerous quantifiable benefits:

- Reduced maverick spend on existing contracts
- Speed up of new contract authoring cycle time
- Increased rebates and discounts
- Reduced penalties

Also offered are important nonquantifiable benefits:

- Decreased contractual risk
- Improved supplier relationships
- Administrative savings by virtue of having a central repository of contracts

Hard and Soft Benefits

A checklist of the major hard and soft benefits that typically play a role in a supply management technology evaluation is provided in Table 16.1. Before presenting the business case, have an understanding of your company's philosophy regarding the handling of some of the soft benefits. For example, at some firms, increased productivity, while assumed to be one of the benefits, is not factored into the economic analysis because eliminating or reducing "parts of people" (or "partial FTEs" in the lingo of big companies) is difficult.

The business case for a contract management tool would incorporate increased productivity benefits and the one-time and ongoing costs into a ROI calculation. ROI is the common denominator for all business cases because it allows the economic aspects of competing alternatives to be evaluated on a comparable basis. As an example of an outstanding ROI, drugmaker GlaxoSmithKline (GSK) won the prestigious *Baseline Magazine* 2005 ROI Leadership Award for its success in implementing a closed-loop technology solution, generating a documented ROI in excess of 5000%. GSK "… was looking to cut costs associated with developing products still in the research and development stage. The aim was to implement a single system to handle spending analysis, negotiation, supplier management, contracts and compliance, and other aspects of its business. The company chose the Emptoris enterprise supply management system to negotiate

Table 16.1. Partial Checklist of Typical Benefits

Hard benefits

Improved enterprise-wide leverage of spend

Improved cost reduction results from new sourcing efforts

Improved compliance with existing contracts

Improved cycle time for new sourcing efforts

Improved selection of categories for sourcing

Optimized contract rebates and discounts

Greater use of consistent contract terms and conditions

Faster contract authoring

Improved inventory strategies

Improved active management of supplier performance and relationships

Improved decision analysis and support

Soft benefits

Improved efficiency of utilizing strategic personnel

Improved credibility of reported results

Improved involvement of user community in supplier performance assessments

Improved "steering" of activities via an executive dashboard

Improved management of multiple efforts via project management features

contracts more quickly with half of the resources, thus cutting administrative costs. The money saved on the project was funneled into R&D and marketing."[1]

Other Considerations

Developing a business case becomes more complex when an integrated, closed-loop system is compared to a collection of stand-alone applications from different vendors, but it can be done. The individual pieces of stand-alone applications will each have a business case, adding up to the gross total benefit, but the costs of integrating the pieces and the impact of potentially less-efficient data sharing among the pieces needs to be estimated. In a presentation to the Conference Board's 2005 Electronic Procurement Conference, Paula Peterson of Hewlett-Packard (HP) indicated that HP ultimately selected the integrated, closed-loop approach for several reasons:

- Increased savings opportunities
- Simplification of systems and common processes
- Increased adoption of best practices and tools
- Access to new benefits, which is only possible with an integrated solution

CLOSING THOUGHTS ABOUT BUSINESS CASE ANALYSIS

Technology suppliers have recently added new pricing methodologies which can complicate business case analysis. Some vendors have introduced a "pay-as-you-go" on-demand pricing formula, which can be a tempting lure for budget-constrained companies. Many other vendors continue to offer the traditional license and maintenance fee method. An ROI calculation can bring out the hidden costs of some of these apparently cheaper pay-as-you-go pricing approaches. Each company's situation will be different. So the pricing option that works in one case may not work in another. Sometimes asking for prices quoted "both ways" enables a situational comparison. The big caution here is to resist the temptation to let factors such as IT integration costs or vendor pricing options influence the technology approaches that are considered. The first step must always be to determine what the strategic objectives of the company are, which is followed by an evaluation of which vendors/tools can effectively address most or all of these objectives. Then, and only then, does the economic evaluation enter the picture as a way make a selection(s) from among the relevant options.

THE SANDBOX TECHNIQUE

A large, global company had been using a series of purchased and homegrown tools to support its supply management objectives. The tools were serving their purpose, but they did not allow the organization to go to the next step in achieving its strategic objectives. The procurement council commissioned a global team to evaluate closed-loop technology system options. The team went through a comprehensive process and finally reduced the list of suppliers under consideration to two. The offerings appeared to be comparable in all major respects. The team leader now faced a quandary—how to make the final selection.

The technique that was chosen is referred to as the "sandbox." The technique is based on the playground sandbox that most people recall from their youth. The idea is simple—allow team members to "play" with the software for a period of time to gain an appreciation of its functionality and ease of use. Functionality and ease of use were deemed

---

THE SANDBOX TECHNIQUE (CONTINUED)

important to evaluate by the company because during the presentation phase of the technology/vendor evaluation process, the demos were typically run by an experienced salesperson from each technology vendor. Each offering looked easy to use, but there was some concern that the apparent ease-of-use was heavily influenced by the expertise of the person who was running the demonstration.

In this case, both vendor finalists agreed to the sandbox technique. In a matter of days, members of the physically dispersed evaluation team logged on and proceeded to "use" the system. The verdict was surprisingly uniform—although the two systems appeared to be comparable during the sales demo process, the sandbox technique demonstrated that one system was significantly more intuitive and easier to use than the other. The business was awarded to that vendor.

LESSONS LEARNED

Do:
- Always link back to your company's strategic role and stretch objectives.
- Quantify how your technology recommendation will help achieve the stretch objectives.
- Involve finance and IT as participants in the process.
- Keep internal clients informed and involved because they are the beneficiaries.
- Talk to other companies who have used the software tools.
- Try the tools yourself (e.g., use the sandbox approach).

Don't:
- Get strategically sidetracked by IT integration concerns.
- Let vendor pricing options cause you to make the wrong technology decision.

Web
Added
Value™

This book has free material available for download from the Web Added Value™ resource center at *www.jrosspub.com*

MASTER PLANNING— CREATING AND FOLLOWING A PRACTICAL BLUEPRINT

The magic is in the weaving.

— **Carol Rubeo,** President
MSE Enterprises

e-Purchasing tools are not cheap. Although the market is maturing and costs have dramatically dropped since the dot.com bust, Fortune 500/Global 2000 companies are still looking at six-figure investments for each of these functionalities/modules (five figures for simpler applications or narrower implementations; seven figures for extremely broad uses). Very few companies in the on-demand business have the deep pockets of a company such as IBM to enable the full range of electronic work flow and supplier engagement capability. The financial size and risk of these implementations (many either fail or simply do not deliver all that they could) means that a poorly thought-out implementation can be disastrous.

THE MASTER PLAN

Hence a master plan is necessary. One would think that the plan precedes the money—but often a "chicken-or-egg" element exists, so sometimes money availability does drive the plan rather than the other way around. This "money before the plan" concept is a bit counterintuitive. Master planning is about more than just the tool investment decision—it holistically looks at the entire picture and is driven by a dozen probing questions about the company's approach to/with its supply base. Several questions build a thought framework for supply e-tool master planning:

- What are we spending?
- Who are we spending it with?
- Where are we spending it?
- Why are we spending it with those suppliers in those places?
- How do we decide with whom and where to spend the money?
- Where could the process we use to decide about all these issues be improved the most?
- What will transform the way we approach those markets/suppliers?
- Where will technology help? ... How much? ... The most?
- Will the technology work? ... Will it work in our organization?
- What are the implications of technology? ... Organizationally? ... In relationships? ... As controls?
- How much will it cost? ... In money? ... People? ... Effort? ... Time?
- Things will not stay the same, so how will the future change?

From these questions a master planning "thought template" will emerge that contains four planning layers, all of which are necessary for success:

- Tools—Choices concerning functionalities/providers to help do what is needed to meet business goals
- Organization—Support, leadership, planning, training, capacity
- Cost—Implementation cost, including initial investment and ongoing budgets, funding, savings/benefits
- Time—Schedules, sequencing

Important: These are interdependent dynamic layers. A rule of thumb about technology transformation master planning is that the plan needs to be redeveloped periodically. The world simply does not stand still—it evolves at a breakneck pace and the plan must evolve with it. Yet, the plan must also resist the temptations of either constantly changing or being paralyzed by uncertainty.

In December 1999, during a leadership meeting about improving the interactions of Procter & Gamble (P&G) with its supply base, realization hit management that P&G was seriously behind the leaders in e-purchasing on several fronts. The result was an urgently assembled "plan" based on three things:

- Well-established and successful worldwide sourcing processes, but weak purchasing IT capability of P&G

- The business priority to improve the ability of P&G to both penetrate supply markets and leverage supplier capabilities
- A naïve belief at P&G (at that time) in the hype of the Web—that e-marketplaces would magically solve volume complexities and create scale on the procurement side

The plan became to:

1. Put data standards in place, particularly for direct material specifications to link with R&D new product design.
2. Access market analysis tools to drive better sourcing strategies and execute them via new go-to-market e-tools, initially a few reverse auctions, but ultimately e-RFXs.
3. Help found and fund Transora, the CPG industry marketplace, seeking to use it for indirect consortium buying (along with numerous sales-side applications that were of real strategic value to P&G). (*Note*: Transora ultimately ceased to exist as an independent organization, merging with UCCnet in May 2005. Today its remnants are part of GS1 US, with P&G still represented on the Board of Governors.)

Comment: Oh well, as the rock n' roll star Meatloaf sang, *Two Out of Three Ain't Bad*. This plan was not master planning—it was a combination of early analysis, luck, and an excellent, very skilled, mature strategic sourcing organization that made two-thirds of a "leap onto the Net" work on the purchasing side. With that background, we will leave P&G and take a closer look at what master planning really is, but we will return to P&G later.

TOOLS—MORE THAN JUST FUNCTIONALITY

Part 1—Determine Focus

Tools planning is not just about what tool suite to buy and the tool module implementation order. Implementing the process described in Chapter 16 (*Money— Making the Business Case*) requires:

- Tool choices—Looking at the range of tools available, tying them to business needs and organizational capability
- Prioritization—Tool implementation order
- Providers—Provider assessment, piloting of "feel" and performance, and final choice

Processes First, Then Tools

Unfortunately, e-tool purchase decisions sometimes precede in-depth thinking. Imposing sourcing tools on an organization hoping the tools will also deliver sourcing processes and expertise is a huge mistake. One can easily be encouraged by the persuasive sales literature from software providers that describes conceptual sourcing and supplier management processes. Buy the tools—get the process, right? Maybe yes, maybe no. Work process change is complex. It is about people, not technology. For example, an IT group at one mid-size company received funding to install their ERP vendor's procurement suite. Meanwhile, procurement was still in the early stages of its development of strategic sourcing processes. Buying tools before installing processes is a recipe for disaster—and the root of procurement/IT conflict in many companies.

Each major work step in the strategic sourcing process typically requires its own tool. Bidding tools do not do spend analysis; contract management tools do not place orders. Hence we have the continued development of closed-loop tool suites encompassing these different but related processes.

Many technology projects fail because of work processes, not faulty software. Too often, procurement leaders focus on the project financials and miss the broader picture because funding is such a battle. At a presentation, Debbie Wilson, former publisher of the *Cool Tools for Purchasing Newsletter* and now research director, Procurement Strategies and Systems, at Gartner, Inc., cautioned that companies must decide where to focus and then apply the tools.[1] Big money has been wasted at corporations that initially went after e-procurement without strong sourcing and compliance processes embedded throughout the organization (see Chapter 7, *P2P—Where e-Procurement Meets Accounts Payable*).

As Chapter 16 emphasized, strategic sourcing processes are first and then e-tool enablement is next. The opening section of this book examines how top companies use the various e-tools available to deliver impressive benefits. Figuring out which tools provide the most business benefit, in what order, is the trick. You cannot do everything. Wilson's advice was to start with sourcing (spend analysis, then bidding tools) followed by supplier portals to make working together efficient and effective. Picking the wrong tool in the wrong order and with the wrong supplier can sap (no pun intended) organizational energy. Most practitioners agree. Still, the planning process at every company has its own personality and its own best roadmap.

Procurement Transformation—The GSK Experience

Pharmaceutical giant GlaxoSmithKline (GSK) began its procurement transformation in October 1999.[2] Gregg Brandyberry took over as vice president of

Global Systems and Operations (the group that supports purchasing processes at GSK) and began a procurement process and system change to enable more effective sourcing. The technology plan was developed to support those processes, not the other way around.

GSK used an intriguing process known as "idealized design" to develop both the processes and their supporting e-tool box. Brandyberry brought in Jason Magidson (now director of Innovation Processes at GSK) as director of Procurement System Development to drive the design. Magidson described idealized design as a way to harness people's "wish mode" through imagination and creative imagery to form a high-level vision of what is needed.

In the GSK case, contracts emerged as the biggest priority. The contract management system was so "cumbersome that the procurement staff prepared their own contracts and stored them in desk drawers. When people left the company, contracts were lost, requiring embarrassed calls to suppliers for replacements."[3, 4] A group of users redesigned the process first; only then did work on the IT tool become the focus. The effort was so successful that it was reapplied to create the e-tool master plan to support the entire procurement transformation.

Over a weeks-long period, stakeholders (about 60 including Sourcing Group managers and leadership representatives from the Accounts Payable, Legal, Purchasing, and IT Departments—as the technology supplier, not the expert telling users what they needed) held a series of meetings to design the ideal tool set. The need for a range of tools became clear when the Sourcing Group managers, when asked to compare the existing tools to what they needed using a transportation analogy, declared the current IT system to be a bicycle and their need to be a rocket ship. Within 3 to 6 months a 3- to 5-person core team identified a set of about a dozen tracking tools, which was ultimately dubbed "galaXy" (more about the name later). The process included moving from the envisioned total to clear priority setting. Four items rose to the top—spend analysis, contract management, savings tracking, and reverse auctions.

Magidson was clear about several things. He said, "To use idealized design the first thing is to think big and get a broad design specification. You want to get people to use their imaginations. Then work toward implementation by designing structures and processes that get you what you need most. For e-tools the design process needs to be renewed every 2 to 3 years, because things change, and totally reconceptualized every 5 to 6 years to keep up with what's happening in technology and the business." The galaXy suite provides sourcing staffers with a range of tools including Ariba Buyer modules and homegrown tools that are hooked to an ERP backbone for data access. Modules are upgraded or changed as technology or needs require and funding/resources allow. GSK recently went through the reconceptualization step. One outcome was a "virtual supplier master" to allow movement across tools to have integrated views rather than in-and-out toggling between different systems. Idealized design techniques give GSK procurement a true master plan that, with renewal, has sustained and evolved for 6 years. The planning process or tool choices at each company might be different, but the point is to do the planning and set the priorities for your unique situation (Table 17.1)

Part 2—Choose Tool Providers

The other half of tool planning includes making provider decisions:
- Evaluation of the types of software suppliers—ERP suites, best-of-breed suites, point solutions, or homegrown applications (A mix of all four could be an option too. The choice whether or not to standardize on one tool across the company also falls here.)
- Determination of whether to buy an enterprise license or use software as a service "on demand" (more about tool pricing later)
- Selection of reliable providers

These provider elements are highly intertwined and require collaborative focus on company business results from both procurement and IT stakeholders, not functional turf.

There is no one right answer for all companies. Hallmark uses mostly homegrown tools; Colgate is an SAP house; and Hewlett-Packard blends homegrown and best-of-breed suite applications that are overlaid on their ERP backbone. There is no single answer—but the master planning process should be the constant. It creates a forum for deciding which tools will most positively impact the company's business.

Pros and Cons

Tradeoffs must be weighed against benefits—best-of-breed tools typically provide superior functionality and user friendliness, but require integration and the management of more than one supplier (ERP and the tool provider). ERP applications eliminate integration, but can miss user satisfaction and elements of leading-edge functionality. Point solutions deliver unique capabilities, but must create significant value with easy implementation to overcome the need for training, support systems, and integration (where required). Contrary to popular belief, many niche tools do not require integration with base systems to get the job done—it all depends on what is being done and the work process used to do it.

Table 17.1. Master Planning — Deciding Tool Priority Based on Functionality, Value, and Urgency of Need

Tool	Functionality/Source of Value
1. Spend analysis	Analyze transactions, identify leveraging opportunities, cost reduction
2. Supplier identification/analysis	Supplier analysis, scorecarding, performance measurement, cost reduction delivery, and supply management process efficiency
3. Sourcing	Competitive bidding, supplier selection, competitive price discovery, deal definition, cost reduction, some process efficiency
4. Contract management	Deal documentation and compliance, process efficiency
5. Procurement/ordering	Transaction management, process efficiency
6. Delivery/receipt/payment	Supply and settlement, accounting, process efficiency
7. Controls	Sarbanes Oxley Act compliance, asset protection, process efficiency, risk reduction
8. Operational risk	Supplier perfect order management, supplier viability/reliability tracking, process efficiency, cost avoidance
9. Supplier innovation/PLM	New product costing, commercialization, cost management/avoidance, revenue enhancement
10. Cost analysis	Should cost, target cost, price negotiation, cost reduction/avoidance, process efficiency
11. Complex service management (e.g., specialized software for managing travel and entertainment, temporary labor, telecom, MRO, capital projects, etc.)	Efficient cross-functional process control and supplier management, process efficiency and cost reduction (each service area represents a separate software investment)

Due Diligence

Software providers can quickly become critical to a company's operation. Due diligence, prior to any commitment and ongoing once a relationship is established, is another "must do" in this part of the master plan. At the 2006 Conference Board e-Procurement Conference in Chicago, Andrew Bartels, Forrester Research vice president, made the point that the e-purchasing software market continues to contract, from a high of 53 providers in 2001 to 37 in 2005.[5] ERP provider market share is steadily increasing as suite functionality is upgraded (Oracle and SAP are up about 15 points over 5 years). The market share of the next ten best-of-breed vendors fell steadily from 2000 to 2004, but increased significantly in 2005. Net is that the top 12 providers are slowly taking market share away from the rest—a sign of continued consolidation. In 2006 Emptoris acquired diCarta, D&B purchased Open Ratings, and SAP acquired Frictionless, to name a few. Weakened software suppliers represent a major risk to a company's operation and data should these suppliers "go under." Even when acquired by another provider, relationships can change when products, priorities, and people are absorbed into the acquiring company. Avoiding (or anticipating and coping with) a hit to the adoption of a tool that is caused by a change in provider ownership, business strategy, or customer prioritization requires continued monitoring of e-tool suppliers.

Comprehensive due diligence should include commercial, functionality, and technical aspects of the supplier. Strong collaboration between procurement and IT substantially improves the effort, but requires ongoing internal relationship building. As mentioned in Chapter 16 (*Money—Making the Business Case*), many providers (other than the ERP players) are privately held, so due diligence can be challenging and supplier viability can shift quickly with cash flow and revenue changes. Today's e-purchasing market is a tough one. Many of the Fortune 1000 companies already have suite suppliers, so providers jockey to sell individual modules or to take business away from each other. Financial health can vary considerably between suppliers—hence the need to *know* where a supplier stands. Until the supply software industry consolidation is complete or a mid-market software cost breakthrough occurs to tap that revenue pool, today's tough market will require ongoing due diligence (see Tables 17.2A and B for a summary of due diligence suggestions).

COSTS—PRICE THE TOOLS, GET THE ROI, MANAGE THE COSTS

Chapter 16 described many of the financial considerations, focusing on a strong financial case. Expanding on that theme, consider the following:

1. When evaluating and prioritizing tool value, remember that normally only two sources of hard savings exist—process efficiency and purchased goods/services cost reduction. Cost avoidance also matters in never-before-purchased components and one-time capital projects. Two "watch outs" apply—one for each type of savings. *Process savings* are often measured in time, but if headcount reductions or lowered overhead costs do not occur, these savings will never get to the bottom line. *Purchased goods savings* can sometimes be achieved without e-tool investment. Integrate these factors into the ROI evaluation.

2. Software suppliers offer pricing options, most of which boil down to either on-demand use or traditional enterprise licenses. Fundamentally, as one software executive put it, "You can either buy the tools by the drink or buy the whole bar." On-demand pricing, also called "software as a service," rents customers the tool to do the work at hand, with payment for each use. Versus more traditional enterprise licenses with an up-front license and ongoing maintenance charges of up to 20 % of the annual license cost (for upgrade development and ongoing support), "software as a service" lowers initial and ongoing costs for companies that do not conduct many events. Forrester's Bartels sees the breakeven point between "software as a service" and traditional licensing at the event-per-day usage rate, after which the license clearly pays off. Most experienced practitioners tend to agree with Bartels, citing a shift from event-based use to a license when a tool is widely utilized.

3. Remember total cost of ownership (TCO)! e-Tool TCO includes not only direct tool costs, but also ongoing internal support (e.g., help desks, dedicated internal staff, etc.).

4. Tool investments are not one-time expenses. Because procurement often sits in staff budgets which are frequently facing severe spending limitations or reductions, understanding and planning for the budget squeeze that occurs as technology tools are added to the organization's repertoire is a vital part of the planning process. This is especially true for the central support staff that develops and executes the master plan which, as best practices throughout this book show, can extend for several years. Existing tool maintenance cost and version upgrade TCO largely become "fixed costs" in future budgets. Sometimes process efficiencies must be turned into real headcount reductions elsewhere in the organization (versus redeployments) to pay for out-year maintenance costs without gutting

Table 17.2A. Provider Due Diligence—Commercial/Operational

Commercial

- Company size, history, financials, product range—ongoing access to changes
- Software and maintenance costs, pricing options; willingness to review as market costs change?
- Estimate of implementation cost and timing
- Option to "rent first" and test?; at discount?

Software capability

- Functionality and range of tools versus customer needs
- Ability to handle multiple spends/languages/etc.
- Ease of use, level of intuitiveness
- Level of flexibility in software to deal with unique customer needs; cost?

Support capability

- Training support for rollout—number of people, geographic footprint, etc.
- Versioning support
- User network access

References

- Customers—penetrate company culture not just tool use
- Privately held companies—bank, investors
- Analyst assessment of financials, sales, products, etc.
- Press releases and trade magazine research
- Direct CFO-to-CFO or finance-to-finance contact and review if deal is imminent or existing supplier
- Benchmark other companies on their tool implementations; compare their vendors' capabilities with the vendors company is considering

the support staff. (*Comment*: Short-sighted central expertise overhead cuts fly in the face of every success the authors found—not an excuse for "fat" central groups, but rather recognition that sustaining the infrastructure is neither simple nor automatic.)

Table 17.2B. Provider Due Diligence—Technical

Software

- History of software, previous versions
- Resources allocated to develop the product, to support the customer
- Number of production environment installations
- How can customer influence the versioning and enhancement process?
- What software/hardware are required at the customer?

Data/volume

- Size of a typical installation—number of users, number of records, number of client servers, etc.
- What level of stress testing has been done? What stress testing will be done at the customer?
- Known hardware or software limitations, processing speed, etc.
- Ability to tie into company's back end system; support for that implementation
- Training for customer IT
- Data configuration requirements

References

- Access to current customer technical resources
- Analyst assessment of software and support
- Press releases and tech trade magazine research

THE ORGANIZATION AND TIME—ABSORPTION AND PROMOTION

Chapters 18 (*Adoption—The Real Measure of Success*) and 19 (*Education— Training the Tools and Tools for Training*) examine organizational planning in more detail, but two other elements are important. As noted above, virtually every best-practice company staffs a central cadre of e-purchasing experts to assess the constantly changing technology landscape, to drive training and adoption, to provide ongoing user support, and to justify the funding to keep the system competitive externally. Staffing such a center of expertise is a prerequisite for success in these areas. Delegation of these decisions to IT or to multiple-line purchasing groups simply does not work.

Having a comprehensive marketing plan is also a necessity and includes the basics—management support, publicized successes, and recognition/rewards for pioneers. Companies that go beyond the basics to "brand" their process and technology initiatives can achieve amazing success. Recall the GSK galaXy tool set? As the tools were added (ValueTrak, SourceTrak, ConTrak, PlanTrak, etc.), the design team realized that organizing the tools in memorable way would harness user enthusiasm, which is a key to adoption. During one of the idealized design sessions, the problem of "tracking the Traks" surfaced. Richard Hollingsworth, Sourcing Group manager, came up with the galaXy screen (a play on GSK and a visual of the Milky Way), which had tool links along the galaXy swirls of stars.

Even more impressive is the transformation effort that Richard Henderson, CPO at Limited Brands, accomplished after his arrival from Dell.[6] Almost from scratch, he built a top-notch procurement organization by investing in people, process, and technology. Three years later spend is down 10% and efficiency is up substantially (a 31% reduction in transactions) using Ariba's tool suite, including reverse auctions, P-Cards to reduce transactions, and an SAP data platform. Included was a major rebranding of the procurement organization that captured people's imagination and sold management on the technology investments that also were needed. In a company with icons such as Victoria's Secret, Bath and Body Works, and The Limited, tapping into corporate branding expertise reinvented the procurement team under the banner:

$ RE-SOURCE, Transforming Procurement

e-Purchasing technology has helped enable coverage of all spends, better supply agreements, increased efficiency, and internal trust based on good internal user experiences.

Holistic technology master planning recognizes that tool expansions easily falter if any of a number of elements goes wrong—money, people, functionality, and results—hence the high incidence of underperforming IT project failure.

CLOSING THOUGHTS—THE REST OF THE STORY

Meanwhile, back at P&G, in 2002 Carol Rubeo (now president of MSE Enterprises, a small consulting company) became director of Purchases Innovation. Rubeo initiated a rigorous master planning effort, building on the positives of the earlier "leap onto the Net."[7] The written purpose, principles, and plan all flowed logically:

- Purpose—Create capability to deliver and measure sourcing results.

- Principles—Enable buyers to use supply networks to save money and reduce complexity while dealing in dynamic markets via improved tool access.
- Leverage scale, mastery, and technology.

So did the resulting project list—optimization of complex spend pools (see Chapter 5, *Optimization—Going to Market with Complexity*); connectivity to enable sourcing supplier innovation; savings tracking and cost forecasting; and SOX compliance.

Reality however was much more complex. Rubeo recalled: "Master planning requires selling abstract concepts supported by numbers to people unfamiliar with purchasing. Your pitch needs both words and pictures because your audience includes individuals that relate to each. You have to balance top-down givens—at the time SAP, Transora, and budget constraints—with grass roots enthusiasm for new tools that work and get results. Hang the innovations on the unchangeable backbones. You blend business sense—ROI, efficiency, and effectiveness—and then include a few 'pet ducks' of influential leaders." (*Note:* Pet ducks are favorite projects with legitimate potential.)

Rubeo continued, "The challenge becomes standardizing in a customized world and then creating a way to fit it together. It requires creative thinking, not following a rote process. Funding becomes a 'tin-cup' exercise, gathering money from overhead budgets to get huge savings in separate operational budgets. Finance support and the pet ducks get buy-in across multiple business units by breaking cost into smaller chunks and encouraging everyone to put 'skin' in the game. The other challenge is balancing near-term reality with long-term technology promises so you get savings without much throw away. Technology changes so fast that people always want to wait for the next promised upgrade" (Figure 17.1).

Rubeo summed it up: *Weaving all these things together is what master planning is all about. The magic is in the weaving.*

Plan Component	Current Business Model	Near-Term Business Model	Long-Term Business Model	Benefits	
				Near Term	Long Term
• Tool • Process • Requirement	What do we do today? What are current results?	1–3 years What does current technology provide?	3–5 years What is technology potential? How is what technology delivers different than near-term?	Cost Benefit ROI Disposal cost Degree of difficulty Payback	Cost Benefit ROI Uncertainty Time line Degree of difficulty

Figure 17.1. Master Plan Outlook Grid.

LESSONS LEARNED

- Master planning is about balancing stakeholder wants with corporate givens, selling abstract concepts with supporting numbers, and balancing near-term reality with long-term promise—and weaving it all together.
- Build a thought template with four layers—tools, organization, cost, and time.
- Choose tools, prioritize them, and continuously check out the health of providers.
- Understand the benefits and how they will reach the bottom line.
- Think past today's cost justification to anticipate the future cost structure of the tool set and how it will be paid for.
- Market the effort to help enthuse people and sell the managers who must buy in.
- Have a best-in-class budget for a central cadre of experts who drive the continuous evolution of the tools and their support. Only the short sighted eliminate expertise in order to pay for the tools (called "spending your seed corn," which often leads to starvation).

This book has free material available for download from the Web Added Value™ resource center at *www.jrosspub.com*

ADOPTION—THE REAL MEASURE OF SUCCESS

Failure lies not in falling down. Failure lies in not getting up.

— **Traditional Chinese proverb**

Money is how a business keeps score, therefore delivering business results as measured by money and seeking a good ROI for e-supply tools are "top of mind" for C-level management. Supply reward systems usually scream "show me the money" as well. Too often, however, ROI is viewed as the only success criteria for these investments—but it is just the price of entry. As author Rogers once said at Procter & Gamble (P&G), "A positive ROI does not necessarily equate to success—it only pays back the bill for the software."

The price of excellence is employee adoption. Given the power of many of these tools, especially the e-sourcing ones, a small percentage of dedicated, enthusiastic users can deliver a positive ROI. Real excellence is driven by wide usage that embeds the technology into the psyche and work processes of the organization. That is real adoption and it can drive ROI to incredible levels beyond any project's economic justification target.

CULTURAL CHANGE

Dennie Norman, global strategist for supply chain intelligence at software supplier SAS, has described a major manufacturing and services multinational that consistently achieved a positive return from its supplier management software investment through the sustained efforts of about 10% of the targeted users.[1] Unanswered is how much more could have been achieved if even 75 to 80% had used the tools? Company efforts to raise adoption rates have typically met with little success. As noted in the discussion in Chapter 7 (*P2P—Where e-Procurement Meets Accounts Payable*), driving employee adoption is the number two challenge for e-procurement that is cited by 55% of companies, despite compelling economics.[2] Why is this? Is there anything that can be done about it?

Barbara Ardell, an independent training consultant and former vice president at software supplier Procuri, makes the point that adoption is about cultural change—an intervention that requires *behavioral change*. There will be resistance, but the final result will emerge from a series of both successes and failures. According to Ardell, "Adoption is nothing more than the outcome of change management. Change management, however, isn't easy."[3] Net—"If it weren't for people, change would be easy."

Financial logic and human nature do not always match because humans have a "logic" known as "emotion" that brings outcomes that are unanticipated by an unemotional planning process. Turf wars, power, egos, fear, personality traits, resistance to change, the need for control—the list of potential barriers to adoption is long and varied.

Too often, executive support and change mandates are simplistically cited as the keys to success. Are they important? Yes! Are they enough? Absolutely not! Many companies are not "mandate" companies. Leadership support is not a given, and even when it is, there is no guarantee that rank-and-file work patterns will actually change to include e-tools.

The other mistake is to assume that rolling out an excellent training plan will ensure adoption. Again—wrong! Training is important (see Chapter 19, *Education—Training the Tools and Tools for Training*), but alone, it too is not enough.

Adoption has two stages—initiation, when new tools are launched (the first 6 to 12 months of usage), and reinforcement, when usage must be sustained through leadership and personnel turnover or through a strategic organizational priorities shift (this stage means years not months). These two stages represent very different challenges, and failure in either one can spell disappointment—hence the view that adoption is the *true* measure of excellence.

THE INITIATION STAGE

Early adoption is about getting leadership and the organization on board, making the business case, training the change, and supporting successes. This phase combines alignment, marketing, education, and organization with several elements—all of which address people and culture:

- Leadership support and alignment
- Selection of user friendly tools
- Training and rollout (see Chapter 19)
- Capturing the organization's emotion
- Support structure for the change
- Measures that matter
- Leveraging successes and managing failures
- Manageable tool expansion
- Breaking down resistance

Leadership Alignment

Leadership alignment is more than "managing up" to get agreement for software funding from senior/financial management. Supply management leaders must have it as well. When P&G was on the cover of the June 2002 issue of *Purchasing* magazine,[4] the story made the point that P&G took its time moving to e-purchasing tools. There were several reasons, but one was significant internal debate within the GPLT (Global Purchases Leadership Team, made up of all purchasing directors and vice presidents worldwide) about the use of auctions versus more traditional RFQs (albeit electronically delivered). Various leaders and business units had different views, driven by the nature of their business needs, spend categories, and supplier relationships. Bridging this philosophical gap required rationales for, and a level of choice about, using the various tools. Without consensus, rapid deployment across the organization was not really sustainable.

Even more important than leadership alignment is alignment between supply management and other "power functions." IT is of special importance. Too often, purchasing and IT do not engage or align early on in the tool selection process. (Recall the caution in Chapter 16 to not become sidetracked by IT integration issues. Although this caution is true, if issues are never really tackled, problems will ensue.) The problem is that eventually, support and integration of buy-side tools into the corporate IT infrastructure plan *will* entail purchasing and IT getting on the same page—so the earlier the better. The process may require some "bloody" infighting, but emerging so that both parties support the platform is critical to avoid problems later. In the long term, if the IT budget does not support the "pet" tool choices of purchasing, inefficiency will raise overhead cost.

- **Passion**—Give early adopters who are eager to try new things the latitude to do so.

- **Pain**—Where traditional approaches do not work, organizational pain will encourage innovation to fix a problem.

- **Pride**—Let people who feel good about their results tell their story and spread the word.

- **Progress**—Steadily encourage natural extensions of functionality that build momentum with existing users and meet priority needs of new users without overwhelming organizational change capacity.

Figure 18.1. The 4-P Adoption Leveraging Approach.

Tool Selection

Choosing the tools that users want to use is a time when procurement and IT goals can be pitted against each other. Selecting user-preferred tools seems obvious, but IT budgets, purchasing preferences, and procurement system internal customers often interpret "obvious" very differently. Dialogue becomes extremely important because in the end if users hate the system, IT infrastructural savings will be wasted because purchasing benefits (typically the backbone of the ROI) are never delivered due to adoption shortfalls. Sometimes these deliberations require senior management arbitration, but at a minimum, the discussion needs to include feedback on user friendliness/intuitiveness and external benchmarking about how choices impact IT infrastructure and user compliance/enthusiasm at other companies. *Remember*: Adoption is about users, not infrastructure. Intuitive tool use makes ongoing adoption far more manageable. Too often user perspective never "makes it" into the decision process. When technical infrastructure considerations and user preferences coincide—seize the opportunity quickly! (Remember the sandbox from Chapter 16?)

Organizational Emotion and Success

Capturing the organization's emotion and structuring for success are two elements that leverage people with energy to expand the tools. Emotion typically falls into three "P" categories—passion, pain, and pride (Figure 18.1):

- Passion develops when users are eager to try new or existing technology tools. Early adopters and mainstream people who are "sold" on the tools should be allowed to "do their thing" and push the change.

- Pain refers to areas in which traditional approaches are not working well, which has resulted in complexity, conflict, and missed results. If a tool looks like it will help, skeptics in these situations can be converted.

- Pride develops from feeling good about results and drives reapplication on another spend or event.

A less emotional fourth "P" is progress, which also plays a role. This "P" entails gradual, steady addition of modules and tools that extend the range of functions (and results) that are achievable from electronic platforms. This concept, which is behind suite offerings, encourages one module to be a natural extension of another, building momentum with existing users while meeting the unique needs of new users and widening the support base.

Structuring for success entails strategically locating e-purchasing tool experts across the spend pools, business units, and geographies of the organization. These people, with organizational credibility, build an effective "shadow organization" to leverage peer interaction by coaching other users and pushing the tool skill envelope toward ever more sophisticated market interventions (Figure 18.2). (*Comment*: Authors Rogers and Rudzki have used this approach during their corporate careers.)

Terms such as "Master Users, Champions, and Super Users" are typically used to describe these hands-on leaders. Ensuring an ongoing supply of these people is vital for long-term success.

Expert user networks are often spread thin because they are the front lines of adoption, helping those who are less skilled to become comfortable with the tools. Sometimes there are just too many tool functionalities that can deliver impressive results competing for users. The organization's ability to absorb the new skills necessary for effective use becomes a key consideration in the adoption effort.

Adoption Measures

Measures drive results, which become the basis for success stories that expand tool usage. The adage "what gets measured gets done" certainly applies here. The nature of the specific measures can vary by company and almost always evolve over time. Early in the adoption journey, measures tend to capture activities (e.g., number of tool uses, number of people using the tools, people trained, etc.). Over time they evolve away from activities toward results (cycle time and cost savings, headcount efficiency, etc.).

For example, Texas Instruments uses a cascading set of measures to drive procurement team and individual results, linking results back to individual development plans.[5] Both quantitative and qualitative measures are part of the system. Customer and user satisfaction, total cost of ownership reduction, deployment schedule targets, percent increase in automated transactions, and talent recognition are just some of the measures in the annual scorecards.

Long term, however, adoption is measured by the percent of total company external spend put through the tools—percent of spend, percent of contracts, percent of orders placed, etc. Unless these numbers grow toward 100%, adoption is at risk because e-tools only represent an alternative approach to conducting

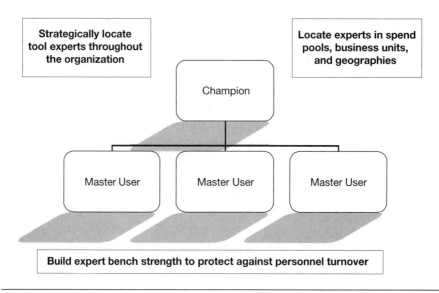

Figure 18.2. e-Tool Expert Shadow Organization.

company business. Different tools can have different targets—sourcing tool adoption levels of 80% might be OK, although purchase order placement tool adoption rates must be closer to 100% to be acceptable.

Sean Devine, director of Consulting Services for leading provider Emptoris, Inc. has emerged as something of an adoption guru. His lengthy e-sourcing experience ranges from the basics to advanced optimization. His adoption approach uses a sophisticated understanding of measures (and quantitative analysis) to focus the efforts of clients by using a framework with four levels of thinking about adoption challenge:[6,7]

- Metrics in three dimensions—Breadth (percent of spend), depth (number of modules used), and efficiency (resources per use) applied to projects (individual sourcing events) and the program (across sourcing projects). Valid metrics must have an impact on business objectives.

- Measurement types—Observations, artifacts, and interviews. Observations come from sitting in on the process and the events; artifacts represent documentation, or evidence, of events such as software data, meeting notes, business awards, etc.; interviews rely on the interviewer's discipline to force specifics and examples, not opinions, that deliver structured output.

- Constraints—People, processes, systems, controls, incentives, and knowledge that can impact project or program metrics.
- Levers—Actions that can improve results or reduce constraints as defined by the metrics.

The conceptual framework stresses accountability and quantitative linkage to deal with the behavioral change that is needed. Objective goals are formed from the four levels—use *levers* to relieve *constraints* by an amount as defined by *measures* that impact *metrics* to deliver *objectives*.

Perhaps more importantly, Devine applies the framework to a client by collecting data broadly across that company. Most programs experience wide variations in adoption across a big, widely dispersed organization. Collection of information allows both data-driven improvement and data-driven program management tailored to the situation. However, regardless of the particulars, centralized process compliance, key decision control (do not let the wrong people use bad data), and comprehensive activity measurement managed from a central program office breed success.

THE REINFORCEMENT STAGE

Ongoing adoption faces different challenges. Therefore different steps are required to sustain adoption:

- Constancy of purpose
- Tool-by-tool focus and suite-wide support
- "Eternal" training
- Managing the impact of organizational turnover and tool changes
- Usage evolution, tool additions
- "Elephant" memory
- Sustaining measures

Maintain Constancy of Purpose

Constancy of purpose describes the nature of ongoing adoption—a job that is never completed because tools continue to change (software releases, new functionality modules, and innovative ways to use existing tools), people change (promotions, transfers, resignations , and terminations), and business changes (new challenges, priorities, acquisitions, and divestitures). Without ongoing attention to the foundations, adoption can simply drift away. Today's business people are so mobile that "shadow organizations" of trained e-procurement users, many who are lower or midlevel employees, can quickly be decimated by personnel turnover.

Anticipate and Manage Expertise Erosion

Training is an ongoing, almost eternal, task if the "invisible erosion of expertise" is to be avoided. Continuing software upgrades that change tools and the addition of new tools make the problem even tougher. Worse, some organizations change providers as sales pitches, price incentives, and improved capabilities result in new sourcing decisions. Companies that change tool suppliers often experience an unexpected adoption hit, underestimating what it takes for behavior change and user comfort with the status quo that rivals the original shift from spreadsheets to e-sourcing—no small adjustment.

The flip side of invisible expertise erosion is the "elephant memory syndrome." Sometimes a software provider dramatically improves its offerings, providing a compelling reason for a customer to change tools. However, past customer experience has "poisoned the well." Stories of past tool failures never seem to go away, even when clear evidence supports the new version as a winner. An Oracle representative lamented this issue in a conversation with one of the authors. Despite major improvements to its e-procurement suite, acknowledged and praised by several analysts, earlier versions "live on" in the minds of people who have never experienced the original tools because of negative war stories. Overcoming human emotional issues must constitute a part of ongoing adoption efforts.

Adopt Sustaining Measures

Mature measures such as percent of spend through the tool help sustain adoption by promptly calling out erosion so action plans can quickly deal with setbacks. The longer tools are in place and used at high adoption rates, the more likely e-purchasing tools are to become culture, sustained by expectation, not just hard work. Still, details such as the loss, without strong replacement, of a respected champion or a tool change without adequate training can undermine months and even years of work. Because this is culture change, holding people accountable—particularly managers more than "doers"—causes adoption to be a human resources responsibility, not a technology effort.

As an example, Sun Microsystems uses classic SMART e-sourcing goals (specific, measurable, achievable, results oriented, time bound) to drive its program, with a goal of ongoing self-sufficiency.[8] Each step (full service, medium service, coached service, and self-service) has "percent-of-events" goals each year, with full service and self-service increasing over time. This migration to self-sufficiency is the ongoing effort needed to make e-sourcing an organizational core competency that embeds sourcing tools into everyday work process. Adoption becomes habit.

Another example of world class execution is the global adoption of e-sourcing by GlaxoSmithKline (GSK). Recall from Chapter 17 (*Master Planning—Creating and Following a Practical Blueprint*) that GSK included reverse auctions as a key sourcing tool part of the plan (in late 2002, auctions were expanded to include other types of e-RFXs in general). By 2006, led by a small central team called the Technology Work Cell (TWC), GSK performed about 3700 e-RFxs (of which 1500 were reverse auctions) in 59 countries (700 e-RFxs in India alone). Nearly 20,000 suppliers participate in the GSK e-sourcing program. Gregg Brandyberry, vice president of Procurement, Global Systems, and Operations at GSK said, "It's amazing how the creation of a transparent electronic bidding environment consistently promotes enhanced competition, and transcends geographic, cultural and political boundaries." This illustrates how constancy of purpose in driving adoption gets results and embeds tool usage into company culture.

CLOSING THOUGHTS—USING TOOLS TO DRIVE TOOL CHANGE MANAGEMENT

One final thought about adoption—the software supplier can be a major asset in an adoption effort beyond the normal contracted "initial training rollout" support. Negotiating to "put supplier skin in the game" to the extent possible for both initial and reinforcing-stage adoption improvement via performance incentives is an innovative approach that engages the supplier long after the sale. The best providers, however, know that adoption is excellence and they will work to help customers to become better.

Software suppliers can monitor a company's use of their tool suite to map adoption levels across the customer's organization. As an example, the Frictionless Commerce "Momentum" program provides usage metrics across suite modules, including an individual's log in history, the number and frequency of sourcing events, new and edited contracts, etc. These usage statistics are mapped to the organization and identify pockets of resistance or low adoption as well as islands of strong adoption so remedial or reapplication steps can be taken to address resistance and reward enrollment.

Pinpointing and overcoming resistance to change is the role of leaders in any change management process. Once "low using" groups are identified, leadership can focus in on the problem. Instead of the traditional approach of concentrating on the resistors—which often fails—using e-tool diagnostic capabilities, segmenting the organization into advocates, "undecided but influence-ables," and resistors becomes possible. Management energy can flow toward the advocates and the undecided, targeting open-minded thought leaders in the undecided camp, who can become sources of honest feedback and be enlisted as supporters of proven benefits. These peer leaders are a powerful force to bring along the remaining undecided (almost always the majority of the organization) and isolate resistors by undermining their credibility. The middle of the typical organizational "bell curve" will decide the battle. The key is nudging it toward progress.

Occasionally, however, a leader is the resistor, creating a "cone of darkness" in his/her organization where the ranks fear participation. This situation, especially in non-mandate companies without forced compliance, obliges e-purchasing initiative leaders to "step up." This type of confrontation can result in significant conflict, but the use of leadership peer pressure (comparison of results), involvement of corporate leadership (finance, especially when ROI is at risk due to a leader's resistance), or ongoing persuasion are all possible approaches short of direction from above. Leadership resistance is the worst barrier to overcome, but forcing this issue out into the open so the resistance is transparent to management makes a clear choice possible. Either insist on adoption or publicly recognize the negative implications of partial implementation. Transparency makes the consequences of leadership resistance quite apparent—one way or the other.

LESSONS LEARNED

- ROI measures financial success, but adoption measures true excellence.
- Adoption is about change management and cultural change, which requires behavioral change.
- At the initial stage, address leadership, alignment, education, and organization.
- Procurement and IT need to reach consensus early on.
- Strategically disperse e-tool experts throughout spend pools, business units, and geographies.
- Measures matter. Measure at both program and project levels using process observation, event artifacts/evidence, and interviews.
- Reinforcing adoption entails a constancy of purpose that combines tool-by-tool focus and suite-wide support.
- Beware of personnel turnover and tool changes. Although sometimes necessary or unavoidable, turnover and tool changes cause training needs to be ongoing. Build e-tool bench strength.
- Tool providers can be important allies in an adoption effort. They provide adoption expertise and software-based usage data for analysis.
- Focus on the early adopters and the "open-minded undecided" group to move the organization forward. When leaders resist, confronting and making the implications of the leadership resistance apparent is necessary.

This book has free material available for download from the
Web Added Value™ resource center at *www.jrosspub.com*

EDUCATION—TRAINING THE TOOLS AND TOOLS FOR TRAINING

I hated every minute of training, but I said, "Don't quit. Suffer now and live the rest of your life as a champion."

— **Muhammad Ali**

Organizational training receives a lot of lip service, but when a crunch hits— either time or money—training is the area where organizations often look to make cuts or to transfer resources elsewhere. An organization can cut back, go remote (e.g., automated e-training to avoid travel costs), or outsource. In the e-tool world, however, training is pivotal, and those who do it well, tend to also use the tools well. Training has three sides:

- Training the e-tool itself—rollout and ongoing
- Using tool providers to increase an organization's sourcing skills
- Using e-tools to train people on non-e-tool subjects

TRAINING THE TOOLS

At the National Association of Purchasing and Payables conference in 2006, Patti Whitehouse, senior director of Procurement Global Performance Solutions at pharmaceutical giant Merck & Company, said it best: "Installation is not realization."[1]

Merck is moving along an "installation path" of several additional Ariba modules into their existing tool suite to enable a long-term procurement transformation effort (remember the constancy of purpose discussion in Chapter 7?). Successful installation of technology is not sufficient to obtain results. Embedding the tools into organizational thinking and habits is just as critical—which requires training. Merck understands this.

Using Dr. W. Edwards Deming's classic PDCA (Plan–Do–Check–Act) cycle, Merck is leveraging its earlier experiences in rolling out other e-tool modules to design a top-notch training effort that is not just a blanket immersion. This more-methodical plan includes:

- Becoming clear on the target audience—Each module may have different key stakeholders, not only procurement people. For example, train the lawyers on any contract creation/management module, not just the purchasing people.

- Assessing and understanding the needs that the tool meets and using them to identify the learning objectives of the training—This is not just about training the tool. Prethinking the purpose, requirements for use, span of use, and ongoing support is vital (procurement, internal stakeholders, and suppliers). A contract module must be accurate, even to the smallest detail, although a category management strategy module covering a higher-level process can probably "live with" more variation in use at the individual level.

- Assembling the implications for training design that are outcomes of the learning objectives and e-tool purpose evaluations—This involves behavioral change, so the training must also deal with that aspect. Individual desktop e-training of operational aspects simply will not change behaviors (something many companies have learned the hard way). Again, each module has its own implications and design criteria, including hands-on practice, global scope, and navigation across related modules.

- Developing, designing, piloting, and revising the training—The key question here is "if we build it, will they come?" The blend of classroom, long-distance classes, individual e-training applications, quick-reference tools, and stakeholder training are all part of the design. Also included in design is determining if instructors will come from in-house or outside. If they come from outside, what are the implications in 2 years—when 20% of the people in the organization are new and were not present for the initial rollout immersion and the instructors have moved on to another client? Will the tool provider or an outside consultant still be willing to provide training for the tailored version the company is now using—and at what cost to the company?

All of this reads like "motherhood and apple pie"—the discipline to actually plan training is critical, but planning is not the end of the task. The training program must be implemented. At Merck the combination of visibly tracking and reporting class enrollment and having a staged approach for developing and certifying instructors, ongoing involvement of a dedicated learning cadre (core group), stakeholder trainer development, schedule efficiency (e.g., combining multiple module classes where and when it makes sense), and a two-tier help desk (corporate IT for base-level issues and a learning cadre for advanced issues) result in the expansion being sustainable.

Implementation means both installing and sustaining the platform. Whitehouse's team at Merck insists that any upgrades be "stable" (not always the case with software), be accompanied by sustaining and recurring training, and have help desk renewal and self-study support (PowerPoint "on steroids").

The last and perhaps most vital aspect is staying connected to the students and tracking their results. Is training working? At Merck five levels of evaluation are used to understand the results of training:

- Did they like it (use of student satisfaction ratings and verbatim comments)?
- Did they learn from it (monitoring of whether the tool is being used correctly and installing tracking tools to allow issue analysis)?
- How long did it take (time to rollout, e.g., 7 months per course at Merck)?
- What did it cost (fully loaded costs including materials, travel, etc.)?
- Is it being used (number of real users measured per application and relative to the number of users trained)?

These measures address the human (like it?), quality (learn from it?), time (how long?), cost (loaded), and results (use it?) impacts of the training as a subcomponent of overall business results (Figure 19.1).

TOOL SUPPLIERS AS KNOWLEDGE EXPANDERS

Having tools is a far cry from *leveraging* them. *Remember*: e-Tool results are highly dependant on the skills of the people who use them. Software providers offer real opportunities to help increase their customers' purchasing skill levels. However, doing so requires strategy and structure, not just "showing up" at a provider's user conference.

Training Attributes	Questions Asked
Student enjoyment	Did they like it?
Training quality	Did they learn it?
Delivery time	How long did it take to design and roll out?
Cost	What did it cost?
Effectiveness/results	Is the knowledge being used?

Analyze and incorporate the answers to these questions into future training design improvements.

Figure 19.1. Training Evaluation Questions.

Barbara Ardell, an independent training consultant, is well suited to speak about this opportunity. Over her successful career, Ardell has managed sourcing and accounts payable (at Procter & Gamble), run her own training company (Strategic Resources), and supported e-sourcing software utilization at customer locations (as vice president of Strategic Sourcing Support at Procuri Inc.).[2] The key to leveraging an e-purchasing provider is about having two parallel infrastructures at the using company—the provider's infrastructure and the infrastructure *inside* the using company.

Provider Infrastructure

Use the provider's infrastructure to help build the company's organization. Typically this includes user conferences, networks, and geographical forums, plus telephone conferences about targeted topics (e.g., adoption, "how to" practices, and learning from experience). "So what, we expect it," you say. We answer, "The point is to leverage it, not just know about it!"

User Infrastructure

The second infrastructure, which is far more important than the provider's infrastructure, is *inside* the using company. The internal infrastructure concerns mindset, structure, leadership credibility, discipline, and deployment ability:

- Mindset is a willingness to give and to receive. Provider forums are fairly public. If a good provider has been selected, expect many other companies, some of which are competitors, to also participate. Reluctance to participate in forums means walking away from obtaining best practice insights. Keep in mind that best practices include a heavy cultural component, so implementation is not a given when you give or receive, but gaining insight certainly is.

- *Internally*, the infrastructure entails how the roles in the organization that interface with the provider's user network and the organization's internal network are staffed. *Externally*, the key is having a "master user"—the internal focal point of the tool expertise (i.e., the expertise coach, the communicator) and the owner of the relationship with the software supplier—be the user network representative. (There can be an IT relationship owner as well, but the purchasing relationship is critical to obtain hard number results—which is another oversight at many companies where IT is made the designated player.) As discussed in Chapter 18 (*Adoption—The Real Measure of Success*), the master user needs to have a network of skilled users ("super users") that fans out across the company's purchasing centers to coordinate e-events or ongoing implementation efforts.

- Leadership credibility concerns the level of thought leadership and peer respect for master and super users throughout the organization, coupled with reasonable organizational stature. The e-"geek" who every one snickers at or the "toolies" who could not source "their way out of a paper bag" are the wrong people for these jobs. Technology skill is not domain expertise—do not forget that!

- Discipline and deployment involve documenting (the discipline part) both what is learned from the provider's user network and what is discovered by the best of the internal users. Discipline and deployment also concern cultural openness and delivery rigor (the deployment part) to take learning and spread it throughout the organization despite turf and NIH (not invented here) issues. Be honest with yourself—realize the amount of work that will be required in the company's culture. Taking best practices from other companies is more than a simple transplant. It requires a mature gardener who understands how to plant and nurture new ideas in an environment that is foreign to the one in which the best practice was developed.

Provider Training Options

Several e-sourcing software suppliers also provide process training that uses multiple delivery methods. Each company's strategic sourcing process is "generic" enough that some of the training will help build skills in the customer's organization even if the training is not a perfect match for the customer's tailored methodologies.

One example is Procuri University, which addresses strategic sourcing, the contract life cycle, and supplier management processes using online tutorials, Web-based training, and classroom training at Procuri facilities or on-site at a customer's facility—even a strategic sourcing paperback primer is available upon request. These courses qualify for Institute for Supply Management (ISM) accreditation toward CPM (certified purchasing manager) continuing education.

Process training is a logical extension of software and represents an important service element, especially for companies just beginning the on-demand journey, as long as these companies recognize that they need to own and *drive* the process. Too often a company expects the software supplier to be the process driver, not the buying company itself—a major mistake.

TOOLS AS TRAINERS

The marriage between sourcing skills, e-learning systems, and the intranet greatly enhances a practical training menu. Educating a sourcing organization requires administration (the college dean and registrar) and education (the content and faculty).

The Administrative Side

e-Learning tools heavily support administrative tasks. Anyone who runs a purchasing training system knows that enrolling people, tracking attendance, reporting to managers, maintaining skill level records, assessing course feedback, and having workable distance-learning classes cannot be taken for granted. These tasks are an enormous administrative time sink. Tapping into a corporate learning system (e.g., Saba-Centra) greatly increases efficiency versus using manual and spreadsheet efforts. Alone, a purchasing department cannot justify this, but if human resources has such a system, by all means, leverage it.

The Content Side

On the content side, education includes both "thinking" and "doing"—two very different challenges.

"Doing" training is well suited for self-paced electronic training. Students learn and conduct knowledge checks (tests) using PC or handheld access to the company intranet. Course completion is automatically monitored. However, the somewhat "static" nature of the e-class environment is limiting. Policy reinforcement (training in standard purchasing policies, SOX reporting, supplier ethics, or supplier compliance audits) or work processes with minimal user flexibility are good candidates for this approach. Convenience, lower cost/travel requirements, and push delivery to students (policy and compliance training) and pull from them (training for company systems and tools) are all benefits—as long as students are allocated enough time to "attend" amid their daily work pressures (another overlooked requirement).

For "thinking" training however, face-to-face, classroom, and team case study interactions are superior—despite the hype of distance learning—because there are no specific "correct" answers. Best-in-class companies recognize the situational nature of supply decisions and use senior supply leader teaching, mentoring, and coaching to instill sourcing and supplier relationship management thought processes, experience, and even wisdom into the organization.

Intranet Tools

Intranet tools can reinforce and embed methodologies and the rationale behind them by using templates that trigger mental connections. The best recognize that "a picture is worth a thousand words" by laying out thought-process diagrams (e.g., a strategic sourcing process) with embedded links to templates, training documents, and market-tracking websites. Some e-procurement suites have helpful modules, but most companies use homegrown tools that are uniquely tailored to their processes and that are developed without a major resource investment.

A few years ago Rolls Royce (a jet engine manufacturer) created a visual "strategic sourcing main menu" with a pictorial workflow and embedded templates, tools, training, and approval formats. Sourcing people used the menu to embed the overarching process and the thinking behind it—on which they had been formally trained—into their work.[3] Hallmark has a similar tool (Global Procurement Strategic Sourcer), which has all of its templates (over 50) consolidated into a single tool that houses 90% of any sourcing project's documentation needs along with training capabilities. The tool allows significant user customization via common Microsoft Excel capability in the Hallmark procurement intranet site. What is important is that tools of this type reinforce common processes inside purchasing which make communication with non-purchasing internal stakeholders consistently repeatable. These processes can be relatively easy to create (e.g., low IT resourcing, but no real software cost) in weeks/months, not months/years. The prerequisite, of course, is having sourcing processes and templates to populate the "visual" and the links.

LESSONS LEARNED

- Training is an important element for both rollout and sustaining support for e-tools.
- e-Tools are an important element for administering and conducting training on a range of content, including both e-tools and non-e-tools.
- Think through the plan for the training design—target audience, training objectives and their implications on training design, training pilot tests, and revisions based on those tests.
- For training execution, consider the full range of delivery options (classroom, online, help aids, etc.) and get student evaluations for incorporation into continuous improvement changes.
- Software providers know about sourcing and procurement. Use their resources and augment them with your own.
- Use e-training for the "doing" training aspects of your skill development plan. Use more-interactive, team, and face-to-face methods for the "thinking" training aspects.
- Intranet sites can be used to reinforce sourcing processes using process diagrams with templates to spur thinking and data collection/evaluation.

This book has free material available for download from the
Web Added Value™ resource center at *www.jrosspub.com*

GOALS AND MEASUREMENTS— DEFINING WINNING

First, have a definite, clear practical ideal; a goal, an objective. Second, have the necessary means to achieve your ends; wisdom, money, materials, and methods. Third, adjust all your means to that end.

— **Aristotle**
Greek Philosopher and Scientist

"It's all about leadership"—a point we made in Chapter 16, but it is a point worth repeating as we begin discussing goals and measurements. Also remember from Chapter 16 that the starting point for any supply management technology evaluation and plan must be consideration of the overall business strategy for supply management at that company. Also as discussed in Chapter 16, if a company has relegated supply management to a very tactical role, that decision will have a fundamental impact on the technology debate—and the ensuing goals and metrics. If supply management has a tactical role, you are encouraged to think principally of tools that support the efficient processing of purchase orders and not much beyond that.

Alternatively, if sound principles of procurement and supply base management are followed at your firm,[1] senior management likely understands the value of supply management and has given it the strategic role that it deserves. If this is the case, you will have an opportunity to focus on the tools to help the organization to achieve the overarching corporate objectives that senior executives really care about.

THE GOALS AND MEASUREMENTS DISCUSSION

Sometimes, the discussion of goals and measurements—if poorly organized—can complicate the more strategic discussion and prioritization that should be taking place. As an example, our good friends and partners in the accounting department care about numerous important topics, including the processing costs of purchase orders and invoices. However, an overriding emphasis on optimizing the per-item processing cost of purchase orders or invoices can quickly derail a discussion of technology strategy and draw it into a tactical focus. Yet these tactical and operational considerations are also very important—they should not be ignored.

Organizing the Topics

How, then, can the subject of goals and measurements be organized in such a way that achievement of the right objectives and the right priorities will be facilitated—and not inadvertently cause strategy to suffer? A useful framework is recognizing that there are three major categories of objectives, which cascade downward from each other (Figure 20.1).

At the top are the overarching business-level or strategic objectives. These objectives are the ones that your corporation's senior executives and business unit leaders think about regularly. They are also the objectives that tend to receive the focus of shareholders and Wall Street. Prime among them are return on invested capital (ROIC) and earnings per share (EPS). ROIC and EPS tend to heavily drive stock price performance, which of course is of prime interest to stockholders.[2]

In the middle, and supporting the business-level, strategic objectives, are process-level objectives. These objectives provide indications about whether (or not) core business processes are performing well, in support of strategic objectives. Examples include quality, cost, and delivery performance.[2]

If the metrics relating to processes indicate some amount of unhealthiness or a degree of suboptimization, then the third level of metrics, sometimes referred to as "diagnostic" metrics, should be introduced. Diagnostic metrics enable management to identify and analyze underlying problems or root causes that are having an adverse effect on the process-level metrics (and which, in turn, impact the strategic objectives). Diagnostic metrics are also helpful during the early stages of innovation or process change, when monitoring adoption rates and measuring

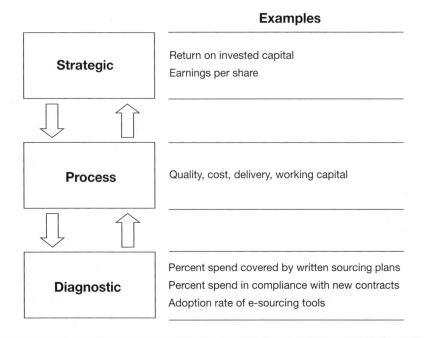

Figure 20.1. The Hierarchy of Metrics. (Source: *Beat the Odds: Avoid Corporate Death and Build a Resilient Enterprise*. With permission.)

how individual activities are changing are desirable to gage how well the transformation is progressing).[2]

What Should Be Measured?

A common challenge, particularly in large organizations, is the tendency to measure virtually everything—all the time—which can cause confusion among employees (not to mention administrative burden). As an example, in one large corporation, a cross-functional team convened to develop a high-level, balanced scorecard. After much debate, the "short list" for the corporate balanced scorecard was comprised of 72 *different* metrics. With no means to prioritize the metrics, the effort came to a standstill and confusion reigned.

If goals and measurements are organized as suggested by Figure 20.1, the chances of a multitude of lower-level metrics unduly influencing your strategy and plans will be minimized. All activities should drive toward strategic, business-level objectives. Everyone—regardless of department or business unit affiliation—should act as if they belong to the same organization, with common, shared objectives. All enabling technology must first answer the question: how does it help achieve the strategic objectives? This becomes the foundation for the business case for an enabling technology (as discussed in Chapter 16).

IMPLEMENTATION AND METRICS

Discussions regarding strategic goals, leadership, structure, and other critical dimensions and a "prescription" are available for successful transformation.[1] Let us assume you have followed that prescription, have appropriately involved senior management, and have been awarded a strategic role for supply management. Let us further assume that you have followed the recommendations in this book and have built a successful business case for supply management technology—which incorporates many of the elements in Table 20.1—and have received a budget. What is next?

As noted earlier in this chapter, during the initiation of change or transformation, employing diagnostic metrics to monitor adoption and implementation of enabling technology can be very helpful. For example, in the context of the closed-loop technology functionality (see Figure 1.3 in Chapter 1), two categories of metrics, sometimes referred to as key performance indicators (KPIs), can be developed:

- Metrics that monitor the effectiveness of each process (e.g., spend analysis, strategy development, sourcing and negotiating)
- Metrics that monitor for the occurrence of "leakages" between processes

As an example, an important KPI for measuring the effectiveness of the sourcing process is the percentage of cost reductions achieved vis-à-vis historical costs. As is often the case, however, negotiated results may not "make it" all the way to the bottom line, due to "leakage" between the sourcing, contracting, and compliance processes. As a result, quantifying this shortfall by comparing dollars realized versus dollars negotiated can point to the effectiveness of the linkages among these interlinked processes.

The following are examples of common metrics that apply to select segments of the closed-loop processes:

Spend and strategy:

- Percent of spend under management
- Percent of spend with nonapproved suppliers
- Percent of spend with written sourcing strategies
- Spend concentration (e.g., percent of supply base accounting for 75% of spend)

Table 20.1. Supply Software—Key Areas of Performance Improvements Used to Justify Long-Term Software Strategy

Demonstrably lower TCO

Increased ROI

Faster time to value

Improved cycle times (faster implementation)

Better employee productivity

Reduced errors

Greater penetration/use of applications within an organization

Increased flexibility

Improved functionality of systems

Greater consistency/standardized use of applications

Greater simplicity of systems

Lower cost of upgrades

Stronger support among users

Stronger support from senior management

Easier training

Lower cost of deployment

The ability to scale the system as needed

Ability to tap vendor innovations faster

Ability to focus more on customer needs

Source: Adapted from *Software as a Service*. Study by AMR Research; 2005. With permission.

Sourcing activities:

- Number of sourcing events, by type (e.g., RFI, RFQ, RFP, reverse auction) during the last 12 months
- Percent of total spend e-sourced via each type of sourcing event
- Sourcing efficiency (cycle time per sourcing event)
- Percent of total spend utilizing decision support/optimization
- Benefits negotiated and realized

Contract activities:

- Percentage of spend involved in contracts
- Percentage of contracts captured in the system
- Number of contracts by status (draft, approved, active, expired, etc.)
- Percent of contracts that have automatic renewal features
- Contract efficiency (cycle time from start to finish in preparing a new contract)

Table 20.2. On-Demand Metrics

- Scorecard on customer satisfaction
- Percent of product availability when ordered
- Ease of customer communications throughout supply chain
- Extent of supply chain involvement in customer NPI*
- Percentage of spend covered by "premier" suppliers

*NPI, new product introduction.

Source: From GlobalCPO.com. With permission. Available at: www.globalcpo.com.

Results tracking metrics:

- Percent of active projects with reported results (current)

Supplier performance metrics:

- Number of suppliers that have a completed supplier assessment
- Number of suppliers with sub-par performance

Employee/user activity metrics:

- Number of logins per month
- Number of active projects (total, per employee)

Additional metrics that relate to the on-demand topic are outlined in Table 20.2.

CLOSING THOUGHTS ABOUT MEASURING PROGRESS

Drive procurement and enabling technology activities with the strategic objectives that matter (ROIC, EPS) and reward achievement of those objectives. Use process and diagnostic metrics to monitor adoption and compliance and to highlight areas that need attention. To ensure that key metrics are communicated and regularly discussed, include them in a "dashboard." A dashboard is a visual means of displaying the key metrics that management should be watching. Imagine the dashboard of a car, with its key metrics/dials. That is exactly what a corporate supply management dashboard is intended to be—a few key metrics, displayed in an easy-to-understand fashion, which measure progress toward key objectives (ROIC, EPS, TCO reduction) and also include key process metrics.

Web Added Value™

THE FUTURE—
CRYSTAL BALL GAZING

Even if you are on the right track, you'll get run over if you just sit there.
— **Will Rogers**
Humorist

In the year 2000 futuristic descriptions of "automatic commerce," ranging from supplier selection to financial settlement, promised enormous time and money savings. Visions of freed-up supply managers achieving breakthroughs by sourcing more spends and developing closer supplier relationships were abundant. Indeed more spends are being sourced, but are supplier relationships *better*? The jury is still out, but things are still not all that automatic. People are still busy as hell.

Even today the value creation available from using e-tools to manage a company's supply base can be mind boggling. Companies that do it, sustain it, and build on it, emerge as winners—with one important proviso—their product must remain compelling to their customers. Superb purchasing sells nothing, and great buying organizations that lose sight of their customers can and do stumble. Tapping suppliers for value that goes beyond, but still includes, cost savings (e.g., adding innovation, effectiveness, and speed to the list) keeps supply focus on the business, not the function. Suppliers are drawn into corporate value propositions via efficiency, effectiveness, innovation, responsiveness, and resilience. Supply leverage is pivotal to major turnarounds (e.g., at IBM) and sustained continuous improvement (e.g., at Toyota). Supply e-tools are and will continue to be a part of success.

THE ROLE OF TECHNOLOGY

The power of technology will emerge from four areas:
- Data integration across functions, divisions, and companies
- Mathematics that allow deep analysis across those boundaries
- Economics that allow widespread e-tool use
- Technology applications that extend and integrate supply processes

Data—The Base

The backbone (or the base) will be built on the transfer and use of accurate data within and between companies, which is coupled with selectivity about who gets how much. Those who matter get more; those who do not get the basics. Self-service pull and proactive push from place to place within the supply base will manage material, service, information, financial, and idea flows through to the customer. Advances in software integration—procurement suites connected to ERP systems that feed PLM and should-cost tools—provide a glimpse into a future in which multifunctional information access makes the difference as product design and supply chain flows are linked early on, tapping human resources across companies. Software tools can describe work processes and then enable them through users who "grew up" with e-tools to make commerce flow. RFID and satellite tracking will make supply chains increasingly transparent, so opaque areas are a "red flag" exception rather than the rule.

Mathematical Analysis—The Power of "What If" and "Why"

Chapter 5 (*Optimization—Going to Market with Complexity*), Chapter 9 *(PLM— Everyone Gets Together)*, and Chapter 10 *(Should Cost—From Spreadsheets to Science)* begin to point the way (with an emphasis on the word "begin"). Integrated data platforms will extend the mathematical ability to analyze the world across functions. Joint development tools will create spaces for joint design. Now visualize the integrated supply process of the future as an "up escalator" across multiple product generations, which have been jointly innovated simultaneously across functional and corporate boundaries by suppliers, customers, production, R&D, and logistics, shifting as development roadmaps change. (*Comment*: The authors see the beginnings in electronics original design manufacturers, or ODMs, and private label clothing designers.)

In-depth post-event bidding analysis will drive understanding of how savvy suppliers bid—their strategies and tactics will become clear in hindsight, providing buyers with next-level purchasing skills in supplier bidding psychology. Using technology to link tools for supply chain simulation, supplier risk assessment, and supply base cost optimization to deliver flexibly costed supply network options, complete with switching costs, time lines, and inventory positions, will change from vision to reality. Tying product design, demand management, and supply management together—then applying statistical risk analysis to the ultimate CRM/SRM connection—is tomorrow's vision.

Economics—The Affordability Factor

Big companies have already installed supply side suites. The next growth engine for the software industry should be the mid- and small-market companies. Today these tools are simply too expensive for small companies. Yet as small companies outsource to offshore manufacturers or back office or service operations, the same sourcing risk considerations of lengthy complex supply bases apply to them as well. The next generation of software, simple and affordable for these companies, either as "lite" suites, usage-based pricing (Saas—software-as-a-service), or Web 2.0 applications (more on Web 2.0 later in the chapter), will make the end-to-end sophistication widely available.

Capabilities—Ever Evolving

Today many point solutions are easily integrated into suites. Imagine the rapidly developing search industry (e.g., Google, Yahoo!, Ask, etc.) providing market knowledge on a pull basis, and ultimately fee-based push services, straight to a buyer's desktop dashboard. Blog search engines that track thought leaders in various fields, industries, and companies will tap expert ideas and opinions. Intuitive, user-friendly, almost self-training, applications that reduce adoption challenges will be updated continuously, not in major software releases. Wireless technology advances that result in supply managers who have mobile access to information—anywhere, anytime, seamlessly—will become the norm.

The wide application of the Internet could dramatically change the software world once companies have the integrated data noted above. Web platform software, dubbed Web 2.0 by Tim O'Reilly, an open standards software champion, may signal the next wave of higher-end collaboration and non-price-focused value.[1] This Web software with new application names such as "wikis" (content collaboration sites), "blogs" (expert Web journals), "mashups" (Web applications that combine content from multiple sources), and "folksonomies" (user-developed content-labeling systems) is largely open-source software. The key to its use is the data behind it and the usage level of the site. (Remember the analogies about the Internet and telephones—a single telephone is worthless, two telephones are a curiosity, and a million telephones are a network? It's the same idea.)

Think about a corporate "Wikipedia" that contains each company's key policies, terms, products, etc. Now think about one for the members of a supply chain, a new product development project, or a P2P network. Think about the product development group using mashups to speed the design, testing, and commercialization analysis of a new product. Think about Web 2.0 applications sitting on top of a well-integrated set of Web 1.0 databases. Who knows, maybe software companies will sell tailored tools such as these, making both open-source and software sales a choice for supply managers to purchase/use. Instead of software applications, the keys will be who owns the data and the constants in all of this—the habits, levels of trust, motives, and needs of the people.

Challenges

Furniture maker Herman Miller (HM) realized that the "Achilles heel of our industry (furniture) has been poor reliability."[2] Hence the HM SQA Division (Simple, Quick, Affordable) was designed to solve this problem for small- and medium-sized businesses. The HM Holland, MI factory and 500 suppliers are fully integrated. The suppliers have direct access to the HM Web order system, assembly schedules, and inventories. Each supplier receives daily ratings on delivery punctuality and quality—attributes that drive reliability. Feedback is continuous, so that strong performers do well and those that do not are warned and then, if improvement is not forthcoming, are dropped. Sounds like utopia, right? The key business need of reliability has been met via deep integration with suppliers. Not so fast!

SQA was founded over 10 years ago in 1995. The Web integration occurred in 1999. Numerous magazine articles have described it all. So, after 5 to 10 years why isn't everyone doing it? That's the rub. As you read earlier, the tough part is doing it. It is not about technology, but rather it is about leadership, change management, culture, and people, plus new substantive issues which have been brought to the surface by solving the old ones.

The Web 2.0 tools have real promise for top-end supplier relationships, but their acceptance will be driven by marketplace power structures between buyers and sellers and by the level of trust they allow. These tools are *very* open, so concerns about acceptance of change, information security, competitive preemption, product counterfeiting, benefit distribution, and intellectual property protection will impact the rate and range of their use. Does this remind you of today's issues? That's the point.

RFID provides transparency, but raises privacy and data interpretation challenges. Massive data storage requirements are power intensive and, as energy prices rise, the data centers necessary to handle the data will become more and more expensive, both in terms of capital and operating expense. (*Comment*: This issue is why several new data centers are under construction in the low-cost, hydroelectric-powered grids of the U.S. Pacific Northwest.)

The people side is even more difficult. Surely, after over 10 years, one reason that the HM story still reads like a breakthrough is NIH (not invented here). Many companies benchmark, but successful reapplication is the exception, not the rule. How many supplier ideas simply do not "get traction" because internal players are not open enough to let them? Adoption is about change—but the range of individual people is so wide that one person's "easy" is another person's "incomprehensible." So pockets of resistance and NIH emerge.

Time and Turnover

Today businesses often lack "institutional memory" for two reasons—time and turnover. These factors make supply utopia a "slow burn" proposition. Time—because supply managers are so busy that the time to analyze the past and to think about the future is a luxury few have and because daily tactical efforts enslave people, which is made worse by universal 24/7 connectivity via Blackberries, cell phones, and laptops. Turnover is even more insidious. Easy to rationalize as only impacting the lower levels, turnover also impacts the top level. When it does, company priorities, strategies, and even hierarchies can turn over with top level change. Champions leave and their passion is never replaced. Either the status quo wins out—the path of least resistance, even if it leads to mediocrity—or new priorities usurp partially completed programs.

For example, in June 2003, co-author Smock chaired a meeting of the Editorial Advisory Board of *Purchasing* magazine to discuss the common denominators of great supply organizations.[3] In addition to Gene Richter (former IBM CPO), top supply executives represented nine companies—Harley-Davidson, Hewlett-Packard, Alcoa, Cessna, Motorola, Bayer, Invensys, Intel, and Lucent. A little over 3 years later, only two of these executives are still with the same company, and some have moved more than once! Without leadership continuity, constancy of purpose is tough to maintain. Whether driven by ambition, boredom, conflict with management, frustration with the pace of change, performance shortcomings, mergers and divestitures, sponsor resignations, retirements, or death, new-leader-driven supply management organizational strategy changes inevitably slow down what "was" and initiate a new "what is." That is why the constancy of purpose at IBM, P&G, GSK, and other companies described in this book stand out—and also why sometimes great companies of 3 years ago are average companies 3 years later.

Complacency

The flip side of turnover is complacency. Supply and the software industry that supports it are dynamic. Too often, companies decide that they are best in class and stop changing. They stick to past core competencies even as the world changes them into core rigidities, which disable change and adaptation. Some tools and approaches that we have described are timeless—others are not. As Jason Madigson of GSK rightly cautions, a change effort needs renewal every 2 to 3 years to stay up to date. (*Comment*: A chemistry professor once told co-author Rogers' freshman class, "Half of what I will teach you is wrong. The problem is I don't know which half.")

Corporate Culture

Corporate culture and top management attitudes toward suppliers will determine how much of the technology "buffet" makes it onto the plate and, of that, how much is actually consumed. Companies that only see suppliers as places to extract money will probably use one subset of the tools. Those that see suppliers as avenues for performance and innovation will use another broader set. Once chosen, tool effectiveness is driven by adoption, organizational absorption capacity, and user training, which embed new habits, all of which determine whether the change will stick or be a long, slow, failed implementation. Some will make it and some will not. Yet the future will probably not move as quickly as we think because of these basic, yet powerful factors. For every step forward at one company, another company will likely take a half-step back.

CLOSING THOUGHTS ABOUT CHANGE

Through it all, change will continue. There is no one right answer for all companies. Whether it is Mittal (a giant steel maker), with global buyers stationed in London, or HP, which recently moved back to decentralized business unit supply management structures, or P&G, which moved from business units to a more centrally led corporate structure, or the Lucent merger into a French company, or the decision by IBM to headquarter procurement in China—organizations will change, as will markets, corporate needs, and business strategies. Supply management must change with organizational and business climate changes. The use of tools, flexibly wielded, can greatly enhance supply capabilities—if the culture and the people will allow it. Rigid approaches will likely move companies in the opposite direction.

Inevitably the winning companies combine people, processes, and technology. The question is how fast will these companies move relative to their competition? Companies that match their needs with their people, processes, and technology as events change will lead their industries, but every industry will not move in lockstep nor will "on demand" look the same everywhere.

EPILOGUE

PERSONAL WORDS FROM THE AUTHORS

Doug Smock

I have always had a passion to write about business. My father wrote a weekly steel column for the Associated Press from Pittsburgh after he retuned from World War II, and I hung on every word in his clips. I realized my dream when I became a business writer for the *Pittsburgh Post-Gazette* and then moved to *Purchasing* magazine in 1977 to cover industrial markets. Little did I know that I would be a front-seat witness to the greatest transformation in business since the Industrial Revolution.

In the 1970s Big Steel owned Pittsburgh just like the Big Three owned America. "What was good for General Motors was good for America," and what was good for GM was good for American steel. It was hard to argue with that. American workers were the best paid in the world and were rewarded with generous retirement packages. Even if they were laid off by one of the automobile giants, they had to be paid. The prosperity produced arrogance. Steel producers bristled at any notion that it was inappropriate to spew poisonous gases from coke ovens located adjacent to Downtown Pittsburgh in the 1970s. Foreign competition was sneered at. American industrial giants had all of the answers and had little interest in seeking ideas or innovation from suppliers. The paradigm worked in an era of cheap energy for America and in a world order marked by Cold War fears that created giant barriers between countries and whole regions of the world.

The collapse of the Berlin Wall in 1989 was followed quickly by the rise of the Internet, two forces that propelled growth of free market economies, especially in

China and India, and globalization. The American steel industry fell and electronics manufacturing moved to China. The American automobile industry slowly worsened, culminating in bankruptcies and huge shutdowns in 2005–2006. "Supply chains" became a magical term as surviving companies developed manufacturing bases in all corners of the globe. Few companies, however, genuinely changed their view of suppliers, who were still largely treated as sycophants rather than partners. One example was the meteoric rise of electronic reverse auctions from 1999 to 2002 as automated price-reduction tools. Suddenly many CEOs, including highly respected management maven Jack Welch of General Electric, were praising their contribution to corporate performance.

In *Straight to the Bottom Line™: An Executive's Roadmap to World Class Supply Management,* four co-authors (three chief procurement officers and myself) made a case to executive-level officers to take an enlightened view of the role of suppliers and the potential they offer in a global economy. The emphasis was on the role of supply management and improved business processes, including improved integration of purchasing, engineering, manufacturing, and finance.

On-Demand Supply Management: World Class Strategies, Practices, and Technology is a detailed look at how companies that adopt those best practices can employ technology to become better global players. One of the particular goals we examine is "on demand" or the ability of huge, global supply chains to adapt quickly to changes in market conditions or customer demands. Huge unsold inventories of highly customized products were serious, and potentially grave, problems for high-flying tech companies Lucent Technologies and Cisco Systems in 2001, when the booming tech economy collapsed almost overnight. Major equipment producers, such as John Deere, launched major product development projects that were hugely over budget even though they employed large and sophisticated cost-estimating departments. Cell phone producers, such as Motorola and Cisco, had to respond to large and highly specific orders from big-box retailers such as Wal-Mart on extremely short notice, while they were increasing outsourcing and moving production to China. Additionally, big sections of the American industrial base, such as the critical tool and die industry, were completely unprepared to cope with globalization and on demand.

What are the solutions? Sacrifice our manufacturing base? Scream for protection, as American steel producers did in the 1970s? Subsidize our companies through price controls or outright grants?

We think the answers are in this book. Become leaner and smarter. Use technology to improve communications, process integration, relationships with suppliers, and the ability to configure on the fly.

I would like to thank my co-authors—Bob Rudzki, for sticking with me for another massive writing project, and Steve Rogers, for the fresh vision and tremendous energy he has brought to this book. I dedicate my work on this book to my wife Nancy, my children, and all of my grandchildren (born and to be born), who will inherit the problems and the opportunities we are leaving for them.

Robert A. Rudzki

In *Straight to the Bottom Line™: An Executive's Roadmap to World Class Supply Management,* four co-authors (Doug Smock, Shelley Stewart, Mike Katzorke, and myself) collaborated on a long-overdue book for corporate executives and procurement leaders. The book zeroed in on the opportunities to improve top- and bottom-line performance—and described a roadmap of how to achieve significant, lasting results.

Response to *Straight* has been very encouraging and confirms our original belief that a book written for the executive audience on this topic would elevate the discussion—and perhaps make the difference in the performance and survivability of many companies. Some of the most rewarding feedback we have received about the book has been from procurement leaders, who bought a few copies for their senior executive team and found that the book did in fact serve as a catalyst for long-overdue discussion, strategy, and action.

On-Demand Supply Management: World Class Strategies, Practices, and Technology is a very important companion to the first book. If you have made it to this point in this book, you should have recognized the critical *enabling* aspect of technology—and should have a good feel for how to make it work to your company's advantage. "Enabling" is the key word here because you must have something that you are aiming for—some overarching set of objectives that you are trying to enable. But, more on that point shortly.

I have to confess that I really had not intended to become involved in another book on procurement so soon after *Straight to the Bottom Line.* The reason was simple. There was another, long-standing research project that was rapidly approaching final form, and its conversion to finished manuscript was demanding my attention (*Beat the Odds: Avoid Corporate Death and Build a Resilient Enterprise,* which is being published by J. Ross Publishing). However, when Doug Smock, who was aware of my other project, called me to describe his concept for this book, I have to admit I was hooked. The topic of this book is very important for the success of any business, and that, after all, is what we are trying to accomplish by sharing ideas and lessons learned and by authoring a few business books.

The role of technology in our personal lives and our business lives continues to broaden and deepen. There is virtually no aspect of life that we cannot complicate—or potentially simplify—with technology. Whether or not technology serves to *assist* your life can depend on how well you have established your vision and your objectives. With a clear vision and well-defined objectives, technology can be a powerful enabler. In the absence of vision and objectives, technology can certainly seem to complicate and confuse matters, if not outright worsen the situation.

There have been all too many examples of companies that have failed miserably at technology implementation and adoption, with significant financial repercussions. In some cases, companies have come close to failing outright, due to a misguided effort to adopt a "magical solution" for basic business needs. In an ironic twist of fate, one of the "magical solution" companies that visited me in the late 1990s, a software company that promised all sorts of huge "savings" in "supply chain management," nearly went out of business a few years later. At the time, their sales pitch seemed to lack the framework and rigor which we describe in this book as being necessary for successful technology implementation.

On-Demand Supply Management contains a wealth of information to guide you on the journey that most companies will need to take to stay competitive. As a former corporate executive, now an advisor to other companies, I can tell you from personal experience that it is fun to see what the new technology and tools can do. It is exciting. Yet as we have reminded you throughout this book, the journey must first be built on a foundation of several critical ingredients—foremost among them is leadership, a well-conceived and integrated supply management transformation plan, and objectives that are linked to overarching corporate strategy objectives.

Readers, the best of luck to you as you undertake this journey. In the words of Albert Einstein, "The significant problems we have cannot be solved at the same level of thinking with which we created them." We hope that this book helps to provide you with some helpful parts of the solution.

Steve Rogers

After a 30-year career at one company, rare these days, I was starting to figure out the next stage of my work. In college I had been the Sports Editor of the *Purdue Exponent* and a stringer for *The South Bend Tribune* before my business career began. I also had a handful of magazine articles to my credit, so writing seemed to be a part of that next stage, but the idea of writing a book seemed daunting and I kept putting it off. Then the telephone rang. It was Doug Smock, whom I had met for the first time a few weeks earlier at a panel discussion on optimization tools. He asked about my interest in co-authoring a book, but he also cautioned that I could not just write about Procter & Gamble, my old company, because a book must have more depth than that. I could not agree more.

Procter & Gamble (P&G) is a "promote-from-within" company, which while a great strength has also at times in its history limited its perspective. To offset that, finding external perspectives to fertilize the internal organization is a corporate priority. A big part of my last role as worldwide purchasing mastery leader was looking outside our industry to see how others buy and bringing those good ideas into Procter. The Intels, IBMs, Toyotas, BASFs, and American Expresses of the world do great things much differently than the CPG (consumer packaged goods) industry where P&G lives. No company or industry has a lock on all the good ideas.

I signed on as a co-author with trepidations about the subject—electronic purchasing tools. As a practitioner who bought books on the subject, I was amazed and dismayed at how fast "tool books" became obsolete! A 2002 e-tool book sounds quaint today because technology makes new things become old fast. I wanted my first book to stay relevant for a while. Plus, I knew from my own and the experiences of other companies that glowing e-tool success stories only tell half the story. The justification, installation, and adoption challenges are neither easy nor simple. Many fail to meet their targets.

A 4-hour authors' meeting in a quiet corner of a Pittsburgh hotel convinced me. This book is about the timeless struggles of "doing e-tools" through the eyes of people and companies grappling with change management. Although the tools constantly improve functionality and intuitiveness, the other two-thirds of the equation—people and processes that apply the tools to business—are what this book is about, not just the tools.

I learned the importance of people and processes long before e-technology turned the world flat. In the late 1980s, P&G dramatically decentralized a strong central purchasing organization, made it a support group for manufacturing (in one business unit, all the way to brand/plant buyers for whom volume leverage became a lost art), and lost half of the purchasing leaders (who retired or transferred to other functions). It nearly destroyed the sourcing capability of P&G within less than 3 years. All of those transferred leaders (including me) came back to mount a huge skill-rebuilding effort and then to launch global sourcing. Purchasing organizations were fragile even before technology's disruptive force became the third element of world-class performance. People leverage the tools, not the other way around.

My co-authors, Doug and Bob, have my real thanks. They have been instrumental in helping me get over my "fear" of book writing and continue to teach me the ropes of this authoring stuff.

My wife, Susan, deserves a medal. She endured the clutter of my research notes, my laptop sitting on the breakfast table instead of our food, and my preoccupied typing when the muse hit in the middle of a long-awaited 2-month vacation.

Thanks to many past colleagues at P&G—the bosses who coached me, the peers who collaborated and challenged me, and, most of all, my people, who delivered the results. I learned from all of them. There is one person in particular to thank (you might remember Pete Wolf from Chapter 3). Pete took the time to teach a computer-phobic director, two levels above him in a different function, what Lotus Notes and the Internet were all about and, importantly, how technology could become the third powerful force for purchasing competitive advantage—along with processes and people.

I hope this book helps you, the readers, to choose tools to drive your business, combining them with strong processes and creative, proactive people to reinvent your supply system. In the hands of skilled people who understand the art of supplier management, these tools are simply amazing—tough to do, but amazing. Good luck!!

APPENDIX

EXAMPLE OF A REQUEST FOR INFORMATION FOR SUPPLY MANAGEMENT AND PROCUREMENT

As noted in Chapter 16 (*Money—Making the Business Case*), proceeding down the path of technology evaluation and tool selection requires considerable homework plus the ability to build a compelling business case. A request for information (RFI) can be a valuable part of that process.

The following pages provide an example of a comprehensive RFI, compiled from various industry sources, including Emptoris, Inc., and cover many areas of functionality that are of value to the supply management function. Although no RFI should be used "off the shelf" without careful consideration of applicability, the authors believe this example offers a useful, comprehensive checklist that can be used to build your own, tailored RFI.

STRUCTURE OF AN RFI

I. YOUR COMPANY

Provide information on the following (the more detail the better):

A. Company Profile

1. Core business, mission, and vision statements
2. Organization and structure
3. Locations—identifying all locations that will be used to support this project and the operations handled from these locations
4. Total number of employees and contractors (each of the last 3 years)
5. Number of employees and contractors focused on supply management—total and by major department (each of the last 3 years)
6. Strategic milestones achieved by your company (number of new customers, dollars of private financings committed, rate of new bookings, etc.)
7. Strategic relationships with other related suppliers—stating all subcontractors and outsourced services to be used in implementing the supply management solution

B. Long-Term Vision and Strategic Plans

1. What future enhancements are currently planned for product? How do these enhancements position it for market leadership?
2. How do you plan to support emerging technologies and industry standards?
3. What is your primary target market? Does the target market have the right products to be successful against this target?

C. Depth of Experience and Customer References

1. Provide specific examples of industry recognition and customer success that demonstrate a proven track record of successfully providing supply management solutions.
2. Provide a list of reference customers, including contact information.

II. YOUR PRODUCT'S FUNCTIONALITY

Provide detailed information explaining how product addresses each of the following requirements:

A. Spend Analysis

i. Data Cleansing and Normalization
1. Cleanse spend data from different sources to make data capable of being analyzed.
2. Cleanse and classify data regardless of language.
3. Normalize the cleansed spend data to make it comparable.

ii. Data Enrichment and Classification
1. Classify the normalized and cleansed spend data by vendor. What different types of classification does product provide? Can it normalize disparate vendor names into one clean vendor master name automatically on a repeatable basis? How does it handle acquisitions and divestitures?
2. Classify the normalized and cleansed spend data by product category. What core data classification technologies are used for data classification, i.e., (a) artificial intelligence techniques such as neural networks; (b) rules-based mapping; or (c) other? Does product allow spend to be mapped to multiple commodity taxonomies (e.g., UNSPSC and customer internal taxonomy)?

3. Support rules-based classification through which rules may be defined to classify spend data. Does product support user-defined rules precedence hierarchies to automatically resolve conflicts between rules? Can it automatically convert feedback submitted by end users through the system into classification rules for a closed-loop classification feedback mechanism?

4. Support autoclassification and machine learning to automatically capture knowledge for continuous improvement and accuracy of spend classification. Does it allow end users to specify a minimum degree of confidence required for a classification to be applied? How many different classification algorithms does product apply to address variety in the quality and type of data available?

5. Allow end users to review and approve or reject classifications. In the review process, does it allow users to filter and sort the spend classifications to address those with the largest impact first? Is the approval or rejection of spend classifications automatically captured and incorporated in a classification knowledge base that drives auto-classification to provide greater accuracy during future analysis cycles?

6. Provide accurate classifications. On average, what percentage of line items of spend data is accurately classified by product in the first one-to-three analysis cycles? On average, what percentage of line items of spend data is accurately classified by product after the first three analysis cycles? Please note differences, if any, between results for direct materials, MRO, and indirect goods, and services.

7. Allow for manual correction or identification of ambiguous or unclear classifications.

8. Provide for end-user data review and automated feedback of corrections to further enhance quality and establish buy-in.

9. Leverage external data sources (e.g., supplier Web catalogs) to enrich item-level data when deep granularity is required and customer data is lacking.

10. Support enhancing the spend data with additional attributes (e.g., credit, performance, supplier parent-child relationship data, supplier diversity status).

iii. Spend Analysis Reporting

1. Provide reports for analyzing spend patterns. How extensive are product's reporting capabilities? Does it support queries, drill-

down, aggregation, summarization, and summary reports? How many predefined reports does product provide? Does it support analysis of different dimensions, such as market, product, suppliers, and the internal organization and its hierarchies? Can the user create a personalized profile of analytics?

2. Are downloads to Microsoft Excel or Word possible?

3. Are pivot tables provided without having to download to Excel?

4. Automatically identify sourcing opportunities using analytics and generate sourcing events based on spend data. Can product automatically identify high-value savings opportunities based on spend data attributes? Does it support persistence of business rules for opportunity identification across all spend data refreshes?

5. Support the identification of spending with approved versus non-approved suppliers and on-contract versus off-contract spending. Can product analyze transactions for control/process violations, potential fraud, and efficiency? Can product report contract price variances and price discounts that are not captured?

B. Sourcing

i. RFx Creation

1. Enable buyer to create an original RFx from scratch or an RFx from a template:

   a. Allow the creation of RFx templates. Buyer can save an RFx as a template.

   b. Provide a level of authority specific to the creation and maintenance of templates (i.e., Site Administrator).

   c. Allow the maintenance and updating of templates.

2. Allow buyer to add attachments to further define the RFx.

3. Allow RFx to be saved in "Draft" status for future modification, prior to publication.

4. Allow buyer to delete an RFx, if buyer is the "owner" and RFx is in "Draft" status

5. Allow RFxs to be imported.

6. Support multiple RFx types, including RFI, RFQ, and reverse auction.

7. Support multistage negotiations, such as RFI_RFQ_Auction.

8. Support RFxs with hundreds or thousands of individually priced items.

9. Support multiple currencies for bidding.

10. Aggregate demand across multiple items and RFxs to leverage purchasing volume.
11. Provide buyer with a list of RFxs by status (i.e., "Draft," "Open," "Closed," etc.) sorted by date and other fields.
12. Provide buyer with a list of RFxs with "new" bids and other supplier activity.
13. Provide buyer with summary statistics, including number of RFxs by status, etc.

ii. Line-Item Administration

1. Allow buyer to add unlimited number of line items to further specify goods or services to be purchased.
2. Provide buyer with an item template from the category tree that includes prepopulated item attributes.
3. Support creation of multiple bid attributes, other than price:
   a. Allow buyer to specify attributes which contribute to a "total cost" calculation.
   b. Allow buyer to create total cost formulas based on arithmetic operations, logical, and comparison functions.
4. Allow buyer to add an unlimited number of custom line-item attributes. Support multiple attribute types including "Text," "Currency," "Real or Numeric," "Decimal," "Date/Time," "Boolean or Yes/No," "Selection," or "Formula" and allow user to define acceptable values and ranges for each type:
   a. Allow buyer to enter preferred or default values for attributes.
   b. Allow buyer to specify attributes as automatically or manually scored and create scoring schema for automatically scored attributes.
   c. Allow buyer to delete line-item custom "Attributes" while still in "Draft" status.
   d. Allow buyer to assign a weight to "Negotiable" line-item attributes.
   e. Allow buyer to specify negotiable "Attributes" that will be scored manually by buyer.
   f. Allow buyer to specify header attributes as "Required" or not.
   g. Allow "Required" header attributes to be weighed for level of importance to buyer.
   h. Allow buyer to specify attributes, values, and weights, which are not revealed to supplier

     i. Support the ability for different line items to have different attributes.
5. Allow buyer to assign attachments to the line item.
6. Allow line items, definitions, and attributes to be imported.

iii. Supplier Selection

1. Provide buyer with access to a list of suppliers. Allow buyer to select suppliers for participation.
2. Allow buyer to selectively invite supplier to see and bid on entire RFx, specific categories, or specific items
3. Allow buyer to select suppliers based on commodity assignments.
4. Allow buyer to search for suppliers based on profile attributes (i.e., "select or approved," "minority owned," etc.)
5. Allow buyer to invite suppliers from a supplier-qualification RFI based on their scores in that RFI.
6. Allow buyer to view list of supplier performance factors (scorecards) with values and weights to be utilized in scoring process.
7. Provide buyer with a list of supplier users for suppliers selected. Allow buyer to specify specific users for notification and participation.
8. Send an e-mail to all suppler users in the supplier organization to notify of invitation to participate in RFx.

iv. Bidding Rules

1. Allow buyer to specify that partial bids are acceptable and partial awards are possible.
2. Allow buyer to specify that bundled line-item bids are possible.
3. Allow buyer to configure bidding rules based on the auction type, including prebidding, reserve price, starting price and historic price, currency, must-beat best bid, must-beat your best bid, etc.
4. For reverse auction, require bidding to take place in the currency buyer specifies in the configuration.
5. Allow bidders to submit an unlimited number of bids, subject to business rules (i.e., minimum, maximum, etc.).
6. Display bid information to buyer in real time. Allow buyer to see bids in a graphical format.
7. Display bid information to suppliers in real time based on buyer-defined rules.

    a. Ensure that all supplier names are not revealed to other suppliers.

    b. For reverse auctions, allow buyer to specify what will be "revealed" to the supplier, including supplier rank, number of other suppliers, other supplier scores, other supplier bids, etc.

    c. Automatically increment or decrement potential next bid as specified by buyer-defined bid Increment/Decrement.

8. Allow buyer to configure closing time, including date and time of close, extension rules, and duration:

    a. Enable buyer to establish "predefined" extension criteria prior to the auction and automatically extend auction based on criteria.

    b. Open RFx automatically at the given start Date/Time.

    c. Close RFxs automatically at the scheduled Date/Time.

    d. Allow buyer to manually open or close an RFx.

    e. Allow an RFx to be "Suspended," "Revised," or "Closed" once it is scheduled.

    f. Allow an RFx to be "Suspended" halting all activity, with buyer having the ability to "Reactivate" it.

v. Supplier Response and Messaging

1. Provide supplier with a list of RFxs in which supplier is participating by status and sorted by date or some other field.

2. Provide supplier with a list of new RFxs in which supplier has recently been invited to participate.

3. Provide supplier with a list of new "notifications" for all activity.

4. Provide supplier with a list of auctions by status and sorted by date or some other field.

5. Allow supplier to bid only when a RFx has a status of "Open."

6. Allow supplier to view the all aspects of the RFx that have been "revealed" by buyer.

7. Allow supplier to export the RFx and all supporting information.

8. Allow supplier to import bids for the RFx.

9. Allow supplier to create/maintain a bid for any one or many line items.

10. Allow supplier to enter values for any negotiable attributes on each line item on which the supplier is bidding.

11. Allow supplier to bid on bundled line-items as specified by buyer.

12. Allow supplier to create their own line-item bundles.

13. Allow supplier to specify volume discounts at the line-item level.

14. Allow supplier to specify discounts based on the total award volume (units or dollars).
15. Allow supplier to submit mutually exclusive bid sets that allow alternatives to be selected without splitting awards.
16. Allow bids in any currency and support currency translation.
17. Require supplier to bid in the currency specified in the RFx.
18. Allow the supplier to enter free text comments to supplement the bid.
19. Allow supplier to attach documents to the bid at the header and line-item level.
20. Allow supplier to save bid as a "Draft" to modify/submit at a later date.
21. Allow supplier to preview their bid score before submitting it to buyer.
22. Allow supplier to submit bid, sending an e-mail notification to buyer.
23. Allow supplier to view bid activity that buyer has specified to reveal, including number of other suppliers, other supplier bids, etc.
24. Allow supplier to attach documents to supplement the bid.
25. Offer suppliers real-time recommendations to optimize their response considering multiple factors, e.g., price, volume discounting, bundling, etc. (see *Optimization* below).
26. Provide real-time messaging to support online negotiations:
    a. Allow supplier to post a question to buyer.
    b. Allow buyer to post questions to a supplier (private) or all suppliers (public).
    c. Allow buyer to view all questions for an RFx.
    d. Allow buyer to answer a question via an e-mail to supplier.
    e. Send all questions and answers in e-mail to all associated users, in addition to being posted on the site.

vi. Bid Scoring and Comparison

1. Allow multiple buyer users (i.e., the "team") to manually score attributes or line items, which require manual scoring, and allow RFx "Owner" to tabulate individual user scores into an overall score for the bid.
2. Automatically calculate supplier score for each negotiable attribute within a supplier bid.

3. Automatically calculate a rolled-up score for each line item within a supplier bid.
4. Automatically calculate a rolled-up score for the entire supplier bid.
5. Automatically calculate a "total cost" based on the "Attributes" buyer specifies as contributing to the calculation.
6. Calculate a total score for the bid.
7. Allow buyer to perform "what if" analysis by modifying any one or many weights and having the system rescore the bid.
8. Facilitate total score comparison across all or selected suppliers.
9. Facilitate line-item score comparison across all or selected suppliers.
10. Allow buyer to print a RFx with all bids, history, and versions.
11. Allow buyer to export a RFx with all history and versions in text or other formats.
12. Allow buyer and suppliers to print and export a bid report with auction details and history after the auction is completed.

vii. Multistage Negotiation/Iteration

1. Allow buyer to utilize an existing or components of an existing RFx document as the basis for a reverse auction.
2. Allow buyer to utilize the results of a reverse auction in the bid analysis and award of an RFx.
3. Allow buyer to "Suspend" a "Pending" or "Open" RFx, halting any maintenance or bidding activity against the RFx. Notifications are sent by e-mail to all participants.
4. Allow buyer to "Reactivate" a suspended RFx, allowing maintenance and bidding activity to continue. Notifications are sent to all participants.
5. Allow a buyer to "Close" an RFx, preventing any further maintenance or bidding activity.

C. Optimization

1. Provide for sophisticated "what if" analysis of multiple sourcing scenarios. Does the recommendation support complex sensitivity analysis that factors in buyer constraints (e.g., vendor count, vendor type [e.g., supplier diversity, minority vendor], bid data [e.g., color, generic versus brand], supplier performance, and split award allocations)? Does it support alternative price analysis (e.g., virtual rate card) and the incorporation of local requirements or any aspect of category or item into decision criteria?

2. Provide graphical and tabular comparison of items, prices, performance scores, and suppliers.
3. Generate supplier recommendations based on data analysis. Does it optimize supplier recommendations and provide optimization-based feedback directly to suppliers based on an analysis of price factors, non-price factors, and any business constraints and requirements?
4. Allow buyer to create and save one or many "what-if" scenarios.
5. Support the following "what-if" scenarios:
    i. Lowest cost outcome for all items:
        a. Based on standard bids only—excluding bundles, business volume discounts, and alternate bids
        b. Excluding all alternate bids, but including bundles and business volume discounts
    ii. "Cherry picking" scenario, including bundles, business volume discounts, and alternates
    iii. Total cost awarding the entire business to the incumbent suppliers
    iv. Lowest cost for business unit:
        a. No bundles, no business volume discounts, no alternates
        b. By awarding at least 20% to one and at least 30% to another supplier
    v. Lowest cost for enterprise:
        a. No bundles, no business volume discounts, no alternates
        b. By awarding at least 20% to one and at least 30% to another supplier
    vi. Allow buyer to create award constraints for number of suppliers, supplier volume allocation, capacity allocation, geographic coverage, supplier status (e.g., minority or disadvantaged vendor), budget limits, delivery constraints:
        a. Comparative analysis of single sourcing versus multisourcing: awarding business to 1, then 2, then 3, etc. suppliers, each being awarded a minimum of 15%
        b. Comparative analysis for single sourcing with each of the invited suppliers
    vii. Factor in supplier key performance indicators and weights in the total score.
    viii. Allow buyer to exclude supplier profile "Attributes" from scoring for a specific award scenario.

      ix. Allow buyer to modify any one or many weights, having the system rescore the bid and save each with an award scenario.

6. Provide buyer with an overall relative score for each award scenario based on bid scores and buyer-specified constraints.
7. Allow multiple suppliers to fill a single order.
8. Support the partial fulfillment of an order.
9. Automatically provide buyer with the optimal award scenario for each award scenario.
10. Allow buyer to award entire RFx to one supplier.
11. Allow buyer to award entire line item to one supplier.
12. Allow buyer to award multiple suppliers within a given line item.
13. Allow partial awards per line item if specified by buyer
14. Allow buyer to provide comments for an award.
15. Allow buyer to award a "bundled" bid.

D. Contracts

i. Contract Repository

1. Can contracts be grouped by organization, type, project, or other hierarchical structure in the contract repository?
2. Can the contract repository structure be modified on an ad hoc basis?
3. Can contracts be stored as .pdf, .doc, and imaged files within the contract repository?
4. Can a single contract be filed in different folders within the contract repository without replication?
5. Can master and subordinate agreements be linked in the contract repository?
6. How does the contract repository manage contract amendments?
7. Can contracts be searched by business terms?
8. Does the contract repository provide the ability for users to search for specific text within the documents?
9. Is there a file size limit to the number of contracts and other documents that can be stored within the repository? At what point is system functionality or speed compromised?
10. Can legacy contracts be stored in the contract repository?

ii. Contract Creation, Negotiation, and Approval

Contract Control
1. Provide an overview of the contract creation and control processes supported by product.
2. How are contract templates developed?
3. Does product control user access to contract clauses? Does product support alternate clauses? If so, is access to alternate clauses protected by security?
4. Describe the internal contract review and approval processes supported by product.
5. Can terms be captured from contract language in product?
6. Can contract data fields be added "on the fly" and associated with a contract?
7. Describe how master and vendor list properties are tracked by product.
8. Does product support percentage-based pricing?
9. Does product limit the number of line items in each contract?
10. Does product limit the number of fields in each line item?
11. Does product provide any contract configuration capabilities that reduce the level of knowledge and time required to request and create contracts?
12. Does product support the ability to natively manage contracts written on "other people's paper?"

Word Processing Capabilities
1. Does product support contract creation using Microsoft Word?
2. Does product support the ability to automatically send, receive, track, and file completed contracts via Fax?
3. Does product support contract creation through an online editor?
4. Does product support formatting with Microsoft Word?
5. Does product support customers' corporate standards for logos, headers, and footers?
6. Does product manage contract version control and data integrity?

Contract Negotiation
1. Provide an overview of the contract negotiation process supported by product.

2. Does product support both online and offline line negotiation with external parties?
3. Is an audit trail of all contract-related activity automatically captured and tracked during the negotiation process?
4. Does product record both internal and external comments during the negotiation process?
5. How does product enable users to manage their contract-related tasks?

Microsoft Word Integration

1. What versions of Microsoft Word are supported by product, if any?
2. Does product support contract negotiation using Microsoft Word?
3. Do edits made in Microsoft Word affect contract approval structures?
4. Does product automatically update terms entered using Microsoft Word?

Contract Execution

1. Can contracts be signed offline as paper contracts?
2. Does system support digital signatures?

iii. Contract Compliance and Reporting

Enforcing Compliance

1. Does product support internal compliance policies? If so, what business controls can be implemented in product?
2. Does product support supplier performance monitoring?
3. Does product enable purchase order and contract price matching?
4. Does product enable users to track the receipt of volume discounts?
5. How does product ensure that transactions comply with contract terms?
6. Does product help companies meet their own contractual obligations?
7. Does product support customers' business rules?
8. Does product provide executive visibility into all contracts company-wide?
9. Does product facilitate compliance with the Sarbanes-Oxley Act?
10. Describe product's ability to help customers identify supplier savings opportunities.

Contract Reporting
1. Provide an overview of product's reporting capabilities.
2. Does product include any predefined reports?
3. Does product have ad hoc query capabilities?
4. Does product provide multidimensional On-Line Analytical Processing (OLAP)-based analysis tools?
5. Does product provide forecasting capabilities?
6. Describe product's report-designing capabilities.
7. Does product enable customers to report on contract risk?
8. Does product allow users to format reports?
9. Is supporting documentation provided?
10. Does product include customized reporting portals for executives and other users?
11. Does product include any reports specifically designed to facilitate the audit process?
12. Can reports be organized in a customizable folder structure?
13. Can reports be scheduled by interval and by date?
14. Are reports compatible with future product releases?
15. Can reports be exported to Microsoft Excel?
16. Does product record key events in the contract life cycle within an activity log?
17. Are plug-ins required to use product's reporting module?
18. Can other reporting tools be used to obtain report data from your company's contracts?

E. Enterprise Application Integration

Describe product's integration framework:

1. Does product offer any prebuilt adapters for integration?
2. Does product provide tools for mapping contract objects to ERP system objects?
3. Does product support Web services?
4. Does product enable extension of Web services beyond standard services that may be delivered out-of-the-box?

Can product trigger actions by other enterprise systems?

1. Can product verify the compliancy of transactions performed by other systems?
2. Does product interface with systems from SAP?

3. Can product operate in an IBM WebSphere environment?
4. Does product guarantee delivery of information sent between systems?
5. Does framework operate in a manner that is noninvasive to integrated applications? Explain.
6. Does product interface with existing middleware technologies?
7. Does product support leading business-to-business standards such as Rosetta and XML (Extensible Markup Language)?
8. Does product support leading Web services standards such as SOAP (Simple Object Access Protocol) and WSDL (Web Services Description Language)?
9. Does product enable single-sign on?
10. Does product support LDAP (Lightweight Directory Access Protocol) password management?

F. Supplier Performance

1. Provide tools for collaborative scoring and evaluation of vendor performance based on KPIs and scorecards.
2. Support the creation of KPIs. Does product provide a KPI that is associated with a particular commodity, so only suppliers providing that commodity are evaluated on the given KPI?
3. Allow users to add an unlimited number of custom KPIs. Support multiple KPI types including "Text," "Currency," "Real or Numeric," "Decimal," "Date/Time," "Boolean or Yes/No," "Selection," or "Formula" and allow user to define acceptable values and ranges for each type.
4. Support the creation of scorecards based on individual KPIs.
5. Provide trend reporting across scorecards and KPIs, allowing users to compare a supplier's performance against other suppliers providing the same commodity.
6. Provide an "always-on" feedback mechanism through which any member of the organization may provide direct feedback regarding supplier performance. Roll this feedback up into KPIs.
7. Incorporate KPIs as factors in sourcing award decision making, and specify the weight they should play in the overall decision (see *Optimization* above).

G. Program Management

i. Program and Category Management

1. Provide an *n*-tier category tree (or model) that provides a centralized view into all information related to a category including: projects, spend, RFxs, items commonly sourced in the category, approved suppliers, suggested suppliers, predefined business terms required in contracts for the category, contracts, and supplier performance key performance indicators.
2. Provide a centralized view into all information related to a supplier, including spend, RFxs, approved categories, suggested categories, contracts, key performance indicators, and performance scorecards.
3. Provide buyer with a list of new "notifications" for all activity.
4. Provide buyer with a summary of and access to reporting.

ii. Profile and User Maintenance

1. Provide a two-tier supplier organizational hierarchy for organization and user.
2. Support specification of supplier geographic coverage in profile.
3. Support company addresses for mailing, shipping, billing, etc.
4. Allow the supplier user to maintain certain aspects of their profile (e.g., address) and not others (e.g., role).
5. Select valid commodities the supplier provides, facilitated by a commodity tree.
6. Provide a publicly accessible "supplier home page."

iii. Project Management

1. Allow buyer to specify a project, RFx, or contract "team," identifying and assigning other users who can/will participate in the process.
2. Support selective invitation of users to see only those items they are invited to see.
3. For projects, support different levels of project team member authorities, including owner (approve/sign-off), member or collaborator (write), and observer (read).
4. Allow project owner to maintain team member authorities.
5. Associate project templates with the commodity tree categories for which they have been created.
6. Allow buyers to search the commodity tree to locate project templates for use.

7. Support the ability for the owner (or team) to define a list of activities or tasks that must take place over the course of the project.
8. Allow tasks to be defined through textual description, dates, and custom attributes.
9. Allow owner to assign team members to tasks for responsibility and maintain those assignments.
10. Allow owner and team members to maintain task status.
11. Allow tasks to be designated as requiring owner and/or team member review or sign off before task is completed.

H. Internationalization

1. Allow for user profile-driven multilanguage capability.
2. Provide product documentation, interfaces, help screens, and error messages in languages X, Y, and Z. Does product support multiple languages and multiple currencies in the same instance for users across geographies? Can both Latin 1 and double-byte Asian languages be deployed in the same instance?
3. Provide (telephone) technical support in languages X, Y, and Z.

I. Integration

1. Allow single sign-on to supporting applications.
2. Allow category taxonomy and items to be populated and validated from external source (catalog).
3. Allow organization profile and information to be populated and validated from external source.
4. Allow user profile and information to be populated and validated from external source.
5. Support the ability to import an RFx document from an external source.
6. Allow award information to be exported to contract management and e-procurement applications.
7. Provide the ability for additional integration via EAI and messaging tools and/or point-to-point interfaces to external systems.

Source: Adapted from Emptoris, Inc. With permission.

SOURCE NOTES

Authors' note: Much of the information in this book is derived from the personal experiences of the authors and from colleagues, who contributed their experiences and insights. Information in the chapters is referenced if it is derived from another source or if, in the opinion of the authors, readers may want further description of the source.

Chapter 2

1. *CPO Interview;* Doug Smock; September 20, 2005. Available at: www.global-cpo.com.
2. Emptoris, Inc., Burlington, MA. White paper: *Achieving Spend Visibility: Benefits, Barriers and Best Practices.* Available at: www.Emptoris.com.
3. Cebula, James M. Comments: at ProcureCon 2005, Phoenix AZ; September 19–22, 2005.
4. Romney, J. Lisa, coordinator of electronic business for defense procurement and acquisition policy. Interview; April 2005.

Chapter 3

1. Larsh, Roger, Director of Procurement, North American Dressings, Sauces, and Oil, Cargill, Inc. Interview; January 17, 2006.
2. Stewart, Russ, Associate Director of Purchases, Procter & Gamble. Electronic interview; January 19, 2006.
3. Cox, Andrew, professor at the University of Birmingham, UK. Electronic interview; January 22, 2006.

Chapter 5

1. Wheatley, Malcolm. Beyond reverse auctions. *CPO Agenda*; Spring 2005.
2. Waugh, Richard. *Success Strategies in Advanced Sourcing and Negotiations: Optimizing Total Cost and Total Value for the Next Wave of E-Sourcing Savings.* Boston: Aberdeen Group; June 2005.
3. Minihan, Tim, Senior Vice President of Marketing, Procuri, Inc. Interview; April 2006.
4. Motorola/Emptoris Edelman. Presentation and submission; April 27, 2004.
5. *OR/MS Today*, New Postings; July 8, 2004.
6. Whyte, Cherish. Motorola's battle with supply and demand chain complexity. *Supply and Demand Chain Executive*; April/May 2003.
7. Jacobs, Jim. Presentation: *Transportation Sourcing at Procter & Gamble.* At the 2005 Conference Board Logistics Conference, Miami, FL; January 29, 2005.
8. Procter and Gamble/CombineNet Edelman. Presentation and submission; April 18, 2005.

Chapter 6

1. Hannon, David. Technology vs. process: another round. Buyers search for the blend of strategy and functionality that is SRM. *Purchasing*; October 6, 2005.
2. Pande, Sunil and Lapidus, David. Chapter 9: Technology tools—supplier relationship management (SRM). In *ePurchasingPlus: A Non-Technical Book to Help Purchasing Professionals Select the "Best Approach" for Transforming Purchasing Organizations through Technology.* Antonette, Gerald, Giunipero, Larry C., and Sawchuk, Chris, Eds. Cincinnati, OH: Jgc Enterprises; 2002, pp. 167–182.
3. Hughes, Jonathan. What is supplier relationship management and why does it matter. Parts I, II, and III. *Vantage Partners Online Journal*; April 2005, July 2005, October 2005.
4. SAS. SAS Customer Success Story: *From Purchasing to Profits—SAS Uses Its Own SAS Supplier Relationship Management to Drive Strategic Sourcing.* Available at: http://www.sas.com/success/sas_srm.html.
5. Porter, Anne Millen. High hanging fruit—how the global strategic sourcing organization at Bristol-Myers Squibb plans to deliver its next billion in cost savings. *Purchasing*; April 3, 2003.
6. Fitzgerald, Kevin R. *The Supplier Performance Benchmark Report—Program Adoption Lags Despite Clear Evidence of Value.* Boston: Aberdeen Group; September 2005.

7. Enslo, Beth. *Supplier Performance Management: What Leaders Do Differently—A Benchmark Report on How Companies Manage Supplier Performance and Supply Disruptions.* Boston: Aberdeen Group; September 2004.

8. Robertson Cox. Case Study: *Adverse Selection*; 2003. Available at: http://www.robcox.com/robcox/case_one.htm.

9. Cox, Andrew. Electronic interview, January 2006.

10. Howell, Brian, Manager of Alliance Clinical Research, Johnson & Johnson Co. Presentation: *Linking Sourcing to the Operational Delivery of Products and Services from Suppliers.* At the Conference Board Supplier Relationship Management Conference, Atlanta, GA; March 10, 2005.

11. Hughes, Jonathan. Interview; February 14, 2006.

12. Vantage Technologies, Inc. Case Study: *Managing a Critical Outsourcing Partnership*; 2005. Available at: http://www.vantagepartners.com/images/dyn/ news_OSQ106.pdf.

13. Lynch, Robert Porter. Interview; February 3, 2006

14. MacLennan, Don, Vice President of Marketing and Product Management, Frictionless Commerce, and Thomas L. Spak, Senior Director of Sourcing and Supplier Excellence, Bristol-Myers Squibb. Presentation: *Supplier Segmentation: One Size Does Not Fit All, Both in Relationships and the e-Tools to Manage Them.* At the Conference Board Supplier Relationship Management Conference, Atlanta, GA; March 8, 2006.

15. Rogers, Steve, Senior Consultant, Cincinnati Consulting Consortium. Presentation: *Supplier Value: Where Have We Been and Where Are We Going?* At the National Association of Purchasing and Payables Conference, Orlando, FL; February 6, 2006

Chapter 7

1. Manahan, Tim A. *The e-Procurement Benchmark Report—Less Hype, More Results.* Boston: Aberdeen Group; December 2004.

2. Kraus, Dan, Vice President of Operations, Global Procurement, Hallmark Cards, Inc. Presentation: *Low Cost Country Sourcing and e-Procurement Impact.* At the Conference Board e-Procurement Conference, Chicago, IL; April 7, 2006.

3. Conners, Chris, Director of Global Business Management, Hewlett-Packard. Presentation: *Driving Higher Value from the Procure Lifecycle.* At the NAPP Conference, Orlando, FL; February 6, 2006.

4. Prince-Eason, Pamela, Senior Director of Global Sourcing, Pfizer Corporation. Presentation: *P2P Excellence at Pfizer*. At the NAPP Conference, Orlando, FL; February 6, 2006.
5. Hamm, Steve. The new corporate model—services: taking a page from Toyota's playbook. *Business Week*; August 22/29, 2005, pp. 69–72.
6. Harkness, Kerry Ann, Group Manager of Accounts Payable, AT&T. Presentation: *Ariba Invoicing*. At the NAPP Conference, Orlando, FL; February 6, 2006.
7. Kuhn, Mary Alice, Manager of Strategic Sourcing and Design, Timken Co. Presentation: *The Purchasing Highway: Under Construction*. At the NAPP Conference, Orlando, FL; February 6, 2006.

Chapter 8

1. Rudzki, Robert A., Smock, Douglas A., Katzorke, Michael, and Stewart, Shelley, Jr. In *Straight to the Bottom Line™: An Executive's Roadmap to World Class Supply Management*. Ft. Lauderdale, FL: J. Ross Publishing; 2005, Chapter 18.
2. Aberdeen Group. *White paper: Contract Optimization: A Recession-Proof Strategy for Maximizing Performance and Minimizing Risk*; July 2003.

Chapter 9

1. McIntosh, Kenneth G. *Engineering Data Management*. New York: McGraw-Hill; 1995.
2. Saaksvuori, Antti and Immonen, Anselmi. *Product Lifecycle Management*. New York: Springer-Verlag; 2002.
3. Ayers, Dave, Vice President of Multimedia Network Solutions R&D, Platforms, and Quality Engineering. Lucent Technologies, Murray Hill, NJ. Interview; April 2005.
4. Massetti, Michael, Senior Director of Supplier Management, Lucent Technologies, Murray Hill, NJ. Presentation at ProcureCon 2005. Scottsdale, AZ; September 20, 2005.
5. Vijayan, Jaikumar. Global needs propel product life-cycle management. *Computerworld*, May 16, 2005.
6. Bair, Dan, Director of Worldwide Technology Standards and Systems; as cited in Vijayan, Jaikumar. Global needs propel product life-cycle management. *Computerworld*, May 16, 2005.
7. Bell, Stacey L. Molding an expanded business model. *Medical Product Outsourcing*; June 2005. Available at: mpo-mag.com.

8. Thorenson, Dave, Plant Manager at Medical Molding and Assembly, Phillips Plastics, Hudson, WI. Interview; October 2005.
9. Stichter, Kelly, Vice President of Design Development, Phillips Plastics Corporation, Hudson, WI. Interview; October 2005.

Chapter 10

1. For an expanded discussion of savings at Chrysler as described by Thomas Stallkamp, see Rudzki, Robert A., Smock, Douglas A., Katzorke, Michael, and Stewart, Shelley, Jr. In *Straight to the Bottom Line™: An Executive's Roadmap to World Class Supply Management*. Ft. Lauderdale, FL: J. Ross Publishing; 2005, p. 88.
2. Monczka, Robert, Trent, Robert, and Hanfeld, Robert. *Purchasing and Supply Chain Management*. Belmont, CA: Thomson Learning/South-Western; 2001, p. 429.
3. Corporate Backgrounder. *The Challenge in Manufacturing Industries*. Available at: www.apriori.com.
4. Charkiewicz, Thomas. Interview; January 2006.
5. Kagan, John, former Manager of PC Cost Management at IBM and Lenovo. Interview; January 2006.
6. Azzolino, Frank, President and CEO of aPriori Technologies. Interview; January 2006
7. Holland, Brett, COO at Akoya. Interview; January 2006.
8. Dewhurst, Nick, Boothroyd and Dewhurst. Interview; January 2006.
9. Dewhurst, Nick and Meeker, David G. Paper: *A Case to Consider Before Outsourcing to China*. Interview; January 2006.

Chapter 11

1. Der Hovanesian, Mara. Eagle eye on your T&E. *Business Week*, May 8, 2006.
2. Manning, Christa Degnan, Garf, Robert, and Sweeny, Judy. Workforce management: the imperative to optimize labor. *AMR Research Report*; June 15, 2006.
3. Johnson Controls. Website; as of June 2006.
4. Patton, Mike, former Director of Supply Chain Management for Johnson Controls, Inc. Facilities Management. Interview and background material; June 2006.

Chapter 12

1. Poe, Tom, Practice Director at Hudson (a part of the Hudson Highland Group). Presentation: *Sarbanes Oxley and the Procure to Pay Process*. At the NAPP Conference, Orlando, FL; February 6, 2006.

2. Markum, Robert and Hamerman, Paul. *The Forrester Wave—Sarbanes Oxley Compliance Software Q1-2005*. Cambridge, MA: Forrester Research, Inc.; April 7, 2005.

3. Minahan, Tim A., Senior Vice President of Global Supply Management Research at Aberdeen Group. *The Supply Risk Management Benchmark Report—Assuring Supply and Mitigating Risks in an Uncertain Economy*; Boston: Aberdeen Group; September 2005.

4. Nelson, Dave, Moody, Patricia E., and Stegner, Jonathan. *The Purchasing Machine: How the Top Ten Companies Use Best Practices to Manage Their Supply Chains*. New York: The Free Press; 2001, pp. 238–239.

5. United Technologies. Supplier insight for better business performance, 2005 GL&SCS and CSCMP Supply Chain Innovation Award Finalist. *Global Logistics and Supply Chain Strategies Magazine*; December 2005.

6. Gordon, Sherry, Vice President of Supplier Performance Intelligence, Emptoris, Inc. *Quality Progress: Seven Steps to Measure Supplier Performance*; August 2005.

7. Johnsen, Stephen, Manager of International Trade Compliance, Bayer Corporation and Business Services. Interview; February 22, 2006.

8. Enslow, Beth, Vice President of Enterprise Research, Aberdeen Group. *New Strategies for Global Trade Management: How Enterprises Are Mastering Cross-Border Supply Chains by Synchronizing Logistics, Compliance and Finance*. Boston, MA: Aberdeen Group; March 2005.

9. Smith, H. D. Deployment brief: *Pharmaceutical Wholesaler Leverages RFID to Generate Electronic Pedigree for Schedule II Drugs*. GlobeRanger Website; March 2006.

10. Collins, Jonathon. P&G finds RFID "sweet spot." *RFID Journal*; May 3, 2006.

11. Gomez, Andy, CIO, Finance Operations and Supply Chain Management, Bank of America. Presentation: *Vision to Implementation*. At Procuri Empower 2005 Conference; September 27, 2005.

12. MacLennon, Don, Vice President of Marketing and Product Management, Frictionless Commerce. White paper: *Vendor Management Resources and Interview*; March 2006.

Chapter 13

1. Product Review: i2 Supply Chain Collaborator improves forecasting for Whirlpool. *DM Review Magazine*; July 2003.
2. Stone, Reuben E. Cleaning up Whirlpool's supply chain. *Harvard Business Review*; November 22, 2004.
3. O'Meara, Kevin, Director of Supply Chain Operations at Whirlpool Corporation. Interview; July 2006.
4. Anthes, Gary. Supply chain whirl. *Computerworld*; June 5, 2005.
5. Steve Rush, Vice President of North American Procurement at Whirlpool Corporation. Interview; July 2006.
6. Friscia, Tony. *Innovative IT and the New Economy*. AMR Research, September 27, 2005; as cited in Levi, Michael D. *The Multi-Enterprise Challenge: Management and Control Outside of the Enterprise*. Dallas, TX: i2 Technologies, Inc.; April 2006. Available at: http://www.u2.com/assets/pdf/WPR_mei_ challenge_WPR7371.pdf.

Chapter 14

1. Gerstner, J.V., Jr. *Who Says Elephants Can't Dance?* New York: HarperBusiness; 2002, p. 63.
2. Article: Leading change when business is good: an interview with Samuel J. Palmisano. *Harvard Business Review*; December 2004, p. 63.
3. *Undersupply Irks Wall Street*. Available at: www.reed-electronics.com.
4. Radjou, Navi. *IBM Transforms Its Supply Chain to Drive Growth*. Cambridge, MA: Forrester Research, Inc.; March 24, 2005, p. 2–3.
5. Pruitt, Henry, Procurement IT. Interview in Somers, N.Y; June 2005.
6. Paterson, John M., IBM. Interview; October 2005.
7. Crawford, Ian J., Vice President of Strategic Sourcing at IBM. Interview, April 2005.
8. Paterson, John M., IBM. Interview; June 2005.
9. Nugent, James W., IBM IT. Interview; June 2005.

Chapter 15

1. Gravelle, John, President of Mar-Lee Industries, Leominster, MA. Interview; January 2006.
2. See Rudzki, Robert A., Smock, Douglas A., Katzorke, Michael, and Stewart, Shelley, Jr. Automotive purchasing: a tale of two spenders. In *Straight to the Bottom Line™: An Executive's Roadmap to World Class Supply Management*. Ft. Lauderdale: J. Ross Publishing; 2005, pp. 83–94.

3. Martin, Dave, President and owner, Accu-Mold in Portage, MI. Interview; November 2005.

4. Murray, Charles J. The quest for imperfection. *Design News.* October 10, 2005. Available at: www.designnews.com.

5. Executive Report: *Event-Based Functional Build: An Integrated Approach to Body Development.* Southfield, MI: Auto/Steel Partnership Program/Body Systems Analysis Project Team; 1999, p. iii. Available at: http://a-sp.org/database/custom/bsa/bodydevexec.pdf.

6. Bibber, Donna, plastics engineer, Miniature Tool & Die, Charlton, MA. Interview; January 2006.

7. Knapp, Bruce, Michigan Manufacturing Technology Center, Plymouth, MI. Press release: *The United Tooling Coalition Seeks a New Way of Doing Business.* United Tooling Coalition; 2006.

Chapter 16

1. *Baseline Magazine* website. Available at: www.baselinemag.com.

Chapter 17

1. Wilson, Debbie, Debbie Wilson Consulting and Publisher of the Web newsletter *Cool Tools for Purchasing. Presentation: The State of Supply Chain Management.* At the National Association of Purchasing Management, Cincinnati Chapter; May 9, 2006.

2. Magidson, Jason, Director of Innovation Processes, GlaxoSmithKline, PLC. Interview; May 10, 2006.

3. Ackoff, Russell, Magidson, Jason, and Addison, Herbert J. Chapter 6: Process improvement. In *Idealized Design: How to Dissolve Tomorrow's Crisis Today.* Philadelphia: Wharton School Publishing; April 20, 2006, pp. 103–116.

4. Magidson, Jason. Chapter 9: Shifting your customers into "wish mode:" tools for generating new product ideas and breakthroughs. In *The PDMA ToolBook 2 for New Product Development,* Belliveau, Paul, Griffin, Abbie, and Somermeyer, Stephen M., Eds. New York: John Wiley; October 5, 2004, pp. 235–268.

5. Bartels, Andrew H., Vice President and research analyst, Forrester Research, Inc. Presentation: *The Role of Technology in Driving Strategic Value in Procurement.* At the Conference Board e-Procurement Conference, Chicago, IL; April 7, 2006.

6. Henderson, Richard, Vice President of Procurement, Limited Brands. Presentation: *Procurement Transformation—Beyond Shared Services*. At the Conference Board e-Procurement Conference, Chicago, IL; April 7, 2006.

7. Rubeo, Carol. President of MSE Enterprises. Interview; May 5, 2006.

Chapter 18

1. Norman, Dennie, Director of Supply Chain Intelligence Business, SAS Institute. Presentation: *Evaluating, Selecting and Measuring for "A" Suppliers: Creating a Plan for Your Organization*. At the Conference Board 2006 Supplier Relationship Management Conference, Atlanta, GA; March 9, 2006.

2. Minahan, Tim A. *The e-Procurement Benchmark Report—Less Hype, More Results*. Boston: Aberdeen Group; December 2004.

3. Ardell, Barbara, Vice President of Sourcing Solutions, Procuri, Inc. *Proven Methodologies to Increase Internal Adoption*; February 17, 2005.

4. Hannon, David. P&G leaps on the Net. *Purchasing* magazine; June 6, 2002, pp. 16C4– 6C8.

5. Finley, Hal, Manager of Procurement e-Tool Applications and Decision Support, Texas Instruments Incorporated. Presentation: *You Get What You Measure—Texas Instruments' Guide on Benchmarking Metrics*. At Procuri Empower Conference; September 27, 2005.

6. Devine, Sean, Director of Consulting Services, Emptoris, Inc. Presentation at Driving Adoption Workshop, Emptoris Empower Conference; October 2005.

7. Devine, Sean, Director of Consulting Services, Emptoris, Inc. Presentation: *Measuring, Analyzing, and Improving the Performance of Strategic Sourcing Programs*; May 3, 2006.

8. Leinweber, Ken, Worldwide Operations e-Sourcing Program Manager, Sun Microsystems. Presentation: *Empowering Your Team for Self-Sufficiency and Driving Total Cost of Ownership e-Sourcing Procurement*. At Procuri Empower Conference, Atlanta, GA; September 2005.

Chapter 19

1. Whitehouse, Patricia, Senior Director of Procurement Global Performance Solutions, Merck & Company. Presentation: *Learning for Performance*. At National Association of Purchasing and Payables Conference, Orlando, FL; February 7, 2006.

2. Ardell, Barbara, independent training consultant. Interview; March 18, 2006.

3. Hicks, Charles, Director of Global Purchasing Strategy, Rolls Royce Corporation. Presentation: *Strategies to Decrease Costs and Increase Efficiency*

Through Technology Innovation. Information and Automation. At the Conference Board Supply Chain Management Conference, Chicago, IL, June 11, 2003.

Chapter 20

1. Rudzki, Robert A., Smock, Douglas A., Katzorke, Michael, and Stewart, Shelley, Jr. In *Straight to the Bottom Line™: An Executive's Roadmap to World Class Supply Management.* Ft. Lauderdale, FL: J. Ross Publishing; 2007.
2. Rudzki, R. *Beat the Odds: Avoid Corporate Death and Build a Resilient Enterprise.* Ft. Lauderdale, FL: J. Ross Publishing; 2007. Excerpted with permission.

Chapter 21

1. O'Reilly, Tim. *What Is Web 2.0 Design Patterns and Business Models for the Next Generation of Software?* September 30, 2007. Available at: www.oreilly.com.
2. E-Biz Strategies: Reinventing Herman Miller. *Business Week*; April 3, 2000.
3. Smock, Doug, *Purchasing* magazine Editorial Advisory Board, 2003 Spring Meeting. Top buyers speak. *Purchasing Magazine Online*; June, 19, 2003.

INDEX